OSINT 101 HANDBOOK
EXPERT-LEVEL INTELLIGENCE GATHERING

ADVANCED RECONNAISSANCE, THREAT ASSESSMENT, AND COUNTERINTELLIGENCE

4 BOOKS IN 1

BOOK 1
OSINT FUNDAMENTALS: A BEGINNER'S GUIDE TO OPEN SOURCE
INTELLIGENCE TECHNIQUES

BOOK 2
ADVANCED OSINT STRATEGIES: MASTERING OPEN SOURCE
INTELLIGENCE TECHNIQUES

BOOK 3
DIGITAL FOOTPRINT ANALYSIS: HARNESSING OSINT FOR PROFILING AND
INVESTIGATIONS

BOOK 4
EXPERT OSINT: CYBER RECONNAISSANCE AND THREAT INTELLIGENCE

ROB BOTWRIGHT

Published by Rob Botwright
Library of Congress Cataloging-in-Publication Data
ISBN 978-1-83938-546-9
Cover design by Rizzo

Disclaimer

The contents of this book are based on extensive research and the best available historical sources. However, the author and publisher make no claims, promises, or guarantees about the accuracy, completeness, or adequacy of the information contained herein. The information in this book is provided on an "as is" basis, and the author and publisher disclaim any and all liability for any errors, omissions, or inaccuracies in the information or for any actions taken in reliance on such information.

The opinions and views expressed in this book are those of the author and do not necessarily reflect the official policy or position of any organization or individual mentioned in this book. Any reference to specific people, places, or events is intended only to provide historical context and is not intended to defame or malign any group, individual, or entity.

The information in this book is intended for educational and entertainment purposes only. It is not intended to be a substitute for professional advice or judgment. Readers are encouraged to conduct their own research and to seek professional advice where appropriate.

Every effort has been made to obtain necessary permissions and acknowledgments for all images and other copyrighted material used in this book. Any errors or omissions in this regard are unintentional, and the author and publisher will correct them in future editions.

TABLE OF CONTENTS – BOOK 1 - OSINT FUNDAMENTALS: A BEGINNER'S GUIDE TO OPEN SOURCE INTELLIGENCE TECHNIQUES

Introduction 5
Chapter 1: Introduction to Open Source Intelligence 9
Chapter 2: Setting Up Your OSINT Toolbox 17
Chapter 3: Online Privacy and Ethical Considerations 24
Chapter 4: Basic Search Engine Techniques 30
Chapter 5: Leveraging Social Media for OSINT 37
Chapter 6: Web Scraping and Data Collection 44
Chapter 7: Analyzing Publicly Available Information 51
Chapter 8: Geolocation and Mapping in OSINT 58
Chapter 9: OSINT in Investigations and Research 65
Chapter 10: Future Trends and Advanced Learning Paths in OSINT 73

TABLE OF CONTENTS – BOOK 2 - ADVANCED OSINT STRATEGIES: MASTERING OPEN SOURCE INTELLIGENCE TECHNIQUES

Chapter 1: Review of OSINT Fundamentals 81
Chapter 2: Deep Dive into Advanced Search Queries 88
Chapter 3: Targeted Information Gathering 95
Chapter 4: Advanced Social Media Analysis 104
Chapter 5: Dark Web Exploration and Monitoring 113
Chapter 6: OSINT Automation and Scripting 122
Chapter 7: Ethical Hacking for Intelligence Gathering 131
Chapter 8: Advanced Analysis and Visualization Tools 139
Chapter 9: Threat Intelligence and Cybersecurity 148
Chapter 10: Case Studies in Advanced OSINT Operations 157

TABLE OF CONTENTS – BOOK 3 - DIGITAL FOOTPRINT ANALYSIS: HARNESSING OSINT FOR PROFILING AND INVESTIGATIONS

Chapter 1: Understanding the Digital Footprint 169
Chapter 2: Establishing a Comprehensive OSINT Workflow 175
Chapter 3: Tracing Online Identities and Personas 183
Chapter 4: Analyzing Social Media Trails 190
Chapter 5: Uncovering Digital Artifacts and Metadata 196
Chapter 6: Profiling Individuals and Organizations 202
Chapter 7: Investigative Techniques with Digital Footprints 210
Chapter 8: Legal and Ethical Considerations in Footprint Analysis 217
Chapter 9: Cybersecurity Implications and Threat Assessment 223
Chapter 10: Real-World Case Studies in Digital Footprint Analysis 229

TABLE OF CONTENTS – BOOK 4 - EXPERT OSINT: CYBER RECONNAISSANCE AND THREAT INTELLIGENCE

Chapter 1: Advanced OSINT Recap 235
Chapter 2: Cyber Reconnaissance Fundamentals 241
Chapter 3: Mapping the Digital Battlefield 247
Chapter 4: Advanced Dark Web Investigations 253
Chapter 5: Deep Dive into Attribution and Deception 260
Chapter 6: Threat Intelligence Frameworks and Models 266
Chapter 7: OSINT in Counterintelligence Operations 272
Chapter 8: Advanced OSINT Tools and Techniques 277
Chapter 9: Predictive Analysis and Threat Assessment 284
Chapter 10: Case Studies in Expert Cyber Reconnaissance 290
Conclusion 299

Introduction

Welcome to the "OSINT 101 Handbook: Expert-Level Intelligence Gathering" bundle—a comprehensive and illuminating journey into the captivating realm of Open Source Intelligence (OSINT). In this multifaceted collection, we embark on an exploration of intelligence gathering, reconnaissance, threat assessment, and counterintelligence, spanning four distinct volumes designed to empower both beginners and seasoned professionals alike.

In an age where information is currency and knowledge is power, the ability to harness open source intelligence is not just advantageous; it is indispensable. OSINT has emerged as a cornerstone of modern intelligence operations, offering insights, strategies, and techniques that transcend traditional boundaries and redefining the way we approach intelligence gathering.

"BOOK 1 - OSINT Fundamentals: A Beginner's Guide to Open Source Intelligence Techniques" serves as your entry point into this world of digital espionage and analysis. Here, we lay the groundwork, providing novice learners with an accessible and enlightening introduction to OSINT concepts and methodologies. From understanding the significance of open source intelligence to mastering fundamental techniques, this volume is your gateway to a universe of information waiting to be unveiled.

Building upon this foundation, "BOOK 2 - Advanced OSINT Strategies: Mastering Open Source Intelligence

Techniques" immerses you in the intricate web of advanced strategies employed by seasoned OSINT professionals. Delve into the art of crafting intricate search queries, harness the power of automation, and uncover the secrets of expert-level OSINT tools. With this volume, you'll elevate your skills and unlock the true potential of open source intelligence.

As we delve deeper into the world of OSINT, "BOOK 3 - Digital Footprint Analysis: Harnessing OSINT for Profiling and Investigations" takes center stage. Here, we explore the intriguing realm of digital footprints, behavioral analysis, and extracting valuable insights from social media activity. Profiling and investigations become your domain as you uncover the secrets hidden within the digital trails left by individuals and organizations.

Finally, "BOOK 4 - Expert OSINT: Cyber Reconnaissance and Threat Intelligence" catapults us into the heart of cyber reconnaissance and threat intelligence. Real-world examples of expert-level operations reveal the intricate processes by which cyber adversaries are identified, malicious infrastructure is disrupted, and critical assets are safeguarded. This volume immerses you in the dynamic and ever-evolving world of cybersecurity and intelligence.

As you embark on this extraordinary journey through the "OSINT 101 Handbook" bundle, remember that OSINT is not just a collection of techniques; it's a mindset. It's about curiosity, adaptability, and an unquenchable thirst for knowledge. It's about embracing the world of open source intelligence as a canvas upon which you can paint a detailed portrait of the digital landscape.

Each volume within this bundle equips you with the tools and knowledge needed to navigate the complex terrain of information, uncover hidden threats, and make informed decisions. It's a journey that leads you to a deeper understanding of the power and potential of OSINT—a journey where learning never ceases, and expertise is earned through dedication and practice.

The "OSINT 101 Handbook" bundle is an invaluable resource that empowers you to excel in the realms of intelligence gathering, reconnaissance, threat assessment, and counterintelligence. It is a guide that illuminates the path forward, a beacon that pierces the darkness of the digital world, and a trusted companion as you embark on your quest for knowledge.

With each turn of the page, you'll delve deeper into the art and science of open source intelligence, gaining insights that will not only enhance your professional capabilities but also shape your perspective on the world of information. Welcome to the world of OSINT, where the pursuit of knowledge is endless, and the potential for impact is boundless.

BOOK 1
OSINT FUNDAMENTALS
A BEGINNER'S GUIDE TO OPEN SOURCE INTELLIGENCE
TECHNIQUES

ROB BOTWRIGHT

Chapter 1: Introduction to Open Source Intelligence

In this chapter, we will delve into the fundamental concepts of Open Source Intelligence, commonly referred to as OSINT. OSINT is a crucial discipline in the world of information gathering, and comprehending its core principles is essential for anyone venturing into the field of intelligence analysis and research. OSINT, at its core, is about collecting information from publicly available sources. These sources encompass a wide array of mediums, ranging from websites, social media platforms, news articles, and more. The primary distinction lies in the fact that OSINT relies solely on open, unclassified information, readily accessible to anyone with an internet connection. It's a valuable resource for understanding various aspects of individuals, organizations, and events.

At the heart of OSINT lies the principle of openness, which distinguishes it from other forms of intelligence. Unlike classified information or classified intelligence methods, OSINT operates in the public domain. This openness presents both opportunities and challenges, making it a captivating and complex domain of study. In essence, OSINT is the art of extracting meaningful insights and actionable intelligence from publicly available data.

One critical aspect of OSINT is the emphasis on ethical and legal considerations. While the information gathered is openly accessible, it is vital to respect privacy rights and adhere to ethical guidelines. OSINT practitioners must tread carefully to ensure they do not infringe upon individuals' privacy or violate any applicable laws. Understanding these ethical boundaries is fundamental for responsible and effective OSINT.

Another pivotal concept in OSINT is the notion of information triage. Information triage involves the process of filtering and prioritizing data based on relevance and reliability. Given the vast amount of publicly available information, OSINT analysts must develop the skill of discerning which sources and data points are credible and valuable. This discernment enables them to focus on the most pertinent information for their analysis.

Furthermore, OSINT encompasses various techniques for data collection and analysis. These techniques range from basic web searches to more advanced methods like web scraping, social media analysis, and geospatial analysis. The ability to harness these techniques effectively is a hallmark of a proficient OSINT practitioner. Each method serves a distinct purpose, allowing analysts to paint a comprehensive picture of the subject under investigation.

In our exploration of OSINT concepts, we must also acknowledge the ever-evolving nature of the field. The digital landscape constantly changes, and with it, the sources of publicly available information. New platforms, websites, and communication channels emerge regularly, providing fresh avenues for OSINT practitioners. Staying updated with these developments is essential for maintaining the relevance and accuracy of OSINT efforts.

As we move forward in this book, we will delve deeper into the practical aspects of OSINT. We will explore the tools and techniques that enable effective information collection and analysis. Additionally, we will address the ethical considerations that underpin responsible OSINT practices. By the end of this journey, you will have a solid foundation in OSINT and be equipped to leverage its power for a wide range of purposes, from research and investigations to cybersecurity and threat assessment.

Chapter 2: Setting Up Your OSINT Toolbox

In the previous chapter, we discussed the fundamental concepts of Open Source Intelligence (OSINT). Now, as we embark on this journey to master OSINT techniques, we must equip ourselves with the essential tools and resources. Your OSINT toolbox is the key to effective information gathering and analysis. In this chapter, we'll explore the components of this toolbox and how to set it up for success.

The OSINT toolbox consists of a collection of software, applications, and online resources that facilitate the various stages of OSINT work. Whether you're an investigator, researcher, journalist, or security professional, having the right tools at your disposal is paramount. These tools not only enhance your efficiency but also enable you to extract valuable insights from the vast ocean of publicly available information.

One of the first tools you should consider adding to your OSINT arsenal is a web browser with extensions tailored for intelligence work. Extensions like data scrapers, search engine modifiers, and privacy-focused add-ons can significantly enhance your browsing experience. They allow you to extract data, refine your search queries, and protect your privacy while conducting OSINT activities.

Next, a good note-taking and organization tool is indispensable. Effective data management is crucial in OSINT, as it helps you keep track of your findings, sources, and analysis. Tools like Evernote, OneNote, or specialized OSINT notebooks can aid in this aspect, allowing you to maintain a structured and accessible repository of information.

Beyond web browsing and note-taking, specialized OSINT tools play a vital role. These tools cater to specific OSINT functions, such as social media analysis, domain information retrieval, or geolocation. For example, social media intelligence platforms like Maltego can help visualize relationships and connections among individuals and entities. Domain research tools like WHOIS databases provide information about website owners and their registration details. Geolocation tools allow you to pinpoint the physical location of IP addresses or devices. These tools are invaluable for OSINT practitioners, offering precision and depth in their investigations.

Furthermore, a solid understanding of advanced search operators is essential. Search engines like Google offer a plethora of operators that enable you to refine your queries and extract more relevant results. Learning to use operators like site:, filetype:, and intitle: can greatly improve the efficiency of your OSINT searches.

In addition to software tools, consider the importance of online resources and communities. OSINT practitioners often rely on forums, blogs, and social media groups to exchange knowledge and stay updated on the latest developments in the field. These communities offer valuable insights, share tips and techniques, and foster a sense of camaraderie among OSINT enthusiasts.

As you assemble your OSINT toolbox, keep in mind that flexibility is key. The field of OSINT is dynamic, and new tools and resources emerge regularly. Therefore, it's essential to adapt and experiment with different tools to determine which ones align best with your specific needs and objectives.

In the subsequent chapters, we will dive deeper into the practical aspects of OSINT, where we'll use these tools and techniques to gather and analyze information effectively. So, let's get ready to explore the world of open source intelligence, armed with our OSINT toolbox.

Open Source Intelligence, or OSINT, plays a pivotal role in the world of information gathering, offering a unique and valuable approach. OSINT is the art of collecting and analyzing information from publicly available sources, and it operates on the principle that a wealth of data exists in the open domain. In today's digital age, where information is abundant and accessible, OSINT has become an indispensable tool for various purposes, including research, investigations, cybersecurity, and threat assessment.

The significance of OSINT lies in its ability to provide insights and intelligence from sources that are open to anyone with an internet connection. Unlike classified information, which is restricted and often concealed, OSINT relies on openly accessible data from websites, social media, news articles, public records, and other public sources. This openness allows OSINT practitioners to gather a wide range of information about individuals, organizations, events, and more, without the need for special permissions or clearances.

OSINT serves as a powerful force multiplier for intelligence gathering efforts. It complements other forms of intelligence, such as Human Intelligence (HUMINT), Signals Intelligence (SIGINT), and Geospatial Intelligence (GEOINT). While these intelligence disciplines have their strengths, they often operate in classified environments and deal with information that is not readily available to the public. OSINT, on the other hand, can fill critical gaps by providing context and background information that enhances the overall intelligence picture.

One of the key strengths of OSINT is its versatility. It can be applied across a wide spectrum of domains and disciplines. Researchers can use OSINT to gather data for academic studies or market research. Journalists can employ OSINT to uncover facts and verify information for news articles. Law enforcement agencies can use OSINT to support investigations and track down suspects. Cybersecurity professionals rely on OSINT to identify potential threats and vulnerabilities. Additionally, OSINT has a vital role in national security and defense, helping governments monitor and assess international developments.

Ethical considerations are paramount in OSINT. While the information gathered is publicly available, practitioners must adhere to ethical guidelines and respect privacy rights. OSINT professionals should operate within legal boundaries and ensure that their activities do not infringe upon individuals' privacy or violate any applicable laws. Ethical OSINT practices are essential for maintaining trust and credibility in the field.

The process of conducting OSINT involves several key stages. It begins with defining the objectives and scope of the investigation. OSINT practitioners must have a clear understanding of what information they are seeking and why. Next, they embark on data collection, which involves searching, accessing, and retrieving information from various sources. This phase requires the use of specialized tools and techniques to extract relevant data.

Once the data is collected, the analysis phase begins. OSINT analysts sift through the gathered information, looking for patterns, connections, and insights. This analytical process may involve data visualization, link analysis, and the identification of significant trends or anomalies. The goal is to transform raw data into actionable intelligence that can inform decision-making.

The final stage of OSINT involves reporting and dissemination. Analysts compile their findings into reports, briefings, or presentations, tailored to the needs of the intended audience. These reports convey the insights gained from OSINT analysis and provide recommendations or conclusions based on the data. Effective communication of OSINT findings is crucial for informing stakeholders and facilitating informed decision-making.

In addition to its role in investigations and research, OSINT also plays a pivotal role in cybersecurity and threat assessment. Organizations and cybersecurity professionals leverage OSINT to monitor the digital landscape for potential threats. By analyzing publicly available information, such as online forums, social media posts, and hacker chatter, cybersecurity experts can identify emerging threats, vulnerabilities, and attack trends. OSINT enables proactive measures to be taken to protect networks, systems, and sensitive data.

Furthermore, OSINT is a valuable tool for tracking and assessing geopolitical developments and global events. Governments and intelligence agencies use OSINT to monitor international news, social media activity, and online discussions to gain insights into global trends and potential threats. OSINT can help anticipate emerging crises, assess the intentions of state actors, and enhance national security.

In summary, OSINT is a critical component of modern information gathering and intelligence analysis. Its role extends across a wide range of fields and disciplines, from academia and journalism to law enforcement, cybersecurity, and national security. OSINT's ability to harness publicly available information and transform it into actionable intelligence makes it an indispensable tool in the digital age. As we delve deeper into this book, we will explore the practical aspects of OSINT, including the tools, techniques, and methodologies used to conduct effective information gathering and analysis.

Chapter 2: Setting Up Your OSINT Toolbox

In our journey to master Open Source Intelligence (OSINT) techniques, we must familiarize ourselves with the essential tools and software that empower OSINT practitioners. These tools are the backbone of effective information gathering and analysis in the world of OSINT. Whether you're a newcomer or an experienced analyst, having the right OSINT tools at your disposal is crucial for success.

Let's start by exploring some of the fundamental software and applications that can enhance your OSINT capabilities. At the core of any OSINT operation is your web browser. While standard browsers like Chrome, Firefox, or Safari are commonly used, it's essential to equip them with extensions and add-ons tailored for OSINT work. These extensions can provide advanced features such as data scraping, search query optimization, and privacy protection.

One such extension is Maltego, a powerful OSINT and data visualization tool that enables you to explore relationships and connections among individuals, organizations, and entities. Maltego's ability to generate interactive graphs and charts from OSINT data simplifies the process of identifying key players and their associations.

For those diving into the world of domain research, WHOIS databases are indispensable. Tools like WHOIS Lookup allow you to retrieve information about domain names, including ownership details and registration history. This information is valuable for understanding the background and affiliations of websites and online entities.

When it comes to social media analysis, tools like Social Mention and Mention can help you monitor online conversations, track brand mentions, and identify trends in real-time. These tools provide insights into social media activity and sentiment analysis, making them invaluable for OSINT practitioners focused on social media intelligence.

Furthermore, geospatial analysis plays a significant role in OSINT. Tools like Google Earth and Google Maps offer geolocation capabilities, allowing you to pinpoint physical locations, track movements, and visualize data on a map. Geospatial analysis is particularly useful for understanding the geographic aspects of OSINT investigations.

For data collection and web scraping, solutions like Octoparse, Import.io, or BeautifulSoup (for Python enthusiasts) can automate the process of extracting data from websites. These tools streamline the retrieval of structured data and save time, especially when dealing with large volumes of information.

To manage the vast amount of data collected during OSINT operations, consider using note-taking and organization tools like Evernote or OneNote. These applications help you structure your findings, create research notebooks, and maintain a systematic repository of information for future reference.

When conducting in-depth analysis, data visualization tools like Tableau or Gephi can help transform raw data into visual representations. Visualizations provide a clearer understanding of relationships, patterns, and trends within the data, enhancing the overall analysis process.

For monitoring online discussions and forums, tools such as Hootsuite and TweetDeck allow you to track hashtags, keywords, and specific accounts across various social media platforms. These social media management tools facilitate real-time monitoring and engagement with online communities relevant to your OSINT objectives.

In addition to software tools, OSINT practitioners often rely on specialized search engines. Google, for instance, offers a plethora of advanced search operators that allow you to refine your queries and access more precise results. Understanding and mastering these operators can significantly enhance the effectiveness of your OSINT searches.

Now that we've explored some essential software and tools, it's important to highlight the role of online resources and communities in the OSINT ecosystem. OSINT enthusiasts and professionals often engage in forums, blogs, and social media groups dedicated to the field. These communities serve as valuable platforms for knowledge exchange, sharing tips and techniques, and staying updated on the latest developments in OSINT.

It's worth noting that the OSINT landscape is dynamic and continuously evolving. New tools, techniques, and resources emerge regularly. As an OSINT practitioner, it's essential to remain adaptable and open to experimenting with different tools to determine which ones align best with your specific needs and objectives.

In our journey through this book, we will delve deeper into the practical application of these tools and software. We will explore how to leverage them effectively for data collection, analysis, and reporting in various OSINT scenarios. By the end of our journey, you'll have a comprehensive understanding of the OSINT toolkit and how to harness its power for a wide range of purposes, from investigations and research to cybersecurity and threat assessment.

As you delve deeper into the world of Open Source Intelligence (OSINT), one of the critical aspects to consider is the configuration of your OSINT workspace. Your workspace serves as the foundation for your OSINT operations, providing the environment where you collect, analyze, and organize information effectively. In this chapter, we will explore the key elements and best practices for configuring your OSINT workspace to optimize your productivity and ensure efficient information management.

One of the first considerations when configuring your OSINT workspace is the choice of hardware. While OSINT can be conducted on various devices, including desktop computers, laptops, and even mobile devices, it's essential to select hardware that meets your specific needs. A computer with sufficient processing power, memory, and storage capacity is advantageous for handling large datasets and running resource-intensive OSINT tools and applications.

Operating system selection is another critical decision. The choice of the operating system often depends on personal preferences and the software tools you intend to use. Many OSINT practitioners prefer using Linux distributions due to their flexibility, security features, and compatibility with a wide range of OSINT tools. However, Windows and macOS also support OSINT activities, and you can configure them to meet your requirements.

The software tools you select for your OSINT operations play a pivotal role in your workspace configuration. As discussed in previous chapters, OSINT tools encompass web browsers with extensions, data scraping applications, data analysis software, geospatial tools, and more. Ensure that you have these tools installed and properly configured on your system to streamline your OSINT workflow.

Effective data management is crucial in OSINT, and your workspace should reflect this. Consider using dedicated note-taking and organization tools like Evernote, OneNote, or specialized OSINT notebooks to structure your findings, maintain source references, and create a systematic repository of information. Proper organization ensures that you can easily access and reference data during your OSINT investigations.

To enhance your workspace's functionality, consider setting up virtualization software like VirtualBox or VMware. Virtualization allows you to create isolated virtual machines (VMs) for different OSINT tasks. For example, you can have a separate VM for web scraping, another for data analysis, and yet another for online investigations. This isolation helps maintain a clean and organized workspace, preventing cross-contamination of data and applications.

Maintaining privacy and security is paramount in OSINT, particularly when dealing with sensitive or confidential information. Configure your workspace with security in mind by using virtual private networks (VPNs), encryption tools, and secure communication platforms. These measures protect your identity and data integrity while conducting OSINT activities.

An often overlooked aspect of workspace configuration is ergonomic considerations. Ensure that your workspace is set up in a comfortable and ergonomic manner. Ergonomic chairs, keyboard placement, and monitor positioning can contribute to your overall well-being during long OSINT sessions. A comfortable workspace reduces physical strain and enhances your focus and productivity.

Backup and data recovery strategies are essential components of workspace configuration. Regularly back up your OSINT data to external storage devices or cloud services to prevent data loss in case of hardware failures or unforeseen circumstances. Familiarize yourself with data recovery procedures to retrieve information in case of accidental deletions or system issues.

Furthermore, consider the integration of automation and scripting into your OSINT workspace. Scripting languages like Python and tools like AutoIt can automate repetitive OSINT tasks, saving you time and effort. By configuring your workspace to accommodate automation, you can increase the efficiency of your OSINT operations and reduce manual workload.

Collaboration is often part of OSINT projects, and configuring your workspace to facilitate teamwork is essential. Utilize collaboration and communication tools like Slack, Microsoft Teams, or encrypted messaging apps to collaborate with colleagues or share findings securely. Properly configured communication tools enhance information sharing and decision-making within your OSINT team.

In summary, configuring your OSINT workspace is a critical step in your journey to becoming an effective OSINT practitioner. Consider factors such as hardware, operating systems, software tools, data management, privacy and security measures, ergonomic setup, backup strategies, automation, and collaboration tools. Tailoring your workspace to meet your specific needs and objectives will significantly contribute to your success in the field of Open Source Intelligence. In the upcoming chapters, we will delve deeper into practical OSINT techniques and methodologies, allowing you to put your well-configured workspace to good use in real-world OSINT scenarios.

Chapter 3: Online Privacy and Ethical Considerations

In an era where our lives are increasingly intertwined with the digital world, protecting your digital footprint has become a matter of paramount importance. Your digital footprint, often referred to as your online presence, is the trail of information you leave behind while engaging with digital technologies and platforms. It includes your interactions on social media, the websites you visit, the data you share, and the digital traces of your activities.

Why is protecting your digital footprint crucial, you may wonder? Well, your digital footprint is more than just a collection of data; it's a reflection of your identity, preferences, and behaviors in the online realm. It can be a valuable resource for individuals and organizations seeking to understand you, target you with advertisements, or even exploit your personal information for malicious purposes.

One fundamental step in protecting your digital footprint is safeguarding your personal information. This includes details such as your full name, birthdate, address, phone number, and email address. Avoid sharing this information freely on public platforms unless it is absolutely necessary. Cybercriminals often scour the web for such data to engage in identity theft or phishing attacks.

Social media plays a significant role in shaping your digital footprint. The content you post, the photos you share, and the comments you make contribute to your online persona. It's essential to think twice before sharing personal or sensitive information on social media platforms. Adjust privacy settings to control who can view your posts, and be cautious about accepting friend requests or connections from unknown individuals.

Regularly review and update your social media profiles. Remove outdated or irrelevant information, and be mindful of the content you post. What you share online can have lasting consequences, and potential employers, colleagues, or acquaintances may view your online presence. Maintaining a professional and responsible online persona is key to managing your digital footprint effectively.

Your online activities, such as web searches and website visits, also leave traces. Search engines, like Google, often collect data about your search history to personalize search results and advertisements. To mitigate this, consider using private browsing modes or search engines that prioritize user privacy, such as DuckDuckGo. These measures help reduce the data that companies collect about your online behavior.

The use of cookies and tracking technologies by websites is another aspect to be aware of. Cookies are small pieces of data that websites store on your computer to remember your preferences and track your online activities. While some cookies are harmless, others can be used for tracking and profiling. You can manage and delete cookies through your browser settings to minimize their impact on your digital footprint.

Email is a common communication tool, and your email address is often used as a primary identifier for various online accounts. Protecting your email account is crucial, as it can serve as a gateway to other aspects of your online presence. Enable two-factor authentication (2FA) for your email account to add an extra layer of security. Be cautious of phishing emails that may attempt to steal your login credentials.

Your digital footprint extends beyond the personal realm; it also encompasses your professional and financial information. Secure your work-related accounts and financial accounts with strong, unique passwords. Use a password manager to help you generate and store complex passwords securely. Regularly monitor your financial statements for any unauthorized transactions or unusual activity.

Consider using virtual private networks (VPNs) when accessing the internet, especially on public Wi-Fi networks. VPNs encrypt your internet connection, making it more challenging for cybercriminals to intercept your data. They also mask your IP address, enhancing your online privacy.

Educating yourself about online threats and scams is an essential part of digital footprint protection. Stay informed about the latest cybersecurity threats and best practices. Be cautious about clicking on suspicious links, downloading unknown attachments, or sharing personal information with unsolicited contacts.

When it comes to mobile devices, apply security measures such as PINs, fingerprints, or facial recognition to lock your phone or tablet. Install security updates promptly to patch vulnerabilities that could be exploited by malicious actors. Additionally, review and adjust app permissions to limit the data apps can access.

In essence, protecting your digital footprint is about being mindful of your online activities and taking proactive steps to safeguard your personal and sensitive information. Your digital presence is a valuable asset, and by implementing these measures, you can maintain control over your online identity and reduce the risks associated with a vast and interconnected digital world.

Ethical guidelines are the cornerstone of responsible Open Source Intelligence (OSINT) practices, ensuring that OSINT practitioners conduct their activities in an ethical and responsible manner. OSINT, by its nature, involves collecting and analyzing information from publicly available sources. However, ethical considerations are paramount, as OSINT practitioners must adhere to principles that protect privacy, respect legal boundaries, and maintain the trust of the public and stakeholders.

One fundamental ethical principle in OSINT is the respect for privacy. OSINT practitioners should always be mindful of individuals' rights to privacy when gathering information. This means avoiding the collection of personal information that is not publicly available or engaging in activities that could intrude upon someone's privacy. It's essential to strike a balance between the need for information and respecting personal boundaries.

Another key ethical guideline is the principle of transparency. OSINT practitioners should be transparent about their intentions and activities when interacting with individuals or organizations. If inquiries are made, they should clearly identify themselves and the purpose of their information gathering, whenever possible. Maintaining transparency helps build trust and credibility in the OSINT community.

Respecting copyright and intellectual property rights is crucial in OSINT. Practitioners should be cautious when using and sharing information obtained from copyrighted sources. Whenever possible, attribute the source and ensure that the use of such information falls within the boundaries of fair use or other applicable legal exceptions. Unauthorized use of copyrighted material can lead to legal consequences and damage the reputation of the OSINT community.

Another ethical consideration relates to the dissemination of OSINT findings. OSINT practitioners should be responsible and consider the potential impact of the information they share. Avoiding the spread of unverified or false information is critical. Verifying the accuracy and reliability of information before sharing it is an ethical duty. Disseminating inaccurate or misleading information can have serious consequences and harm the reputation of the OSINT practitioner.

Respect for cultural and social norms is another aspect of ethical OSINT practices. Practitioners should be sensitive to cultural differences and avoid making assumptions or judgments based on cultural or social biases. Conducting OSINT in a culturally sensitive manner is essential when dealing with global issues or diverse communities.

An often-overlooked ethical guideline in OSINT involves consent. While OSINT relies on publicly available information, OSINT practitioners should be cautious about using information in a way that goes against the intent or consent of the source. For example, if an individual's social media profile is set to private, respect that choice and avoid circumventing privacy settings to access their information.

The ethical use of automation and data collection tools is also a matter of concern in OSINT. While automation can enhance efficiency, it should be used responsibly. Avoid engaging in automated activities that may disrupt websites, violate terms of service, or overwhelm servers. Responsible automation ensures that OSINT activities do not harm the availability or functionality of publicly available sources.

In OSINT, the importance of data retention and deletion cannot be overstated. OSINT practitioners should establish clear policies and practices for the retention and deletion of data obtained during their activities. Ensure that data is kept secure and protected to prevent unauthorized access or data breaches. Additionally, establish procedures for securely deleting data when it is no longer needed for legitimate OSINT purposes.

An ethical OSINT practitioner should always adhere to the law. This includes local, national, and international laws and regulations that govern information collection and dissemination. Practitioners should avoid engaging in activities that could violate applicable laws, such as hacking, harassment, or unauthorized access to restricted information.

In summary, ethical guidelines are a crucial foundation for responsible OSINT practices. They serve as a compass, helping OSINT practitioners navigate the complex landscape of information gathering while maintaining the highest standards of integrity, privacy, and respect for the rights of individuals and organizations. By embracing these ethical principles, OSINT practitioners contribute to a positive and trusted OSINT community, where the pursuit of information is balanced with ethical considerations.

Chapter 4: Basic Search Engine Techniques

Mastering effective keyword search strategies is essential in the world of Open Source Intelligence (OSINT). Keywords serve as the gateway to unlocking valuable information from the vast ocean of publicly available data on the internet. Whether you're conducting research, investigations, or monitoring online discussions, the way you craft and deploy keywords can make a significant difference in the success of your OSINT endeavors.

Understanding the power of keywords begins with recognizing that they are the terms or phrases you use to instruct search engines and databases to retrieve relevant information. These words act as queries, guiding search algorithms to identify and present content that matches your specified criteria.

When selecting keywords, it's crucial to start with a clear understanding of your objectives. What specific information are you seeking? Who or what is your target? Having a well-defined goal helps you choose keywords that are precise and relevant. For instance, if you're investigating a cyber threat, your keywords may revolve around malware names, threat actors, or indicators of compromise.

To enhance the effectiveness of your keyword search strategies, consider variations and synonyms. Different people or sources may use varying terminology to describe the same concepts. By including synonyms and alternative phrasings in your keyword list, you broaden the scope of your search and increase the likelihood of discovering relevant information. For example, if you're researching cybersecurity, include terms like "cybersecurity," "information security," and "infosec" in your keyword list.

The use of Boolean operators can significantly refine your keyword search results. Boolean operators, such as AND, OR, and NOT, allow you to combine or exclude keywords to tailor your searches more precisely. For example, using "AND" between keywords ensures that search results contain both terms, narrowing down the focus. Conversely, "OR" broadens the search by including results containing either of the specified terms. "NOT" can be used to exclude specific terms from the search, reducing irrelevant results.

Another valuable technique is the use of quotation marks around phrases. When you enclose a phrase in quotation marks, the search engine will look for that exact phrase, ensuring more accurate results. This is particularly useful when you're searching for specific names, titles, or verbatim text.

Consider the importance of wildcards and truncation in keyword search strategies. Wildcards, such as the asterisk (*) or question mark (?), can replace one or more characters within a word. Truncation allows you to search for variations of a keyword by using a symbol, often an asterisk (*), at the end of a word root. For example, searching "hack*" would yield results containing "hacker," "hacking," and "hacktivist."

Furthermore, exploring advanced search operators provided by search engines can unlock additional search capabilities. Search engines like Google offer a range of operators that allow you to refine your queries further. Operators like "site:" restrict the search to specific websites or domains, while "filetype:" narrows results to specific file types, such as PDFs or Excel spreadsheets.

Remember to adapt your keyword search strategies based on the sources you're exploring. Different platforms, websites, and databases may have their own search rules and syntax. Familiarize yourself with these nuances to maximize the effectiveness of your searches on each platform. Additionally, stay updated on changes in search algorithms and functionalities as they evolve over time.

Boolean operators, quotation marks, wildcards, and truncation are just a few of the tools at your disposal. As you become more proficient in OSINT, you'll develop a nuanced understanding of when and how to employ these techniques effectively. The key is to remain flexible and willing to experiment with different keyword combinations and search approaches.

In OSINT, time is often of the essence, and the timely discovery of information can be critical. To stay ahead, consider setting up alerts or notifications based on your keyword search strategies. Many search engines and online platforms offer alert services that can notify you when new content matching your keywords is published. This proactive approach ensures you receive real-time updates, especially in fast-paced or rapidly evolving situations.

Additionally, don't underestimate the power of iterative searches. It's rare to find all the information you need with a single search. As you gather initial results, review them, refine your keywords, and conduct follow-up searches to dig deeper. The iterative process allows you to uncover hidden gems of information that may not have surfaced in your initial search.

Lastly, consider leveraging specialized OSINT tools and platforms that are designed to streamline keyword searches. These tools often provide advanced capabilities, including deep web searches, social media monitoring, and sentiment analysis. Familiarize yourself with these tools and incorporate them into your OSINT toolkit for more comprehensive searches.

In summary, effective keyword search strategies are a fundamental skill in OSINT, enabling you to harness the vast information available on the internet. By understanding your objectives, using Boolean operators, employing quotation marks, utilizing wildcards, and adapting to different sources and platforms, you can refine your keyword searches to yield more precise and valuable results. Embrace a proactive approach with alerts, iterate your searches, and explore specialized OSINT tools to enhance your capabilities in the dynamic world of open source intelligence.

In the ever-expanding landscape of Open Source Intelligence (OSINT), precision and accuracy are paramount. To elevate your OSINT capabilities to the next level, it's crucial to master advanced search operators. These operators are like tools in your OSINT toolkit, allowing you to fine-tune your searches, uncover hidden information, and gain a deeper understanding of your subjects or topics of interest.

One of the most versatile and powerful advanced search operators is the "site:" operator. By using "site:" followed by a specific website or domain, you can narrow your search to results from that particular source. For example, if you're researching a company, using "site:companywebsite.com" will retrieve information exclusively from that company's website, helping you access official documents, press releases, and other valuable resources.

To dig deeper into a website, consider combining the "site:" operator with keywords relevant to your search. For instance, "site:companywebsite.com financial reports" will bring up financial reports specifically from the company's website. This targeted approach can save you time and provide highly relevant results.

If you're looking for specific file types, the "filetype:" operator is your ally. When you use "filetype:" followed by an extension (e.g., PDF, DOC, XLS), the search engine will return results containing files of that type. This is particularly useful when you're searching for documents, spreadsheets, presentations, or other file formats related to your OSINT objectives.

To fine-tune your search further, consider the "intitle:" operator. By using "intitle:" followed by a keyword or phrase, you instruct the search engine to look for webpages with titles that contain that specific term. For example, "intitle:cybersecurity best practices" will return results where the phrase "cybersecurity best practices" appears in the page title.

The "inurl:" operator focuses your search on web addresses (URLs) containing a particular keyword or phrase. When you use "inurl:" followed by a term, the search engine will return results with URLs that include that term. This operator can be especially valuable for OSINT investigations targeting specific website directories or sections.

For more advanced OSINT inquiries, the "related:" operator is a gem. Typing "related:" followed by a URL will yield websites that are related to the specified URL. This operator helps you discover additional sources and references connected to a particular website or topic, expanding your research horizon.

If you're seeking information within a specific timeframe, the "daterange:" operator is your ally. Using "daterange:" followed by two dates (e.g., "daterange:20220101-20220331") narrows your search to results published or updated within that date range. This is particularly useful when you need to access recent information or historical data for your OSINT activities.

To uncover specific types of content, such as discussions or forums, the "inanchor:" operator can be invaluable. By using "inanchor:" followed by a keyword, you can find webpages where the keyword appears in the anchor text of links. This operator is particularly helpful when investigating online communities or forums related to your OSINT subject.

The "cache:" operator allows you to access cached versions of webpages. When you use "cache:" followed by a URL, the search engine will retrieve the most recent cached version of that webpage. This can be useful when a webpage has been modified or taken offline, but you still need access to its content for your OSINT research.

Lastly, the "info:" operator provides a summary of information about a specific webpage. When you use "info:" followed by a URL, the search engine will display a brief overview of the webpage, including its title, description, and related links. This operator can help you quickly assess the relevance of a webpage without visiting it directly.

Incorporating these advanced search operators into your OSINT toolkit empowers you to conduct more precise, targeted, and efficient searches. By combining these operators, adapting them to your specific research goals, and exploring their full potential, you'll unlock a new level of precision in your OSINT endeavors. Keep experimenting, stay curious, and harness the power of advanced search operators to uncover valuable insights and information on the open web.

Chapter 5: Leveraging Social Media for OSINT

Understanding how to profile individuals effectively on social media is a crucial skill in the realm of Open Source Intelligence (OSINT). Social media platforms have become treasure troves of information, offering insights into the lives, interests, and activities of individuals from all walks of life. Profiling individuals on social media allows OSINT practitioners to gather valuable data for various purposes, from investigations and research to threat assessment and cybersecurity.

To begin the process of profiling individuals on social media, it's essential to select the right platforms. Different individuals may have a presence on various social media networks, so identifying which platforms your target uses is the first step. Popular platforms include Facebook, Twitter, LinkedIn, Instagram, and TikTok, among others. Each platform caters to different types of content and interactions, making it important to choose those most relevant to your OSINT objectives.

Once you've identified the social media platforms of interest, the next step is to conduct a comprehensive profile analysis. This analysis involves collecting information from the individual's social media accounts, including their profile details, posts, photos, and connections. Pay close attention to profile bios, which often contain valuable information such as names, locations, job titles, and interests.

Photos shared on social media can reveal a wealth of information. Analyze photos for clues about the individual's activities, hobbies, travels, and relationships. Facial recognition technology can assist in identifying individuals in photos and cross-referencing them with other online sources.

When reviewing an individual's social media posts, look for patterns and themes. What topics do they frequently discuss or share? Are there recurring keywords or hashtags? Analyzing the content they engage with and the communities they participate in can provide insights into their interests and affiliations.

Connections and followers are another critical aspect of social media profiling. Examine the individual's list of friends, followers, and connections. Who are they connected to, and what roles do these connections play in their life? Investigate mutual connections to uncover potential associations or networks of interest.

In addition to the content an individual shares, pay attention to their engagement with others. Review comments, likes, shares, and interactions with other users. This can help you gauge their level of activity, the nature of their relationships, and their online behavior.

Geolocation data is a valuable tool in social media profiling. Many social media posts include location tags or check-ins. Analyzing geolocation information can help determine an individual's travel history, frequented places, and potential routines.

Social media timeline analysis is a methodical approach to understanding an individual's digital footprint over time. Start by reviewing their earliest posts and progressively work your way through their timeline. This process can reveal changes in interests, affiliations, and life events.

Keep in mind that individuals may attempt to maintain different personas or use pseudonyms on social media. Be vigilant in cross-referencing information and verifying the authenticity of profiles. OSINT practitioners should be cautious about relying solely on information from social media, as it may not always be accurate or complete.

As you gather information from social media, it's crucial to maintain ethical standards and respect privacy boundaries. Avoid invasive or harmful practices, such as doxxing or harassment. OSINT practitioners should adhere to ethical guidelines and legal regulations when profiling individuals on social media.

Social media profiling can extend beyond the individual's own accounts. OSINT practitioners often explore connections and relationships to identify potential associates, organizations, or communities of interest. This network analysis can provide a more comprehensive view of the individual's online footprint.

To organize and manage the data collected during social media profiling, consider using note-taking and analysis tools. Create a structured repository of information, including profile details, posts, images, and relevant links. This organized approach streamlines the analysis process and ensures that critical data is readily accessible.

Advanced search operators, as discussed in previous chapters, can be invaluable in social media profiling. Use operators like "from:", "to:", and "mentions:" to search for specific content or interactions involving the individual of interest. These operators allow you to filter social media content for more focused analysis.

In summary, profiling individuals on social media is a multifaceted process that requires a combination of skills, tools, and ethical considerations. By selecting the right platforms, conducting comprehensive profile analyses, cross-referencing information, and respecting privacy boundaries, OSINT practitioners can gather valuable insights into the lives and activities of individuals. Social media profiling is a powerful tool for various OSINT objectives, providing a deeper understanding of subjects and their digital footprints in the ever-evolving landscape of online communication.

Analyzing social media networks and trends is a fascinating and valuable aspect of Open Source Intelligence (OSINT). Social media has become an integral part of our lives, and it serves as a rich source of information and insights into various topics, individuals, organizations, and events. In this chapter, we will explore the techniques and strategies for effectively analyzing social media networks and trends to gather valuable intelligence.

Social media networks are vast and diverse, encompassing platforms like Facebook, Twitter, Instagram, LinkedIn, TikTok, and more. Each of these platforms has unique features, user demographics, and content types. To begin your analysis, it's essential to select the relevant social media platforms that align with your OSINT objectives. For instance, Twitter is known for its real-time updates and trending topics, making it valuable for monitoring breaking news and public sentiment.

The first step in analyzing social media networks is identifying the key players or entities of interest. These entities could be individuals, organizations, influencers, or even hashtags related to a specific topic. Once you have identified the primary subjects, you can start collecting data related to their activities, connections, and interactions on social media.

One of the fundamental techniques in social media analysis is content analysis. Content analysis involves examining the posts, comments, and media shared by individuals or entities on social media. This analysis can reveal valuable information about their interests, opinions, affiliations, and activities. Pay attention to the language, tone, and sentiment expressed in their content.

Another important aspect of content analysis is sentiment analysis. Sentiment analysis tools can help you gauge the overall sentiment of social media content, whether it is positive, negative, or neutral. This information is particularly useful when monitoring public opinion, brand sentiment, or reactions to specific events.

Social network analysis (SNA) is a powerful method for examining the relationships and connections within a social media network. SNA allows you to map the connections between individuals or entities, identifying influencers, communities, and patterns of interaction. By visualizing the network structure, you can gain insights into the dynamics of information dissemination and influence within the network.

To perform social network analysis effectively, consider using network analysis tools and software that can help you create visual representations of the network. These visualizations can highlight central figures, clusters of connected users, and the flow of information within the network.

Hashtags are a prominent feature of many social media platforms, and they play a crucial role in categorizing and trending topics. Analyzing trending hashtags can provide insights into the current interests and discussions within a specific community or social media platform. Tools like hashtag tracking software can help you monitor the popularity and usage of specific hashtags over time.

Geospatial analysis is another valuable technique for social media analysis. Many social media posts include location data, such as geotags or check-ins. By analyzing geospatial information, you can gain insights into the geographic distribution of social media activity and identify trends specific to particular regions or locations.

Time-series analysis is essential when tracking trends on social media. By analyzing data over time, you can identify patterns, spikes in activity, and recurring events. Time-series analysis is particularly useful for monitoring the evolution of discussions, public sentiment, or the impact of events on social media.

Network sentiment analysis combines sentiment analysis with social network analysis. This technique involves analyzing the sentiment expressed within a social network to identify influential users or groups with specific sentiments. By understanding the sentiment dynamics within a network, you can tailor your OSINT efforts to engage with influential users or track sentiment shifts.

It's important to remember that the ethical considerations discussed in previous chapters apply to social media analysis as well. Respect individuals' privacy, adhere to platform policies, and avoid invasive or harmful practices. Always be transparent about your intentions and activities when engaging with social media content.

Social media monitoring tools and software can streamline the data collection and analysis process. These tools often offer features like data scraping, sentiment analysis, trend tracking, and customizable dashboards.

Evaluate and choose the tools that best align with your OSINT objectives and budget.

When analyzing social media networks and trends, the human element remains essential. Algorithms and tools can provide valuable data, but human interpretation and contextual understanding are crucial for making sense of the information. OSINT practitioners should possess critical thinking skills and domain expertise to derive meaningful insights from social media data.

In summary, analyzing social media networks and trends is a multifaceted process that involves content analysis, sentiment analysis, social network analysis, geospatial analysis, time-series analysis, and more. By selecting the relevant social media platforms, identifying key entities, and using appropriate analysis techniques and tools, OSINT practitioners can uncover valuable intelligence, monitor public sentiment, and track emerging trends. Social media analysis is a dynamic field, and staying informed about the latest tools and methodologies is essential for successful OSINT endeavors in the digital age.

Chapter 6: Web Scraping and Data Collection

Exploring the world of web scraping opens up a wealth of opportunities in the realm of Open Source Intelligence (OSINT). Web scraping, the process of extracting data from websites, allows OSINT practitioners to collect valuable information for research, analysis, and investigations. In this chapter, we'll delve into the tools and techniques for web scraping, equipping you with the skills to harness the power of web data.

At the heart of web scraping are web scraping tools and frameworks. These tools are designed to automate the process of collecting data from websites, making it faster and more efficient than manual data extraction. While there are numerous web scraping tools available, some of the most popular and widely used ones include BeautifulSoup, Scrapy, and Selenium.

BeautifulSoup, a Python library, is a versatile tool for parsing HTML and XML documents. It simplifies the process of navigating and extracting data from web pages. With BeautifulSoup, OSINT practitioners can easily locate specific elements, such as headers, paragraphs, or links, and extract the desired information.

Scrapy, another Python-based framework, is a powerful choice for more complex web scraping tasks. Scrapy offers a structured approach to web scraping, allowing users to define the data they want to extract by creating custom spiders. These spiders crawl websites and follow predefined rules to scrape data efficiently.

Selenium, often used for web automation, is ideal for scenarios where web scraping requires interaction with dynamic web pages. Selenium can simulate user interactions, such as clicking buttons and filling out forms, making it suitable for scraping data from websites that rely heavily on JavaScript for content loading.

When starting a web scraping project, it's crucial to understand the website's structure and the data you want to extract. This involves inspecting the website's HTML source code to identify the HTML elements containing the desired information. Web browsers, such as Google Chrome or Mozilla Firefox, offer built-in developer tools that make it easy to inspect page elements and determine their structure.

Once you've identified the target data and its location within the HTML structure, you can use web scraping tools like BeautifulSoup or Scrapy to create scripts that extract the data. These scripts typically involve specifying the HTML elements to scrape, defining data extraction rules, and storing the extracted data in a structured format.

To avoid overwhelming a website's servers and adhering to ethical considerations, it's essential to implement web scraping responsibly. Avoid aggressive scraping that could disrupt the website's performance or violate its terms of service. Implement rate limiting to control the frequency of your requests, and always check a website's robots.txt file for guidance on what can and cannot be scraped.

Authentication and handling cookies are necessary when scraping websites that require user logins or sessions. Tools like Selenium can assist in automating login processes and maintaining session cookies to access restricted content.

Proxy rotation is a technique used to hide your IP address and avoid IP bans when scraping websites that impose restrictions. By rotating through a pool of proxy servers, you can distribute your requests across different IP addresses, reducing the risk of being blocked.

Web scraping tools often support the use of user-agent headers to mimic different web browsers or devices. This can be useful when websites serve different content based on the user-agent information. Adjusting the user-agent string in your scraping requests can help you access content tailored for specific platforms.

Crawling and scraping large websites or multiple pages can be resource-intensive. To optimize your web scraping process, implement features like URL deduplication to avoid revisiting already scraped pages, and prioritize the order in which pages are crawled to collect the most relevant data first.

Data storage is a critical consideration when web scraping. Decide whether you want to store the scraped data in a local file, a database, or a cloud storage solution. Choosing the right storage method depends on the volume of data, your analysis requirements, and data retention policies.

Regularly testing and debugging your web scraping scripts is essential to ensure their reliability and accuracy. Be prepared to adapt and modify your scripts as websites undergo changes in structure or functionality.

When scraping websites, it's crucial to respect copyright and intellectual property rights. Avoid scraping and using copyrighted material without proper authorization or adherence to fair use principles.

Web scraping is a dynamic field, and staying updated on the latest tools, techniques, and legal considerations is essential for successful OSINT endeavors. Engaging with the OSINT community and forums can provide valuable insights and support for your web scraping projects.

In summary, web scraping is a powerful technique for collecting data from websites, enabling OSINT practitioners to access valuable information efficiently. By selecting the right web scraping tools, understanding website structures, responsibly implementing scraping practices, and staying informed about best practices and legal considerations, you can harness the power of web data for your OSINT activities. Web scraping opens up a world of possibilities for data-driven insights and intelligence gathering in the digital age.

Data cleaning and transformation play a pivotal role in the realm of Open Source Intelligence (OSINT) and data analysis, allowing practitioners to turn raw, noisy data into actionable insights. Imagine you've gathered a vast amount of data from various sources, including web scraping, social media analysis, and public records. While this data holds the potential to uncover valuable intelligence, it often arrives in a messy and unstructured form, riddled with inconsistencies, errors, and irrelevant information.

The process of data cleaning begins with data validation, which involves checking the integrity and quality of the collected data. This step ensures that the data is accurate, complete, and conforms to the expected format. Common data validation tasks include verifying the presence of required fields, checking data types, and identifying missing or duplicated records.

Once data validation is complete, data cleaning focuses on rectifying errors and inconsistencies within the dataset. This can involve handling missing values, correcting typos, standardizing formats, and addressing outliers. Missing values are particularly common and can distort analyses, so strategies for dealing with them are essential.

Imputation, the process of filling in missing values, is a common approach in data cleaning. Imputation methods range from simple techniques like replacing missing values with the mean or median to more complex methods like regression-based imputation or predictive modeling. The choice of imputation method depends on the nature of the data and the research objectives.

Outlier detection and treatment are crucial for maintaining data integrity. Outliers are data points that deviate significantly from the majority of the data. Identifying and addressing outliers is essential to prevent them from skewing analysis results. Common techniques for outlier detection include visualizations like box plots and statistical methods like the Z-score or the modified Z-score.

Data transformation is the next step in the data cleaning process. Transformation involves reshaping, reformatting, or aggregating data to make it suitable for analysis or modeling. One common transformation is converting categorical data into numerical format through techniques like one-hot encoding, which assigns binary values to categories. This transformation enables machine learning algorithms to work with categorical data effectively.

Normalization is another data transformation technique that scales numerical data to a standard range, typically between 0 and 1. Normalization ensures that features with different units or scales have equal influence on the analysis, preventing biases in algorithms that rely on distance measures.

Data aggregation is often required when dealing with large datasets. Aggregation involves grouping data by specific attributes or criteria and summarizing them to reduce complexity. For example, you may aggregate sales data by month or customer segment to analyze trends or identify patterns.

Data merging or joining is essential when integrating data from multiple sources. Merging combines datasets based on common identifiers or keys, such as customer IDs or timestamps. This process allows you to create a comprehensive dataset that combines information from various sources.

Data filtering is a transformation step that involves selecting a subset of the data based on specific criteria. Filtering allows you to focus on relevant portions of the data while excluding irrelevant or noisy observations. Filtering criteria can be based on values, date ranges, or other attributes.

Feature engineering is a more advanced data transformation technique that involves creating new features or variables from existing ones. Feature engineering aims to improve the performance of machine learning models by providing them with more informative input data. Techniques like polynomial features, interaction terms, and dimensionality reduction can enhance the predictive power of models.

Data standardization is important when dealing with data measured in different units or scales. Standardization scales data to have a mean of 0 and a standard deviation of 1, making it easier to compare and interpret results. Standardized data ensures that variables contribute equally to analyses like clustering or principal component analysis.

Data cleaning and transformation are iterative processes, and it's not uncommon to revisit these steps multiple times as you uncover new insights or encounter challenges during analysis. Keeping a clear and well-documented record of data cleaning and transformation steps is crucial for maintaining data lineage and ensuring the reproducibility of analyses.

In summary, data cleaning and transformation are foundational steps in the data analysis process, enabling OSINT practitioners to work with raw data effectively. These processes involve data validation, cleaning, transformation, and standardization to prepare data for analysis or modeling. Whether you're dealing with missing values, outliers, or the need to reshape and aggregate data, data cleaning and transformation are essential skills for deriving meaningful insights from messy datasets in the world of OSINT.

Chapter 7: Analyzing Publicly Available Information

In the world of Open Source Intelligence (OSINT), data analysis is the cornerstone that transforms raw information into actionable insights. OSINT practitioners gather vast amounts of data from diverse sources, including web scraping, social media monitoring, public records, and more. Yet, the true value of this data emerges through the methods and techniques employed for analysis.

One fundamental method for data analysis in OSINT is exploratory data analysis (EDA). EDA involves examining the dataset to gain a preliminary understanding of its characteristics, structure, and potential patterns. This process includes generating summary statistics, visualizing data distributions, and identifying outliers or anomalies. EDA helps OSINT practitioners form hypotheses and guides subsequent analysis steps.

Descriptive statistics are essential tools in EDA. They provide a snapshot of key summary measures, such as mean, median, and standard deviation, which offer insights into the central tendency and variability of the data. Box plots, histograms, and scatter plots are valuable for visualizing data distributions and relationships between variables.

Hypothesis testing is a critical method for drawing conclusions from data in OSINT. OSINT practitioners use hypothesis testing to assess whether observed patterns or differences in data are statistically significant or if they could have occurred by chance. Common hypothesis tests include t-tests, chi-square tests, and analysis of variance

(ANOVA). These tests help validate hypotheses and make informed decisions based on data.

Regression analysis is a powerful technique for modeling relationships between variables in OSINT. Linear regression, for example, allows OSINT practitioners to assess the linear association between a dependent variable and one or more independent variables. Regression models can be used for prediction, trend analysis, and identifying factors that influence outcomes.

Cluster analysis is employed to group similar data points together based on their characteristics or attributes. This method is useful in OSINT for identifying patterns or clusters within large datasets. K-means clustering and hierarchical clustering are common techniques used to segment data into meaningful groups.

Time series analysis is crucial when dealing with data collected over time, as is often the case in OSINT. Time series analysis methods, such as autoregressive integrated moving average (ARIMA) modeling and exponential smoothing, help OSINT practitioners uncover temporal patterns, trends, and seasonal variations in data.

Text analysis is indispensable in OSINT, especially when analyzing textual data from sources like social media, news articles, or online forums. Natural language processing (NLP) techniques, including sentiment analysis, topic modeling, and named entity recognition, enable OSINT practitioners to extract insights from unstructured text data.

Social network analysis (SNA) is a method for studying relationships and interactions within networks, such as social media platforms. SNA helps OSINT practitioners identify influential nodes, detect communities, and understand the flow of information or influence within a network.

Geospatial analysis is essential for OSINT practitioners working with location-based data. Geographic information systems (GIS) and spatial analysis techniques allow for the visualization and analysis of data on maps. Geospatial analysis is valuable for tracking events, identifying geographic patterns, and understanding the spatial context of data.

Machine learning and artificial intelligence (AI) are increasingly leveraged in OSINT data analysis. These techniques, including supervised and unsupervised learning, classification, and anomaly detection, enable OSINT practitioners to automate tasks, make predictions, and uncover hidden insights within large and complex datasets.

Data visualization is a critical component of data analysis in OSINT. Visualizations, such as charts, graphs, heatmaps, and geospatial maps, help convey complex information in a comprehensible and actionable format. Effective data visualization aids in storytelling and decision-making.

Ethical considerations are paramount in data analysis within the OSINT context. OSINT practitioners must prioritize privacy, data protection, and responsible data handling. Anonymizing data and adhering to ethical guidelines are essential to ensure the responsible use of data in OSINT.

Collaboration and knowledge sharing are valuable aspects of data analysis in OSINT. OSINT practitioners often work in teams, and sharing insights, findings, and methodologies fosters collective intelligence and enhances the quality of analysis.

Continuous learning and staying updated on the latest data analysis techniques and tools are crucial for OSINT practitioners. The field of data analysis is dynamic, with new methods and technologies emerging regularly. OSINT practitioners should invest in ongoing education and skill development to remain effective in their roles.

In summary, data analysis is the backbone of OSINT, transforming raw data into actionable intelligence. Methods such as exploratory data analysis, hypothesis testing, regression analysis, clustering, time series analysis, text analysis, social network analysis, geospatial analysis, machine learning, and data visualization are essential tools in the OSINT toolkit. Ethical considerations, collaboration, and continuous learning are integral to responsible and effective data analysis in OSINT, ensuring that practitioners can uncover valuable insights and make informed decisions in the ever-evolving landscape of open source information.

Visualizing OSINT data is like painting a picture that tells a story, a story hidden within the vast sea of information we gather from open sources. It's a journey through the world of data, where we use charts, graphs, and other graphical representations to make sense of the complex web of information at our disposal.

One of the primary purposes of visualizing OSINT data is to make it more accessible and understandable to the human mind. Our brains are wired to process visual information quickly and efficiently, so a well-crafted visualization can convey insights and patterns that might be challenging to discern from raw data alone.

Bar charts are a popular choice for visualizing categorical data in OSINT. They provide a clear and straightforward way to compare different categories or groups. Imagine you're analyzing social media mentions of various topics. A bar chart can show you which topics are most frequently discussed, giving you a quick overview of the current trends.

Line charts, on the other hand, excel at showing trends and changes over time. When monitoring the growth of a particular hashtag on social media, a line chart can reveal how its popularity has evolved, allowing you to identify spikes or declining interest.

Pie charts are ideal for displaying parts of a whole. If you're investigating the distribution of different types of online content, a pie chart can show the proportions of each content type in a visually appealing way.

Heatmaps are a versatile tool in OSINT data visualization, especially when dealing with large datasets. A heatmap can reveal patterns or concentrations within geographical data, helping you identify areas of interest or anomalies. For instance, it could be used to map the frequency of specific keywords mentioned in social media posts across different regions.

Network diagrams come in handy when visualizing relationships and connections within data. In OSINT, you might use network diagrams to depict connections between individuals, organizations, or websites. This type of visualization can help you uncover hidden networks or communities.

Word clouds are a creative way to represent textual data, such as the most frequently used words in a collection of social media posts. The size of each word in the cloud corresponds to its frequency, making it easy to spot keywords that stand out.

Geospatial maps are invaluable for visualizing OSINT data with a geographical component. They allow you to plot data points on a map, revealing geographic trends or hotspots. For example, you might use a map to show the locations of social media posts related to a specific event or incident.

Sunburst charts are a more advanced visualization technique that can display hierarchical data structures. If you're analyzing the organizational structure of a company based on publicly available information, a sunburst chart can help you visualize the hierarchy from top-level executives to lower-level employees.

Interactive dashboards take OSINT data visualization to the next level. These dynamic tools enable you to create custom dashboards that allow users to explore data interactively. Dashboards can incorporate various types of visualizations, filters, and drill-down capabilities, providing a rich and immersive data analysis experience.

Choosing the right visualization depends on the nature of your OSINT data and the insights you aim to convey. It's essential to match the visualization type with your data's characteristics and the questions you're trying to answer. A well-chosen visualization can make complex data more digestible and empower you to draw meaningful conclusions.

Data visualization tools and software make the process of creating visualizations more accessible to OSINT practitioners. Tools like Tableau, Power BI, and Python libraries like Matplotlib and Plotly offer a wide range of options for crafting compelling visuals. These tools often provide templates and customization options, allowing you to tailor your visualizations to your specific needs.

When creating OSINT data visualizations, keep in mind that clarity is paramount. Your goal is to convey information effectively, so avoid cluttered or overly complex visuals. Use appropriate colors, labels, and legends to ensure that your audience can interpret the visualization accurately.

Interpretation is a key aspect of data visualization in OSINT. While the visual representation can make patterns more apparent, it's essential to provide context and analysis alongside the visualizations. Explain the significance of the patterns or trends you've uncovered, and be transparent about the data sources and methodology used.

Collaboration and sharing are crucial when working with OSINT data visualizations. Visualizations can be powerful tools for conveying intelligence to decision-makers or colleagues. Ensure that your visualizations are shareable and accessible to those who need the insights they provide.

In summary, visualizing OSINT data is a creative and essential part of the data analysis process. Through various types of visualizations, such as bar charts, line charts, heatmaps, and interactive dashboards, OSINT practitioners can transform complex data into actionable insights. Choosing the right visualization, using appropriate tools, providing context, and fostering collaboration are key principles in the art of visualizing OSINT data, enabling practitioners to uncover the stories hidden within the data and make informed decisions in the world of open source intelligence.

Chapter 8: Geolocation and Mapping in OSINT

Geospatial analysis in Open Source Intelligence (OSINT) is like having a GPS for information, guiding you to valuable insights through the geographical context of data.

Imagine you're tracking the movements of a prominent individual through their social media posts, and you want to know where they've been and where they might be going. Geospatial analysis can help you map their activities, providing a visual representation of their locations on a map.

Geospatial analysis is all about making sense of data that has a geographic component, such as latitude and longitude coordinates. It allows you to explore patterns, relationships, and trends by overlaying data on maps and using spatial analysis techniques.

One of the fundamental tools in geospatial analysis is Geographic Information Systems (GIS). GIS software enables you to create, analyze, and visualize geospatial data. It's like having a digital mapping toolkit at your disposal.

GIS software allows you to create maps that display various types of geospatial information. For instance, you can create a map that shows the locations of social media posts related to a specific event, giving you insights into where the conversation is happening.

Spatial queries are a key component of geospatial analysis. These queries allow you to filter and extract data based on location. You can ask questions like, "Show me all social media posts within a 5-mile radius of a particular point."

Buffer analysis is another powerful technique. It involves creating a buffer, or a zone of interest, around a specific location. This can be useful when assessing the proximity of certain features or events to a particular point on the map.

Heatmaps are a popular visualization tool in geospatial analysis. They represent data density by using color gradients. For example, you can create a heatmap to visualize the concentration of online mentions related to a specific keyword across different regions.

Network analysis in geospatial context allows you to analyze relationships between geographical entities. You can use it to study transportation networks, social networks, or any other type of network where location matters.

When dealing with large datasets, spatial clustering can help identify groups of data points that are close to each other. For instance, you might use clustering to identify hotspots of criminal activity in a city based on incident reports.

Geospatial analysis extends beyond maps and GIS software. Location-based services and mobile apps also play a role. OSINT practitioners can utilize these services to collect geospatial data from mobile devices, social media check-ins, or geotagged photos.

Satellite imagery and remote sensing data are valuable sources of geospatial information. They can provide high-resolution images of geographical areas, allowing you to monitor changes in the landscape or detect anomalies.

Geospatial analysis in OSINT is versatile and can be applied to various scenarios. For instance, it can be used for tracking natural disasters, monitoring social unrest, assessing urban development, or investigating criminal activities.

Ethical considerations are essential when conducting geospatial analysis in OSINT. Privacy concerns must be respected, and data should be handled responsibly. Avoiding the identification of individuals without their consent is crucial.

GIS tools often provide the ability to create custom maps that can be shared with others. These maps can serve as powerful communication tools when presenting findings to stakeholders or decision-makers.

The integration of geospatial data with other OSINT sources is a valuable practice. Combining geospatial information with textual data, social media posts, or public records can provide a more comprehensive understanding of a situation.

Machine learning and artificial intelligence are increasingly used in geospatial analysis. These technologies can automate the detection of patterns and anomalies in large geospatial datasets, enabling OSINT practitioners to process information more efficiently.

Collaboration is vital in geospatial analysis in OSINT. Sharing geospatial data and findings with colleagues or experts in related fields can lead to more robust analysis and better-informed decisions.

Continuous learning is crucial in the field of geospatial analysis. New tools, technologies, and data sources are constantly emerging. OSINT practitioners should stay updated on the latest developments to leverage the full potential of geospatial analysis.

In summary, geospatial analysis is a powerful tool in the world of OSINT, allowing practitioners to unlock valuable insights by incorporating the geographic context of data. Whether you're tracking social media posts, monitoring events, or studying geographic patterns, geospatial analysis provides a lens through which you can see the world in a new light. With the right tools, techniques, and ethical considerations, geospatial analysis enhances the depth and breadth of open source intelligence, enabling you to navigate the information landscape with precision and purpose.

Mapping tools and Geographic Information Systems (GIS) integration are like the dynamic duo of Open Source Intelligence (OSINT), working in harmony to bring the power of location-based data analysis to your fingertips.

Imagine you're conducting OSINT research on a developing situation, and you need to visualize the locations of key events, social media posts, and relevant points of interest. Mapping tools and GIS integration can help you create interactive maps that provide a spatial context to your data.

Mapping tools are software applications or online platforms that enable you to create, customize, and share maps. These tools are user-friendly and often come equipped with a range of features to enhance your mapping experience.

One of the primary advantages of mapping tools is their ease of use. You don't need to be a GIS expert to start creating maps. These tools provide intuitive interfaces with drag-and-drop functionality, making map creation accessible to OSINT practitioners of all skill levels.

Customization is a key feature of mapping tools. You can personalize your maps by adding layers, markers, labels, and shapes. This flexibility allows you to tailor your maps to your specific OSINT research needs.

Interactive mapping is another highlight. You can embed your maps on websites, share them with collaborators, or use them in presentations. These interactive maps can enhance communication and storytelling by providing an engaging visual experience.

Geocoding is a fundamental function in mapping tools. It involves converting addresses or place names into geographic coordinates (latitude and longitude), which enables you to place data on the map accurately. Geocoding can be a game-changer when working with location-based OSINT data.

GIS integration takes mapping to the next level by combining mapping tools with Geographic Information Systems. GIS is a powerful technology that allows you to analyze, manipulate, and interpret geospatial data in-depth.

GIS integration brings spatial analysis capabilities to your OSINT toolkit. You can perform advanced spatial queries, identify patterns, and uncover hidden insights within your data. For example, you might use GIS to analyze the proximity of social media posts to specific landmarks or to calculate the density of incidents in different geographic regions.

Spatial analysis techniques, such as buffering, routing, and network analysis, become accessible through GIS integration. These techniques enable you to answer complex questions like "What's the nearest hospital to a reported incident?" or "What's the optimal route for a reconnaissance mission?"

Overlay analysis is a key feature of GIS integration. It allows you to overlay multiple layers of geospatial data to identify relationships and correlations. For instance, you can overlay a layer of social media posts with a layer of weather data to explore how weather conditions might impact online conversations.

GIS integration enables you to work with different data types, including raster data (imagery) and vector data (points, lines, and polygons). This versatility is essential when dealing with diverse OSINT data sources.

Spatial data visualization is enhanced through GIS integration. You can create thematic maps that highlight specific patterns or attributes within your data. These maps can reveal trends, hotspots, and spatial distributions that might go unnoticed in tabular data.

Geospatial intelligence (GEOINT) is a valuable application of GIS integration in OSINT. GEOINT involves analyzing geospatial data to gain insights into the physical environment, human activities, and their interactions. It's particularly useful for tracking movements, identifying facilities, and assessing terrain.

Mobile GIS applications extend the reach of GIS integration. OSINT practitioners can collect geospatial data in the field using mobile devices, geotag photos, and annotate maps in real-time. This capability is invaluable for on-the-ground data collection and reconnaissance.

Collaboration is seamless with mapping tools and GIS integration. You can share maps and GIS projects with colleagues, allowing for real-time collaboration and data sharing. This collaborative approach enhances the collective intelligence of OSINT teams.

Ethical considerations are vital when using mapping tools and GIS integration. Privacy and data protection must be respected, especially when working with sensitive location-based information. Anonymizing data and adhering to ethical guidelines are essential practices.

Continuous learning and skill development are encouraged in the realm of mapping tools and GIS integration. While these tools are user-friendly, mastering advanced GIS analysis techniques requires ongoing education and practice.

In summary, mapping tools and GIS integration are essential assets in the OSINT toolbox, enabling practitioners to harness the power of location-based data analysis. These tools provide accessibility, customization, interactivity, and spatial analysis capabilities that enhance the depth and breadth of OSINT research. By combining mapping tools with GIS integration, OSINT practitioners can unlock spatial insights, visualize data effectively, and collaborate seamlessly, ultimately empowering them to navigate the complex landscape of open source intelligence with precision and purpose.

Chapter 9: OSINT in Investigations and Research

Conducting Open Source Intelligence (OSINT) for investigations is akin to being a digital detective, using the vast sea of publicly available information as your investigative playground.

Picture this: You're tasked with unraveling a complex case involving a missing person. OSINT becomes your magnifying glass, allowing you to sift through online breadcrumbs, social media posts, and digital footprints to piece together the puzzle.

The foundation of OSINT for investigations lies in information gathering. It begins with defining your objectives and understanding the scope of your investigation. Are you looking for a person, tracking a cybercriminal, or uncovering corporate wrongdoing? Clarity in your goals is essential.

Keyword searches are your first step. They're like casting a wide net into the digital ocean, searching for mentions of relevant terms, names, or entities across various online platforms. This initial sweep helps you identify potential leads and sources.

Social media platforms are treasure troves of information. Facebook, Twitter, Instagram, and LinkedIn can reveal a person's interests, connections, and recent activities. OSINT practitioners often start their investigations by examining a subject's social media profiles.

But don't stop there. Online forums, blogs, and discussion boards are goldmines of user-generated content. They offer insights into niche communities, discussions, and opinions that can be valuable in understanding a subject's online presence.

Public records are another crucial data source. These include court records, property records, marriage and divorce records, and more. Accessing these records can provide a wealth of information about individuals, organizations, or events.

News articles and media coverage can shed light on significant events or developments related to your investigation. News sources can help you trace the timeline of an incident, understand its context, and identify key players.

Geolocation data plays a pivotal role in OSINT investigations. When people share their locations or tag themselves in photos, you can trace their movements and potentially pinpoint their current whereabouts.

Domain and website analysis is essential for uncovering online footprints. By examining domain registrations, website content, and hosting information, you can identify associations, potential threats, or malicious activities.

Whois databases are valuable tools in domain analysis. They provide information about domain owners, registration dates, and contact details, which can be crucial in investigations involving suspicious websites or entities.

Online image analysis involves reverse image searches. If you have a photo but don't know its origin or subject, you can use image search engines to find instances where the same image has been posted online, potentially leading you to relevant information.

Email addresses and communication patterns are vital elements to consider. OSINT practitioners can analyze email headers and addresses to trace communication networks, identify potential collaborators, or detect phishing attempts.

Metadata within digital files can reveal valuable information. Photos, documents, and videos often contain metadata such as timestamps, geolocation data, and device information that can provide context to an investigation.

OSINT practitioners also leverage advanced search operators to refine their queries. These operators enable you to narrow down search results and find specific types of information. For example, you can use "site:" to search within a particular website or "filetype:" to find specific file types.

The human element in OSINT investigations is irreplaceable. OSINT practitioners often engage in social engineering techniques, such as pretexting or elicitation, to gather information from individuals who may have relevant knowledge or access.

Language and sentiment analysis can help you interpret textual data. Natural language processing (NLP) tools can analyze the sentiment, tone, and context of text, which can be useful in assessing the attitudes and intentions of individuals or groups.

Link analysis involves mapping connections between entities or individuals. By creating visual diagrams of relationships, you can uncover associations, collaborations, or hidden networks.

Collaboration and information sharing are common practices in OSINT investigations. OSINT practitioners often work in teams, sharing findings, insights, and leads to piece together the puzzle collectively.

Ethical considerations are paramount in OSINT investigations. Privacy, data protection, and respect for legal boundaries must guide your actions. Avoiding unauthorized access to information and adhering to ethical guidelines are fundamental principles.

The iterative nature of OSINT investigations means that you may need to revisit and refine your search queries, expand your sources, or adjust your investigative strategy based on new information or leads.

Continuous learning is essential for OSINT practitioners. The field of OSINT is dynamic, with evolving techniques, tools, and data sources. Staying updated and honing your skills is crucial for success.

In summary, conducting OSINT for investigations is a multifaceted and dynamic process. It involves information gathering from a wide range of sources, including social media, public records, news articles, geolocation data, online images, communication patterns, and advanced search techniques. OSINT practitioners use their skills, tools, and ethical guidelines to piece together information, uncover connections, and build a comprehensive understanding of individuals, events, or entities under investigation. Collaboration, language analysis, link analysis, and adherence to ethical principles are integral to successful OSINT investigations, enabling practitioners to solve complex cases and uncover hidden truths in the digital landscape.

Research methodologies and case studies are the backbone of Open Source Intelligence (OSINT), providing a structured approach to gathering and analyzing information for a wide range of purposes.

Imagine you're tasked with investigating a potential cybersecurity breach in a large organization. Research methodologies guide your process, helping you to systematically collect, evaluate, and interpret open-source information to uncover the truth.

One of the fundamental research methodologies in OSINT is the research plan. Think of it as your roadmap, outlining the objectives, scope, data sources, and analytical techniques you'll use to achieve your investigative goals.

The research plan starts with a clear definition of your research question or problem statement. It's essential to articulate precisely what you aim to discover or achieve through your OSINT investigation.

Scope definition is the next step. You need to determine the boundaries of your research. Are you focusing on a specific aspect of a larger problem, or are you conducting a comprehensive investigation?

Data sources play a crucial role in research methodologies. OSINT practitioners leverage a diverse range of sources, such as websites, social media, public records, news articles, and geospatial data. Identifying the most relevant and reliable sources is a critical task.

Data collection methods vary depending on the nature of your investigation. Web scraping, advanced search queries, and data mining techniques are commonly used to gather information from online sources.

Archival research involves the systematic collection and analysis of historical records, documents, and data. It's often used to trace the evolution of events, entities, or individuals over time.

Content analysis is another research methodology that focuses on examining textual or visual content. It's particularly valuable when studying online conversations, social media trends, or user-generated content.

Surveys and interviews can be integrated into OSINT research methodologies to gather firsthand information from individuals or experts who possess valuable insights.

Analysis techniques are essential for making sense of the collected data. Content analysis involves coding and categorizing text or visual content to identify patterns, themes, or sentiment.

Quantitative analysis is used to quantify and measure data, such as tracking the frequency of keywords or conducting statistical analyses of trends.

Qualitative analysis involves interpreting data to gain a deeper understanding of the context, meaning, and implications of the information collected.

Case studies are a practical application of research methodologies in OSINT. They involve in-depth investigations of specific events, entities, or individuals to provide comprehensive insights and lessons learned.

Case studies follow a structured approach. They typically begin with a problem statement or research question that defines the scope and objectives of the case study.

Data collection for case studies involves gathering relevant information from various sources, including primary and secondary data. Primary data may include interviews, surveys, or firsthand observations.

Data analysis in case studies can be both quantitative and qualitative, depending on the research objectives. Researchers aim to uncover patterns, causal relationships, and underlying factors.

The presentation of findings is a critical component of case studies. Researchers use narratives, visualizations, and evidence to construct a compelling story that conveys their insights and conclusions.

Case studies often provide a rich context for understanding complex phenomena. They can be used to examine cybersecurity incidents, corporate fraud, geopolitical events, and many other subjects within the realm of OSINT.

Comparative case studies involve analyzing multiple cases to identify similarities, differences, and patterns. This approach allows researchers to draw broader conclusions and generalize findings.

Ethical considerations are paramount in research methodologies and case studies. OSINT practitioners must respect privacy, data protection, and legal boundaries when collecting and using open-source information.

Transparency is key when conducting OSINT research. Researchers should clearly document their methods, sources, and analytical processes to ensure the reproducibility and credibility of their findings.

Continuous learning and adaptation are essential in the field of OSINT research methodologies. New tools, techniques, and data sources are constantly emerging, requiring practitioners to stay updated and adapt their approaches accordingly.

In summary, research methodologies and case studies provide a structured framework for conducting rigorous and insightful investigations in the world of OSINT. These methodologies guide the research process, from defining objectives to data collection, analysis, and presentation of findings. Case studies, in particular, offer a practical application of research methodologies, allowing OSINT practitioners to dive deep into specific topics, events, or entities and extract valuable lessons and insights. Ethical considerations and transparency are integral to the practice of OSINT research, ensuring that investigations are conducted responsibly and with the utmost respect for privacy and legal boundaries. With continuous learning and adaptation, OSINT researchers can navigate the evolving landscape of information and uncover hidden truths in the digital age.

Chapter 10: Future Trends and Advanced Learning Paths in OSINT

Emerging technologies in Open Source Intelligence (OSINT) are like the latest tools in a detective's arsenal, empowering investigators and analysts to uncover information more efficiently and effectively.

Imagine being in the midst of a high-stakes OSINT investigation, and you need to sift through vast amounts of data in record time. Emerging technologies can provide you with the cutting-edge solutions to navigate this digital maze.

Artificial Intelligence (AI) is a game-changer in OSINT. Machine learning algorithms can analyze large datasets, detect patterns, and make predictions with remarkable accuracy. They can assist in sentiment analysis of social media content, automate data collection, and even recognize faces and objects in images and videos.

Natural Language Processing (NLP) is another essential component of emerging technologies. NLP enables machines to understand, interpret, and generate human language. In OSINT, NLP algorithms can be used to analyze text data, extract key information, and identify sentiment or intent behind messages.

Computer vision is transforming how OSINT practitioners handle visual content. With image recognition and object detection algorithms, computers can identify objects, people, and locations in images and videos, making it easier to extract valuable information from multimedia sources.

Machine translation technologies bridge language barriers in OSINT. They enable real-time translation of text from multiple languages, facilitating the analysis of international content and conversations on the web.

Blockchain technology has implications for verifying the authenticity of digital content. By using blockchain to timestamp and secure data, OSINT practitioners can ensure the integrity of information and prove its origin and modification history.

Big Data analytics is a cornerstone of modern OSINT. With the ability to process and analyze massive datasets, OSINT practitioners can identify trends, anomalies, and correlations that might otherwise go unnoticed.

Social media monitoring tools equipped with AI can sift through vast amounts of social media posts and conversations in real-time, flagging relevant content and potential threats. These tools can be invaluable for tracking breaking news, monitoring brand reputation, and identifying emerging trends.

Dark web analysis tools leverage AI and machine learning to monitor and investigate underground online communities. They can uncover illegal activities, track cyber threats, and help law enforcement agencies in their efforts to combat cybercrime.

Geospatial intelligence (GEOINT) is enhanced through emerging technologies. Advanced satellite imagery, remote sensing, and geolocation technologies enable more accurate mapping and monitoring of geographic locations, making it easier to track movements and assess changes in the physical environment.

Predictive analytics is a forward-looking approach in OSINT. By analyzing historical data and trends, OSINT practitioners can make informed predictions about future events, market trends, or potential threats.

Virtual Reality (VR) and Augmented Reality (AR) are opening new possibilities in OSINT training and simulation. These technologies can create immersive environments for training OSINT professionals and simulating real-world scenarios.

Automation and scripting tools are becoming more sophisticated in OSINT. OSINT practitioners can develop custom scripts and bots to automate data collection, analysis, and reporting tasks, saving time and improving efficiency.

Quantum computing is on the horizon, promising exponential increases in computational power. In the future, quantum computers may revolutionize data encryption and decryption, impacting the security and confidentiality of OSINT data.

Ethical considerations are crucial in the adoption of emerging technologies in OSINT. Privacy, data protection, and responsible use of AI and automation must be at the forefront of OSINT practices.

Interdisciplinary collaboration is encouraged in the realm of emerging technologies in OSINT. OSINT practitioners should work alongside data scientists, AI experts, and cybersecurity professionals to harness the full potential of these technologies.

Training and education are essential for OSINT professionals to stay updated on emerging technologies. Continuous learning and skill development are necessary to leverage these tools effectively.

In summary, emerging technologies are reshaping the landscape of Open Source Intelligence. From AI and machine learning to blockchain and geospatial intelligence, these technologies offer innovative solutions for collecting, analyzing, and interpreting open-source information. OSINT practitioners are equipped with powerful tools that enhance efficiency and accuracy, enabling them to tackle complex investigations and challenges in the digital age. However, ethical considerations, responsible use, and ongoing education are paramount to ensuring that these technologies are harnessed for the greater good while respecting privacy and legal boundaries. As emerging technologies continue to evolve, OSINT remains at the forefront of innovation in the world of intelligence and information analysis.

Advanced training and certification paths in Open Source Intelligence (OSINT) are like specialized roadmaps that guide you to expertise and recognition in this dynamic field.

Imagine you're passionate about OSINT and want to take your skills to the next level. Advanced training and certification can help you achieve that goal, enhancing your knowledge and credibility as an OSINT professional.

Advanced OSINT training programs provide in-depth knowledge and hands-on experience in specialized areas of OSINT. These programs are designed to build on the fundamentals, offering advanced techniques and real-world applications.

One common area of specialization is cyber threat intelligence. Advanced OSINT training in this field equips you with the skills to proactively monitor and analyze cyber threats, identify vulnerabilities, and develop threat intelligence reports.

Social media intelligence is another specialized path. Advanced training in this area delves deeper into the nuances of social media analysis, including tracking online personas, monitoring extremist content, and understanding the impact of social media on public sentiment.

Geospatial intelligence (GEOINT) offers a unique specialization. Advanced training in GEOINT focuses on advanced mapping techniques, geospatial analysis, and the integration of geolocation data into OSINT investigations. Dark web investigations are a niche specialization within OSINT. Advanced training in dark web analysis teaches you how to navigate the hidden corners of the internet, uncover illegal activities, and gather intelligence from underground communities. Advanced training in online reputation management equips you with the skills to help individuals and organizations protect their online image, mitigate online threats, and manage their digital presence effectively. Certification programs provide formal recognition of your expertise in specific areas of OSINT. These certifications are valuable for career advancement and demonstrating your commitment to excellence in the field. Certified Cyber Threat Intelligence Analyst (CCTIA) is a recognized certification for professionals specializing in cyber threat intelligence. It validates your ability to collect, analyze, and report on cyber threats effectively. Certified Social Media Intelligence Analyst (CSMIA) is a certification tailored for experts in social media analysis. It showcases your proficiency in monitoring social media trends, tracking online personas, and conducting sentiment analysis.

Certified Geospatial Intelligence Analyst (CGIA) is a certification for GEOINT specialists. It demonstrates your expertise in geospatial analysis, mapping, and the use of geolocation data in OSINT investigations.

Certified Dark Web Investigator (CDWI) is a specialized certification for professionals skilled in dark web analysis. It certifies your ability to navigate the dark web, uncover illicit activities, and gather intelligence from hidden online communities.

Certified Online Reputation Manager (CORM) is a certification for experts in online reputation management. It highlights your competence in helping individuals and organizations protect their online image and address digital threats.

Training and certification programs often require a combination of coursework, practical exercises, and examinations. They provide a structured learning path that ensures you acquire the necessary skills and knowledge.

Advanced training programs may offer hands-on experience through real-world simulations and case studies. These practical exercises allow you to apply your knowledge in realistic scenarios.

Mentorship and guidance from experienced OSINT professionals can be a valuable part of advanced training. Mentors can provide insights, share best practices, and help you navigate complex OSINT challenges.

Networking opportunities are inherent in advanced training programs. You'll have the chance to connect with fellow OSINT enthusiasts, exchange ideas, and build professional relationships that can be beneficial throughout your career.

Certification exams assess your knowledge and skills in specific OSINT areas. Achieving certification demonstrates your expertise and commitment to the field, enhancing your credibility in the eyes of employers and peers.

Continuing education is essential in OSINT, as the field is constantly evolving. Advanced training and certification programs often include ongoing learning resources and opportunities to stay updated.

Ethical considerations are central to advanced OSINT training and certification. Professionals are taught to respect privacy, adhere to legal boundaries, and use their skills responsibly and ethically.

Employers value advanced training and certifications when hiring OSINT professionals. These credentials can give you a competitive edge in the job market and open doors to exciting career opportunities.

Career advancement is a natural outcome of advanced training and certification in OSINT. You may qualify for higher-paying positions, leadership roles, or specialized positions within intelligence agencies, law enforcement, corporations, or cybersecurity firms.

In summary, advanced training and certification paths in OSINT offer specialized knowledge, skills, and recognition in various areas of the field. These programs provide in-depth expertise, hands-on experience, and formal credentials that enhance your career prospects and credibility as an OSINT professional. Whether you specialize in cyber threat intelligence, social media analysis, geospatial intelligence, dark web investigations, or online reputation management, advanced training and certification can propel your OSINT career to new heights. Continuous learning, mentorship, ethical considerations, and networking opportunities are integral to your journey as you navigate the exciting world of advanced OSINT expertise.

BOOK 2
ADVANCED OSINT STRATEGIES
MASTERING OPEN SOURCE INTELLIGENCE TECHNIQUES

ROB BOTWRIGHT

Chapter 1: Review of OSINT Fundamentals

Revisiting basic OSINT concepts is like going back to the foundation of a house to ensure it's strong and sturdy.

Think of these concepts as the building blocks upon which your OSINT knowledge is constructed, providing a solid framework for your journey in open-source intelligence.

The first fundamental concept in OSINT is information gathering. It's the art and science of collecting data from publicly available sources, which can include websites, social media, public records, news articles, and more.

Understanding the clear distinction between open-source information and classified or restricted data is essential. OSINT relies exclusively on publicly accessible information, ensuring compliance with legal and ethical boundaries.

Another crucial concept is data analysis. Once you've collected data, you need to make sense of it. This involves processing, organizing, and interpreting the information to extract meaningful insights.

Context is key in OSINT. It's not just about collecting data; it's about understanding the context in which the information exists. Context helps you assess the reliability, relevance, and significance of the data you gather.

Verification is a fundamental principle in OSINT. It's crucial to confirm the accuracy and authenticity of the information you collect. OSINT practitioners employ various techniques and cross-referencing to verify data.

Timeliness is a critical concept in OSINT, particularly in fast-paced environments. Gathering and analyzing information in a timely manner can be the difference between reacting to an emerging threat or missing a crucial opportunity.

Source credibility is paramount. OSINT practitioners must assess the reliability of the sources from which they obtain information. High-quality, reputable sources are more likely to provide accurate data.

Corroboration involves cross-referencing information from multiple sources to validate its accuracy. It's a crucial step in ensuring the reliability of the data you collect.

Critical thinking is a foundational skill in OSINT. It involves the ability to question, analyze, and evaluate information critically. OSINT practitioners must be discerning consumers of data.

Data privacy and ethics are essential OSINT concepts. Respecting individuals' privacy, complying with data protection laws, and adhering to ethical guidelines are non-negotiable principles in OSINT.

The principle of non-attribution is another critical concept. OSINT practitioners must avoid actions that could reveal their identity or intentions during investigations.

Open-source intelligence isn't limited to text-based information. Multimedia content, such as images and videos, is equally important. OSINT practitioners need to be skilled in analyzing visual data.

Geolocation is a concept that comes into play when analyzing location-specific information. Understanding geospatial data and mapping techniques is valuable in OSINT investigations.

Social media is a rich source of information in OSINT. Practitioners must be adept at navigating various social platforms, understanding their features, and extracting relevant data.

Link analysis is a concept that involves mapping connections between individuals, entities, or pieces of information. It's a powerful technique for uncovering relationships and networks.

Keyword search strategies are fundamental. Knowing how to construct effective search queries and use advanced search operators can greatly enhance your OSINT capabilities.

The dark web is a concept that OSINT practitioners must be aware of, even if they don't actively explore it. It's the hidden part of the internet where illegal activities often occur. Metadata, the hidden data within files, is a concept that plays a role in OSINT. It can contain valuable information about the origin and history of digital content. Data visualization is a technique that helps make sense of complex data. It involves creating visual representations of information to identify patterns and trends.

Information dissemination is a concept that pertains to how data is shared and spread online. Understanding how information flows can be valuable in tracking trends and assessing influence.

Information overload is a challenge in OSINT. With the abundance of data available, practitioners must develop strategies to filter, prioritize, and focus on the most relevant information.

Continuous learning is a lifelong commitment in OSINT. The field is dynamic, with evolving tools, techniques, and data sources. Staying updated is crucial to maintaining your OSINT skills.

Collaboration is an important concept in OSINT. Practitioners often work in teams, sharing findings, insights, and leads to collectively solve complex puzzles.

Real-world application is the ultimate goal of OSINT. It's about using the information and insights gathered to inform decisions, solve problems, or support investigations.

In summary, revisiting basic OSINT concepts is like revisiting the ABCs of a language. These foundational concepts underpin your proficiency in open-source intelligence, enabling you to gather, analyze, and interpret information effectively and ethically. Whether you're navigating the complexities of social media, understanding geolocation data, or ensuring source credibility, these concepts form the bedrock of your OSINT journey. As you delve deeper into the world of open-source intelligence, remember that continuous learning, critical thinking, and ethical considerations will guide you toward becoming a skilled and responsible OSINT practitioner.

Building on the foundation of OSINT knowledge involves taking your skills and expertise to the next level in this dynamic field.

Imagine your OSINT journey as constructing a sturdy house. The foundation represents the basic concepts and principles you've already learned, providing stability and support for what comes next.

One key aspect of building on the foundation is specialization. OSINT offers various specialization areas, such as cyber threat intelligence, social media analysis, and geospatial intelligence.

Specializing allows you to focus your efforts and expertise in a specific area of OSINT, becoming a subject matter expert in that domain.

Cyber threat intelligence, for example, is a specialization that delves deep into the world of online threats, vulnerabilities, and attack vectors.

As you build on your foundation, you can explore advanced techniques and tools tailored to your chosen specialization. These tools empower you to gather, analyze, and interpret information more effectively in your area of expertise.

In cyber threat intelligence, you might utilize advanced malware analysis tools, hone your skills in identifying advanced persistent threats (APTs), and understand the tactics, techniques, and procedures (TTPs) employed by cybercriminals.

Building on the foundation also involves staying up-to-date with the latest developments in OSINT. The field is ever-evolving, with new tools, techniques, and data sources emerging regularly.

Continuing education is a crucial part of building on your OSINT knowledge. It ensures you're aware of the latest trends and equipped with the most current tools and skills.

Engaging in online forums, attending conferences, and participating in OSINT communities can help you connect with fellow practitioners and experts, further expanding your knowledge base.

Another aspect of building on the foundation is developing a deeper understanding of the ethical and legal considerations in OSINT.

As you gain expertise, you'll encounter more complex scenarios that require a nuanced understanding of privacy, data protection, and legal boundaries.

Ethical dilemmas may arise in your OSINT work, and it's essential to navigate these situations with integrity and responsibility.

Building on the foundation also involves honing your critical thinking skills. OSINT often involves sifting through vast amounts of data, and being able to discern what's relevant, reliable, and significant is crucial.

You'll refine your ability to identify patterns, connections, and anomalies within the data, helping you draw meaningful insights and conclusions.

In your journey to build on the foundation, you may find opportunities for mentorship and collaboration with experienced OSINT practitioners.

Mentors can provide guidance, share their expertise, and offer insights that can accelerate your learning and growth in the field.

Collaboration with peers allows you to tackle complex OSINT challenges collectively, benefiting from diverse perspectives and experiences.

Data visualization is another skill to develop as you build on your OSINT foundation. Creating visual representations of data can make complex information more accessible and actionable.

Whether you're mapping connections between individuals and entities or visualizing geospatial data, data visualization tools and techniques can enhance your ability to communicate findings effectively.

As you build on your foundation, consider exploring advanced OSINT automation and scripting. These skills can save time and improve efficiency in data collection and analysis.

You might develop custom scripts to automate repetitive tasks, such as web scraping or data parsing, allowing you to focus on higher-level analysis.

The concept of threat intelligence feeds into building on your OSINT foundation. Understanding how to gather and analyze threat intelligence data can be invaluable for identifying potential risks and vulnerabilities.

Threat intelligence feeds provide real-time information on emerging threats and attack trends, empowering organizations to proactively defend against cyber threats.

Building on the foundation also means embracing innovation. Keep an eye on emerging technologies, such as artificial intelligence and machine learning, that can enhance your OSINT capabilities.

These technologies can automate data analysis, identify patterns, and detect anomalies at a scale that would be impossible for humans alone.

In your advanced OSINT journey, you may have opportunities to contribute to the field by sharing your knowledge and expertise.

Writing articles, giving presentations, or teaching OSINT courses can help you give back to the OSINT community and inspire others on their journeys.

Building on the foundation of OSINT knowledge is a continuous and rewarding process. It involves specialization, staying updated, ethical considerations, critical thinking, collaboration, data visualization, automation, threat intelligence, and innovation.

By embracing these aspects and continuously refining your skills, you'll become a seasoned OSINT practitioner, equipped to tackle complex challenges and contribute to the ever-evolving field of open-source intelligence.

Chapter 2: Deep Dive into Advanced Search Queries

Mastering advanced search operators is like acquiring a secret key to unlock the full potential of your online searches.

Imagine you're an explorer, and the internet is your vast, uncharted territory. With advanced search operators, you can navigate this digital landscape with precision and find the information you seek more effectively.

At its core, a search operator is a special character or command used in search queries to refine and narrow down results. These operators allow you to tell search engines exactly what you're looking for.

One of the most commonly used search operators is the "site:" operator. It restricts your search to a specific website or domain. For example, "site:wikipedia.org artificial intelligence" would only return results from Wikipedia related to artificial intelligence.

The "filetype:" operator is another handy tool. It lets you filter results based on file types. For instance, "filetype:pdf quantum computing" would yield PDF documents specifically about quantum computing.

Sometimes, you may want to find exact phrases. To do this, you can enclose your search query in quotation marks. For example, "machine learning algorithms" will retrieve results containing that precise phrase.

If you're looking for synonyms or variations of a word, you can use the tilde "~" operator. Searching for "~healthy recipes" will include results with synonyms like "nutritious" or "wholesome."

The "OR" operator, in uppercase, allows you to broaden your search. For instance, "OSINT tools OR techniques" will return results containing either "OSINT tools" or "OSINT techniques."

Searching within a specific range of numbers is possible with the double-dot ".." operator. For instance, "iPhone 12..14" will show results related to iPhone models 12, 13, and 14.

If you're interested in finding content created within a specific timeframe, you can use the "daterange:" operator. For example, "daterange:20220101-20220630 cryptocurrency" will display results related to cryptocurrency from January 1, 2022, to June 30, 2022.

The "intitle:" operator allows you to search for pages with specific words in their titles. For instance, "intitle:OSINT tools" will retrieve pages where "OSINT" and "tools" appear in the title.

To search for content that links to a particular URL, you can use the "link:" operator. For example, "link:nytimes.com" will display pages that link to The New York Times website.

In some cases, you may want to exclude specific terms from your search results. To do this, use the minus "-" operator. Searching for "machine learning -deep" will yield results related to machine learning but not deep learning.

If you want to find content from a specific location, you can use the "location:" operator. For instance, "location:Paris travel tips" will show results about travel tips specifically in Paris.

The "related:" operator helps you discover websites related to a specific URL. For example, "related:github.com" will provide a list of websites related to GitHub.

Advanced search operators are not limited to Google; they work on various search engines and websites. For instance, you can use them on social media platforms, job search sites, and academic databases.

Boolean operators, such as "AND," "OR," and "NOT," can be combined with advanced search operators to create complex queries. These operators allow you to fine-tune your search by specifying logical relationships between keywords.

Mastering advanced search operators opens up a world of possibilities for researchers, analysts, and anyone seeking precise information on the internet.

Whether you're conducting academic research, competitive analysis, or investigative journalism, these operators empower you to find data that might otherwise remain hidden in the vast digital landscape.

By leveraging these tools effectively, you can save time, reduce information overload, and retrieve highly relevant results tailored to your specific needs.

However, it's essential to practice and experiment with these operators to become proficient. Familiarity with their syntax and application will enhance your search skills and help you uncover valuable insights.

As you venture into the realm of advanced search operators, remember that the internet is a dynamic and ever-changing ecosystem. New websites, data sources, and content are continuously being created.

Therefore, staying updated on emerging search operators and trends is an ongoing endeavor. Online search engines and platforms frequently update their algorithms and features, providing users with new tools and capabilities.

In summary, mastering advanced search operators is akin to becoming a seasoned explorer of the digital realm. These operators are your compass, helping you navigate the vast sea of online information with precision and efficiency.

Whether you're conducting in-depth research, competitive analysis, or simply seeking answers to your questions, advanced search operators are invaluable tools in your quest for knowledge.

As you continue your journey, remember that practice and adaptability are key. By honing your skills and staying attuned to evolving search technologies, you'll become a master of the digital frontier, unlocking the hidden treasures of the internet with ease and expertise.

Crafting complex search queries is like being an architect, designing intricate blueprints to construct a precise and refined search experience.

Imagine you're embarking on a treasure hunt in a vast library, and you're equipped with a map of keywords, operators, and search techniques that will lead you to the buried treasure of information you seek.

Complex search queries allow you to dig deeper into the digital landscape, uncovering hidden gems of knowledge that might elude simpler searches.

At the heart of crafting complex search queries is the art of combining keywords strategically. Think of keywords as the building blocks of your query, each one contributing to the overall structure of your search.

To craft an effective complex search query, it's essential to consider the logical relationships between keywords. Boolean operators like "AND," "OR," and "NOT" are your tools for defining these relationships.

The "AND" operator narrows your search by requiring both keywords to be present in the results. For example, searching for "machine learning AND data analysis" will only yield results that contain both of these terms.

Conversely, the "OR" operator broadens your search by allowing either keyword to appear in the results. "Machine learning OR artificial intelligence" will return results that mention either of these terms.

The "NOT" operator excludes specific keywords from your search results. If you're interested in "machine learning" but not "deep learning," you can search for "machine learning NOT deep learning."

Parentheses are invaluable in crafting complex queries, helping you group keywords and control the order of operations. For instance, "(data analysis OR data mining) AND statistics" ensures that your search first looks for results containing "data analysis" or "data mining" and then narrows it down further with "statistics."

Quotation marks are your allies when you want to find exact phrases. "Natural language processing" in quotes ensures that results include that precise phrase, not individual occurrences of the words scattered throughout the text.

Wildcards and truncation characters, such as asterisks (*) or question marks (?), are powerful tools for finding variations of a keyword. "Comput* science" would return results containing "computer science," "computational science," and more.

Proximity operators let you specify the proximity of keywords within the text. "Machine NEAR/3 learning" requires "machine" and "learning" to appear within three words of each other, ensuring they're closely related in the context.

Searching within specific fields or attributes of a document is another dimension of crafting complex queries. You can use field-specific operators like "intitle:" to look for keywords only in the document title or "inurl:" to find keywords in the URL.

Numeric ranges can be defined using operators like "numrange:" to search for documents with numerical values falling within a specified range. For example, "price:numrange(100,500)" would return results for items priced between $100 and $500.

Proximity operators let you specify the proximity of keywords within the text. "Machine NEAR/3 learning" requires "machine" and "learning" to appear within three words of each other, ensuring they're closely related in the context.

Searching within specific fields or attributes of a document is another dimension of crafting complex queries. You can use field-specific operators like "intitle:" to look for keywords only in the document title or "inurl:" to find keywords in the URL.

Numeric ranges can be defined using operators like "numrange:" to search for documents with numerical values falling within a specified range. For example, "price:numrange(100,500)" would return results for items priced between $100 and $500.

Geolocation-based searches are powerful for finding information tied to specific locations. You can use location-based operators to narrow down results by region, city, or even coordinates.

Language-specific searches are valuable when you want information in a particular language. You can use language operators to filter results based on language preferences.

Combining these various techniques and operators enables you to craft complex search queries tailored to your specific needs. Whether you're conducting academic research, market analysis, or investigative journalism, these queries empower you to uncover rich and relevant information.

As you refine your skills in crafting complex search queries, keep in mind that practice makes perfect. Experiment with different combinations of keywords, operators, and techniques to see how they affect your search results.

Also, be aware that search engines and databases may have their own syntax and rules for complex queries. Familiarize yourself with the specific guidelines of the platform you're using to maximize your search effectiveness.

In summary, crafting complex search queries is a skill that opens doors to a wealth of information on the internet. By strategically combining keywords, operators, and techniques, you become a digital architect, designing queries that yield precise and tailored results.

Whether you're seeking answers to intricate questions, conducting thorough research, or uncovering hidden insights, mastering the art of crafting complex search queries empowers you to navigate the vast digital landscape with finesse and precision.

Chapter 3: Targeted Information Gathering

Precision techniques for data collection are like finely crafted tools in the hands of a skilled artisan, allowing you to gather valuable information with accuracy and efficiency.

Imagine you're embarking on a quest to collect data in a vast and intricate landscape. The techniques you employ will determine the quality and reliability of the data you acquire.

At the heart of precision data collection is the understanding that data is the lifeblood of analysis, decision-making, and problem-solving. Collecting data haphazardly or without care can lead to inaccurate conclusions and flawed insights.

One fundamental aspect of precision data collection is defining clear objectives. Before you start collecting data, you must have a clear understanding of what you aim to achieve and the specific information you need.

Imagine you're conducting a market research study. Your objectives might include understanding consumer preferences, evaluating market trends, or assessing competitor performance.

With well-defined objectives, you can tailor your data collection techniques to gather the most relevant and valuable information.

Selecting the right data sources is another critical consideration. Depending on your objectives, you might collect data from primary sources, such as surveys, interviews, or observations, or from secondary sources, like databases, reports, or existing records.

For instance, if you're studying customer satisfaction, conducting surveys and interviews with actual customers can provide primary data directly from the source.

Data collection methods should align with your objectives and sources. Surveys and questionnaires are effective for gathering structured data from a large number of respondents, while interviews allow for in-depth insights through open-ended questions.

Observational techniques involve watching and recording behaviors, which can be useful in fields like anthropology, psychology, and marketing.

Precision data collection also involves designing data collection instruments. If you're using surveys or questionnaires, crafting well-structured questions is crucial.

Questions should be clear, unambiguous, and relevant to your objectives. They should avoid leading or biased language that could influence respondents' answers.

Consider a survey question about smartphone preferences. Instead of asking, "Don't you think the latest model is the best?" you could ask, "Which smartphone features do you value most when choosing a device?"

Sampling techniques play a vital role in precision data collection, especially when dealing with large populations. Sampling allows you to collect data from a subset of the population while still drawing valid conclusions about the whole.

Random sampling, stratified sampling, and cluster sampling are some of the methods you can use to ensure your sample is representative and unbiased.

Data collection instruments can be administered in various ways, such as face-to-face interviews, telephone surveys, online questionnaires, or mailed forms. The choice of administration method depends on factors like accessibility, cost, and respondent preferences.

For instance, if you're conducting a nationwide customer satisfaction survey, an online questionnaire might be a cost-effective and convenient option.

Precision data collection also requires careful consideration of data quality. Data quality assurance involves validation checks, error detection, and measures to minimize inaccuracies.

Imagine you're collecting data on financial transactions. To ensure accuracy, you might implement validation rules to flag entries with suspicious amounts or irregular dates.

Data collection is not limited to numerical data. Qualitative data, such as text, images, or audio, can provide valuable insights. If you're analyzing customer reviews, sentiment analysis tools can help categorize and quantify qualitative data.

Precision data collection also involves ensuring ethical and legal compliance. Protecting respondents' privacy, obtaining informed consent, and adhering to data protection regulations are essential considerations.

If you're conducting research involving human subjects, like medical trials or psychological studies, ethical review boards may need to approve your data collection methods.

Data collection tools and software can streamline the process, making it more efficient and accurate. From survey platforms to data entry software, leveraging technology can enhance precision.

If you're conducting online surveys, tools like SurveyMonkey or Google Forms provide user-friendly interfaces and data analysis capabilities.

Furthermore, data collection should be systematic and well-documented. Keeping detailed records of your methods, procedures, and data sources ensures transparency and replicability.

Imagine you're conducting a scientific experiment. A comprehensive lab notebook detailing every step, from sample preparation to data recording, is essential for other researchers to validate your findings.

Continuous monitoring and quality control during data collection are crucial. If you're conducting a longitudinal study, regular checks and audits can help identify and rectify issues before they compromise the data.

Precision data collection extends to data entry and validation processes. Implementing double data entry, where two independent operators enter the same data and discrepancies are resolved, can minimize errors.

Data cleaning involves identifying and correcting errors, inconsistencies, and outliers in your dataset. Statistical software like R or Python can help automate data cleaning tasks.

While precision data collection emphasizes accuracy and reliability, it's also important to consider the timeliness of data collection. In some cases, waiting too long to collect data can render it less relevant or outdated.

For instance, if you're tracking social media trends, timely data collection ensures you capture real-time conversations and sentiment.

Lastly, consider data storage and security. Protecting your collected data from unauthorized access or loss is paramount.

Data encryption, secure servers, and regular backups are some measures to safeguard your valuable information.

In summary, precision data collection is a meticulous process that requires careful planning, clear objectives, appropriate sources, well-designed instruments, effective sampling, data quality assurance, ethical considerations, technology integration, systematic documentation, continuous monitoring, and security measures.

By mastering the art of precision data collection, you ensure that the information you gather is not just data but a valuable resource that can lead to informed decisions, meaningful insights, and a deeper understanding of the world around you.

Crafting customized data gathering strategies is akin to tailoring a suit, ensuring a perfect fit for your specific information needs.

Imagine you have unique research objectives or business goals, and off-the-shelf data sources and collection methods may not fully address them.

In such cases, customization becomes the key to unlocking valuable insights, enabling you to collect data that is precisely aligned with your requirements.

The journey of designing customized data gathering strategies begins with a clear understanding of your objectives.

Whether you're conducting market research, academic studies, or competitive analysis, defining your goals and the specific data you seek is the foundational step.

Consider a scenario where you're launching a new product and want to understand your target audience better.

Your objectives might include gathering demographic data, identifying consumer preferences, and assessing market trends related to your product category.

With these objectives in mind, you can start crafting a strategy tailored to your needs.

One essential aspect of customization is choosing the right data sources. Depending on your objectives, you might draw data from internal sources, external databases, publicly available information, or a combination of these.

For example, if you're analyzing customer behavior for an e-commerce platform, internal transaction records and user interactions data could be valuable sources.

However, for a broader market analysis, you might integrate external sources like industry reports, government statistics, or third-party data providers.

The granularity of data is another consideration. Customization allows you to define the level of detail you need.

If you're conducting a regional market analysis, you may want data broken down by cities or even neighborhoods, rather than just at the national level.

The timing of data collection is also crucial. Some research requires real-time or near-real-time data, while other projects can be satisfied with historical data.

For instance, monitoring social media trends might necessitate real-time data gathering, while historical sales data analysis could use past quarterly reports.

Choosing the right data collection methods aligns with your objectives and data sources. Surveys, interviews, observations, web scraping, and sensor data are just a few examples of data collection methods.

Customization allows you to select methods that fit your specific research context. For instance, if you're studying user behavior on a website, you might use web analytics tools to gather data about page views, click-through rates, and user paths.

Survey design is another critical aspect of customization. Crafting tailored survey questions that address your research objectives ensures you collect relevant and actionable data.

Imagine you're conducting a survey to assess employee satisfaction. Customized questions could focus on aspects like work-life balance, job security, and career growth opportunities, which are particularly relevant to your organization.

Customized data gathering strategies also offer flexibility in terms of sampling techniques. Depending on your goals, you can choose probability or non-probability sampling methods.

For example, if you want to generalize survey results to a larger population, probability sampling ensures every member of the population has a known chance of being included in the sample.

Non-probability sampling, on the other hand, is useful when you have specific subgroups you want to target.

Consider a scenario where you're conducting a political poll. If you want to ensure representation from various demographic groups, non-probability quota sampling can be customized to your needs.

Quality control mechanisms are integral to customized data gathering. Implementing validation checks, data cleaning processes, and error detection protocols ensures the data collected is accurate and reliable.

If you're collecting data from multiple sources, data integration becomes a crucial step. Customization allows you to design data integration strategies that combine information from various datasets cohesively.

For instance, if you're analyzing global market trends, integrating data from different countries, currencies, and time zones requires a customized approach.

Customized data gathering strategies also extend to ethical considerations. Ensuring compliance with data protection regulations, obtaining informed consent from participants, and protecting sensitive information are essential aspects of customization.

Imagine you're conducting a healthcare study. Customized data gathering strategies would include stringent privacy measures to safeguard patients' medical records and personal data.

Technology plays a significant role in customized data gathering. Leveraging data collection tools, software, and platforms tailored to your needs can streamline the process.

For instance, if you're conducting online surveys, customization allows you to choose survey platforms that offer advanced features like skip logic, branching, and customized reporting.

Furthermore, customization extends to data analysis techniques. Depending on your objectives, you can choose from a wide range of statistical, machine learning, or qualitative analysis methods.

For example, if you're analyzing customer reviews for sentiment analysis, customized machine learning models can be trained to identify nuances specific to your industry.

Iterative refinement is an inherent part of customization. As you collect and analyze data, you may discover new insights or refined objectives, prompting adjustments to your data gathering strategies.

Customization ensures flexibility to adapt and fine-tune your approach along the way.

Finally, communication and reporting are vital in customized data gathering. Tailoring your findings and insights to your audience, whether it's stakeholders, clients, or research peers, ensures the data collected is actionable and meaningful.

Imagine you're presenting research findings to a business executive. Customization involves highlighting key metrics and insights relevant to their decision-making.

In summary, customized data gathering strategies are like personalized journeys to knowledge discovery. They empower you to collect data that precisely aligns with your objectives, sources, granularity, timing, methods, questions, sampling, quality control, ethical considerations, technology, analysis, refinement, and communication.

By customizing your approach, you ensure that the data you collect is not only relevant but also a powerful tool for informed decision-making, innovation, and a deeper understanding of the subject matter.

Chapter 4: Advanced Social Media Analysis

In-depth social media profiling is akin to becoming a digital detective, delving into the online personas and behaviors of individuals and organizations.

Imagine you're embarking on an investigative journey, where the digital footprints left on social media platforms hold clues, insights, and revelations waiting to be discovered.

At its core, in-depth social media profiling involves a meticulous examination of social media accounts, posts, comments, connections, and interactions.

The goal is to gain a comprehensive understanding of the profiled entity, whether it's a person, a company, a brand, or even a political organization.

To embark on this journey, you must choose the right tools and techniques tailored to your profiling objectives.

Consider a scenario where you're conducting background checks on potential employees. In-depth social media profiling would involve a deep dive into their online presence to assess their professionalism, behavior, and alignment with your company's values.

One of the foundational aspects of in-depth profiling is the selection of social media platforms for examination. Different platforms cater to various demographics, interests, and purposes.

If you're profiling a technology enthusiast, platforms like GitHub, Stack Overflow, or Reddit may offer valuable insights into their interests and contributions within the tech community.

For a broader understanding of an individual's online persona, platforms like Facebook, Twitter, LinkedIn, and

Instagram are commonly examined due to their widespread use.

The examination process begins with the collection of digital breadcrumbs. This entails gathering information from the target's social media profiles, including profile pictures, usernames, biographies, and any publicly available posts.

Imagine you're researching a public figure for a news story. In-depth social media profiling would start with collecting information such as their Twitter handle, LinkedIn profile, and any recent tweets or posts related to the story.

Keyword analysis is a fundamental component of in-depth profiling. By identifying and analyzing specific keywords or phrases used by the target, you can uncover their interests, affiliations, and sentiments.

Consider a scenario where you're investigating a political candidate. Analyzing their social media posts for keywords related to policy positions, campaign slogans, or party affiliations can provide valuable insights into their political stance.

Social network analysis is another dimension of in-depth profiling. It involves mapping the connections and interactions within a target's social media network.

For instance, if you're researching a business competitor, mapping their LinkedIn connections and identifying mutual contacts can shed light on potential partnerships, collaborations, or shared business interests.

Content analysis plays a pivotal role in uncovering insights from social media profiles. It involves examining the type of content shared by the target, including text, images, videos, and links.

If you're profiling a lifestyle influencer, content analysis would delve into their Instagram posts, assessing the themes, aesthetics, and brand partnerships present in their visual content.

Sentiment analysis is particularly valuable for understanding public opinion and sentiment toward the target. By analyzing comments and reactions to their social media posts, you can gauge the general sentiment of their audience.

For example, if you're analyzing a company's social media presence, sentiment analysis can reveal how customers perceive the company's products and services based on online discussions and comments.

Behavioral analysis involves scrutinizing the target's online behavior, including posting frequency, engagement patterns, and response times.

If you're researching a customer support account for a brand, behavioral analysis can reveal how quickly and effectively the account responds to customer inquiries, providing insights into the brand's customer service quality.

Visual analysis is essential when profiling entities that heavily rely on visual content. It entails dissecting images and videos for hidden information, such as location tags, facial recognition, and object recognition.

For example, if you're investigating a travel blogger, visual analysis can reveal the destinations they frequent, their preferred photography styles, and their travel companions.

Geolocation tracking is a powerful technique for in-depth profiling. It involves identifying the physical locations associated with the target's social media posts.

Imagine you're researching a suspected criminal. Geolocation tracking can help you pinpoint the locations where their social media posts were made, potentially aiding law enforcement in tracking their movements.

Anonymity and pseudonymity are challenges in in-depth social media profiling. Some individuals or entities may hide behind fake identities or anonymous accounts.

If you're profiling an anonymous whistleblower, unraveling their true identity and motivations can be a complex endeavor that may require advanced investigative techniques.

Ethical considerations are paramount in in-depth social media profiling. Respecting privacy, adhering to terms of service of social media platforms, and obtaining informed consent when necessary are fundamental principles.

If you're profiling a victim of cyberbullying, ethical considerations would require you to handle their social media data with sensitivity and empathy, taking care not to expose them to further harm.

Customization is key in in-depth social media profiling. Tailoring your approach and techniques to match the profiled entity's characteristics and objectives ensures the relevance and accuracy of your findings.

For instance, if you're profiling a tech startup for a potential investment, your approach would focus on assessing their online reputation, market positioning, and investor relations.

Lastly, communication and reporting are vital aspects of in-depth social media profiling. Presenting your findings clearly and concisely to your intended audience, whether it's a client, a newsroom, or a law enforcement agency, ensures that the insights you've uncovered can be put to effective use.

In summary, in-depth social media profiling is an art and science that involves meticulous examination, keyword analysis, social network analysis, content analysis, sentiment analysis, behavioral analysis, visual analysis, geolocation tracking, anonymity challenges, ethical considerations, customization, and effective communication.

By mastering the techniques and principles of in-depth profiling, you become a digital investigator capable of uncovering hidden insights, untangling complex online personas, and revealing the stories concealed within the digital realm.

Behavioral analysis and sentiment monitoring are like the twin pillars of understanding the human element within the vast ocean of data generated by online interactions.

Imagine you're standing at the shore of a digital sea, and you want to navigate the waves of emotions, behaviors, and sentiments expressed by people in the virtual world.

At its essence, behavioral analysis seeks to decode the patterns, actions, and reactions of individuals or groups as they engage with digital platforms, while sentiment monitoring aims to gauge the emotional undercurrents that flow through the digital landscape.

Let's dive into the depths of these two intertwined concepts, starting with behavioral analysis.

Behavioral analysis involves the systematic examination of how individuals or entities interact with online platforms, websites, or applications.

Imagine you're a web developer, and you want to improve user experience on your e-commerce site. Behavioral analysis would entail tracking and analyzing how visitors navigate your website, where they click, what they search for, and where they drop off during the checkout process.

One of the key tools in behavioral analysis is user tracking. It allows you to collect data on user activities, such as page views, clicks, mouse movements, and the time spent on each page.

For instance, if you're optimizing an e-learning platform, user tracking can reveal which lessons students find most engaging, where they struggle, and which parts of the course they tend to revisit.

Heatmaps are another valuable tool in behavioral analysis. They provide visual representations of user interactions, highlighting which areas of a webpage receive the most attention and engagement.

Consider you're managing a news website. Heatmaps can show which sections of an article readers focus on, allowing you to optimize content placement and design for maximum engagement.

A/B testing is a method often used in behavioral analysis. It involves comparing two or more versions of a webpage or application to determine which one performs better in terms of user behavior, such as click-through rates or conversion rates.

For example, if you're an e-commerce retailer, A/B testing can help you decide which product page layout leads to higher purchase rates.

Conversion funnels play a crucial role in understanding user behavior. They visualize the steps users take to complete specific actions, such as signing up for a newsletter or making a purchase.

Imagine you run a subscription-based service. Analyzing the conversion funnel for sign-ups can help identify bottlenecks in the process, allowing you to streamline it for a smoother user experience.

Now, let's transition to sentiment monitoring, which focuses on the emotional tone and sentiments expressed in online content.

Sentiment monitoring employs natural language processing (NLP) techniques to analyze text data from various sources, such as social media posts, customer reviews, or news articles.

Imagine you're a brand manager, and you want to understand how customers perceive your product. Sentiment monitoring would involve analyzing customer reviews to gauge whether they are positive, negative, or neutral.

Sentiment analysis tools utilize algorithms to assess the emotional context within text. They can categorize sentiments as joy, anger, sadness, or other emotions, providing a nuanced understanding of how people feel.

For instance, if you're tracking public sentiment about a new policy, sentiment analysis can help you identify not only whether people are generally positive or negative about it but also the specific emotions driving their opinions.

Topic modeling is a technique often combined with sentiment monitoring. It uncovers the main themes or topics within a large set of text data, allowing you to pinpoint the subjects that trigger certain sentiments.

Consider you're a social media manager for a political campaign. Topic modeling can reveal which campaign issues generate the most passionate positive or negative reactions from voters.

Social listening tools are valuable in sentiment monitoring. They allow you to track mentions of specific keywords or phrases across social media platforms and monitor the associated sentiments.

Imagine you're a public relations specialist, and you want to assess the public's perception of a recent corporate crisis. Social listening can help you gauge how the crisis is affecting public sentiment and identify areas that require reputation management.

Emotion detection is a specialized area within sentiment monitoring. It focuses on identifying and quantifying specific emotions expressed in text data.

For example, if you're a market researcher studying customer feedback, emotion detection can help you categorize responses as joy, frustration, disappointment, or satisfaction, enabling a deeper understanding of customer sentiment.

Sentiment monitoring also extends to real-time sentiment tracking during events or product launches. By monitoring social media conversations in real-time, you can gauge immediate reactions and adjust your strategies accordingly.

Imagine you're launching a new tech gadget. Real-time sentiment monitoring can help you quickly identify any issues or concerns raised by early adopters and address them promptly.

Ethical considerations are paramount in both behavioral analysis and sentiment monitoring. Respecting user privacy, obtaining consent when necessary, and adhering to data protection regulations are fundamental principles.

If you're an educational institution conducting behavioral analysis on students' online interactions, ethical considerations would involve obtaining informed consent from students and ensuring data security.

In summary, behavioral analysis and sentiment monitoring are like the twin lenses through which we can gain insight into the digital world's complex human behaviors and emotions.

By applying behavioral analysis techniques like user tracking, heatmaps, A/B testing, conversion funnels, and sentiment monitoring tools such as NLP, topic modeling, social listening, emotion detection, and real-time tracking, we can navigate the digital landscape with greater clarity.

Ethical considerations are our compass, ensuring that we conduct these analyses with integrity, transparency, and respect for privacy, thereby harnessing the power of data to make informed decisions, enhance user experiences, and gain a deeper understanding of the ever-evolving digital realm.

Chapter 5: Dark Web Exploration and Monitoring

Navigating the dark web safely is akin to embarking on a journey through uncharted territories, where anonymity reigns, and the hidden corners of the internet conceal both opportunities and risks.

Imagine you're stepping into a digital realm where conventional search engines dare not tread, and encrypted networks obscure the identities of users.

At its core, the dark web is a part of the internet that is intentionally hidden and inaccessible through standard web browsers and search engines.

Consider the surface web, where you access websites through common search engines like Google or Bing, and contrast it with the deep web, which comprises web pages that aren't indexed by search engines but are still accessible through direct links or login credentials.

The dark web goes a step further by residing on encrypted networks like Tor (The Onion Router) and requiring specialized software for access.

Tor, designed to protect users' privacy and anonymity, routes internet traffic through a series of volunteer-operated servers, making it challenging for anyone to trace your online activities back to your physical location or identity.

Now, let's explore the essential principles of navigating the dark web safely.

The first and foremost rule is anonymity. When accessing the dark web, it's crucial to maintain your anonymity to protect your identity and privacy.

Imagine you're an investigative journalist researching sensitive topics. Anonymity ensures that your online activities remain untraceable, allowing you to gather information without fear of retribution.

To achieve anonymity, you must use the Tor network or similar anonymizing services. These tools conceal your IP address and encrypt your internet traffic, making it nearly impossible for anyone to trace your online activities back to you.

The second principle is discretion. The dark web is rife with illegal activities, from black markets and hacking forums to cybercriminal enterprises. Therefore, it's vital to exercise discretion and caution when exploring this realm.

For instance, if you're a cybersecurity professional conducting research on dark web threats, discretion helps you avoid attracting unwanted attention from malicious actors.

While the dark web has legitimate uses, such as providing a platform for whistleblowers and activists to communicate securely, it also harbors illegal activities. As a responsible user, it's essential to stay on the right side of the law.

The third principle is secure communication. When interacting on the dark web, communication must be encrypted and secure to protect your conversations from eavesdropping.

Imagine you're a human rights activist coordinating efforts with colleagues in repressive regimes. Secure communication ensures that your messages remain confidential and shielded from surveillance.

End-to-end encrypted messaging services like Signal or secure email providers like ProtonMail are indispensable for maintaining secure communication on the dark web.

The fourth principle is cautious exploration. Navigating the dark web requires a healthy dose of caution and skepticism.

Imagine you're a cybersecurity researcher exploring dark web forums. Cautious exploration means verifying information from multiple sources and avoiding interactions that could lead to compromising your security or privacy.

The dark web is a vast and complex ecosystem, encompassing a wide range of websites, forums, and marketplaces. It's essential to approach each encounter with a critical eye and an understanding of the potential risks involved.

The fifth principle is secure transactions. If you engage in any financial transactions on the dark web, such as purchasing goods or services, it's vital to use cryptocurrencies like Bitcoin to maintain anonymity.

Consider you're a journalist seeking access to confidential documents. Secure transactions ensure that your financial activities can't be traced back to you, protecting both your identity and your sources.

Cryptocurrencies offer a level of anonymity not provided by traditional payment methods, making them the preferred choice for conducting transactions in the dark web's marketplace.

The sixth principle is caution with downloads. When downloading files from the dark web, exercise extreme caution to avoid malware or malicious software that could compromise your device.

Imagine you're a cybersecurity analyst researching malware trends. Caution with downloads involves using virtual machines or sandbox environments to analyze potentially dangerous files without risking your main computer's security.

By isolating and testing downloads in controlled environments, you can safeguard your device against potential threats.

The seventh principle is continuous vigilance. Navigating the dark web safely is an ongoing process that requires constant vigilance and staying updated on the latest security measures and threats.

Consider you're a law enforcement officer tracking down cybercriminals on the dark web. Continuous vigilance ensures that you remain ahead of the curve and can adapt to new challenges and emerging risks.

Dark web marketplaces, forums, and websites are constantly evolving, making it essential to stay informed and adapt your security practices accordingly.

The eighth principle is ethical considerations. While anonymity and privacy are critical on the dark web, ethical considerations should always guide your actions.

Imagine you're an academic researcher studying online communities on the dark web. Ethical considerations involve respecting the privacy and rights of individuals you encounter, even in this hidden digital space.

Responsible exploration of the dark web means not engaging in or supporting illegal activities and respecting the boundaries of privacy and security.

In summary, navigating the dark web safely requires a combination of anonymity, discretion, secure communication, cautious exploration, secure transactions, caution with downloads, continuous vigilance, and ethical considerations.

By adhering to these principles, you can unlock the potential of the dark web for legitimate purposes while safeguarding your identity, privacy, and security. Whether you're a journalist, activist, researcher, or cybersecurity professional, the dark web can be a valuable resource when approached with responsibility and care.

Real-time monitoring and threat assessment form the dynamic backbone of any effective cybersecurity strategy, akin to a vigilant guardian standing watch over the digital realm.

Imagine you're the captain of a ship navigating treacherous waters, and real-time monitoring is your radar, while threat assessment is your compass, guiding you through ever-changing conditions.

At its essence, real-time monitoring involves the continuous observation and analysis of network, system, and application data to promptly identify abnormal or suspicious activities.

Consider you're the IT manager of a multinational corporation, and real-time monitoring ensures that your organization's critical systems and data are safeguarded against emerging threats.

Real-time monitoring tools and technologies collect data from various sources, such as network traffic, server logs, and endpoint devices, to provide a comprehensive view of an organization's digital landscape.

Imagine you're responsible for maintaining the cybersecurity of a financial institution. Real-time monitoring tools would scrutinize network traffic for unusual patterns, detect unauthorized access attempts, and alert you to any anomalies.

One of the key elements of real-time monitoring is intrusion detection. Intrusion detection systems (IDS) are like vigilant sentinels, continuously scanning for signs of unauthorized access or malicious activities.

Consider you're the CISO of a healthcare organization, and intrusion detection is your first line of defense against cyberattacks aimed at stealing patient data. IDS would raise an alarm if it detects any suspicious activity, such as an attempted breach of sensitive medical records.

Anomaly detection is another facet of real-time monitoring. It involves the identification of deviations from established baselines or normal behaviors within a network or system.

Imagine you're the cybersecurity analyst for a tech startup. Anomaly detection tools would alert you if there's an unusual surge in data traffic, which might indicate a distributed denial of service (DDoS) attack or a breach attempt.

Behavior-based monitoring focuses on tracking the behavior of users, devices, or applications within an organization's network.

For instance, if you're managing the cybersecurity of a manufacturing facility, behavior-based monitoring would scrutinize the activities of connected machines to detect any deviations that could indicate tampering or malfunction.

Log analysis plays a pivotal role in real-time monitoring. It involves sifting through vast amounts of log data generated by various systems, applications, and devices to pinpoint security incidents or irregularities.

Consider you're the head of IT security for an e-commerce platform. Log analysis would help you detect any suspicious login attempts, unauthorized changes to product listings, or unusual transactions in real-time.

Threat intelligence feeds are essential in real-time monitoring. These feeds provide up-to-date information on emerging threats, vulnerabilities, and attack patterns.

Imagine you're the cybersecurity manager for a government agency. Threat intelligence feeds would keep you informed about the latest cyber threats, enabling you to proactively adapt your defenses and respond to imminent dangers.

Automated alerting mechanisms are a critical component of real-time monitoring. These mechanisms promptly notify cybersecurity teams or administrators when suspicious activities or security incidents are detected.

Consider you're the security operations center (SOC) manager for a financial institution. Automated alerts would notify your team in real-time if a breach attempt is detected, allowing for swift response and mitigation.

Now, let's delve into the realm of threat assessment, which involves the continuous evaluation and analysis of potential threats to an organization's digital assets and infrastructure.

Threat assessment encompasses a wide range of activities, from identifying vulnerabilities and weaknesses to analyzing the potential impact of specific threats.

Imagine you're the chief risk officer for a telecommunications company. Threat assessment is your compass, helping you navigate the ever-evolving threat landscape to protect critical infrastructure.

Vulnerability assessment is a crucial aspect of threat assessment. It involves identifying weaknesses, misconfigurations, or gaps in an organization's network, systems, or applications.

For instance, if you're responsible for the cybersecurity of an e-banking platform, vulnerability assessment would identify weak points in the system that could be exploited by attackers to gain unauthorized access.

Risk analysis goes hand in hand with threat assessment. It involves evaluating the likelihood and potential impact of specific threats to prioritize mitigation efforts.

Consider you're the IT director for an educational institution. Risk analysis would help you determine the potential consequences of a data breach, allowing you to allocate resources to address the most critical vulnerabilities.

Threat modeling is a proactive approach to threat assessment. It involves systematically identifying potential threats, understanding their tactics and motivations, and devising countermeasures to mitigate the associated risks.

Imagine you're the cybersecurity architect for a technology company. Threat modeling would guide you in designing secure systems and applications, anticipating and countering potential attack vectors.

Incident response planning is an integral part of threat assessment. It involves developing a well-defined strategy and action plan to address security incidents when they occur.

For instance, if you're the incident response coordinator for a cloud service provider, incident response planning would ensure a swift and coordinated response to any security breaches or data leaks.

Continuous monitoring of external and internal threat landscapes is essential in threat assessment. By staying vigilant and proactive, organizations can adapt to evolving threats and vulnerabilities.

Consider you're the head of cybersecurity for a government agency. Continuous monitoring would enable you to stay ahead of nation-state actors and cybercriminals by detecting emerging threats before they manifest.

Collaboration and information sharing are vital in both real-time monitoring and threat assessment. By exchanging threat intelligence with industry peers, government agencies, and cybersecurity communities, organizations can bolster their defenses and respond effectively to shared threats.

In summary, real-time monitoring and threat assessment are like the dynamic duo of cybersecurity, working in tandem to protect digital assets, detect threats in real-time, and adapt to an ever-evolving threat landscape.

By embracing the principles of real-time monitoring, including intrusion detection, anomaly detection, behavior-based monitoring, log analysis, threat intelligence feeds, automated alerting mechanisms, and threat assessment, organizations can safeguard their digital ecosystems from a wide range of cyber threats.

This proactive approach, guided by continuous vigilance and information sharing, ensures that cybersecurity remains a resilient and adaptive defense against emerging threats, allowing organizations to navigate the digital landscape safely and confidently.

Chapter 6: OSINT Automation and Scripting

Imagine having a tireless assistant who tirelessly collects, sifts through, and analyzes vast amounts of data for you, all with lightning speed and unwavering accuracy.

Automating data collection and analysis is akin to harnessing the power of cutting-edge technology to streamline and enhance your decision-making process.

At its core, data automation involves the use of software, scripts, or algorithms to gather, process, and present data without manual intervention.

Consider you're a marketing manager for an e-commerce company, and you want to track customer behavior on your website. Data automation allows you to collect user data, such as page views and click-through rates, in real-time, providing valuable insights for targeted marketing campaigns.

One of the primary benefits of automating data collection is efficiency. It eliminates the need for time-consuming manual data entry and ensures that data is consistently and accurately recorded.

Imagine you're an HR manager handling a large volume of employee data. Automation ensures that employee information, from payroll details to performance evaluations, is updated and maintained seamlessly.

Data automation also enables organizations to work with larger datasets than would be feasible manually. With automation, you can process and analyze extensive datasets, uncovering trends and patterns that might have gone unnoticed otherwise.

Consider you're a financial analyst analyzing stock market data. Automation allows you to handle vast amounts of market data, identify investment opportunities, and make timely decisions to maximize returns.

Real-time data collection and analysis are essential in today's fast-paced digital landscape. Automation tools can continuously monitor data sources, providing up-to-the-minute insights and alerts.

For instance, if you're a cybersecurity expert, real-time automation can help you detect and respond to security threats as they occur, rather than after the fact.

Predictive analytics is another valuable application of data automation. By using historical data and machine learning algorithms, organizations can automate the process of forecasting future trends and outcomes.

Imagine you're a supply chain manager optimizing inventory levels. Predictive analytics can automate demand forecasting, ensuring that your organization maintains the right stock levels to meet customer demands.

Data automation can also enhance decision-making by presenting data in visual formats that are easy to understand. Dashboards and data visualization tools allow you to grasp complex information at a glance.

Consider you're a business owner analyzing sales performance. Data automation can generate interactive dashboards that display sales trends, helping you identify areas for improvement and make informed decisions.

The first step in automating data collection and analysis is defining clear objectives. Understand what data you need and what insights you want to gain from it.

Imagine you're a research scientist studying climate change. Defining your research questions and data requirements is crucial before you embark on data automation to collect and analyze climate data.

Once you have clear objectives, the next step is selecting the right automation tools and technologies. These tools can vary widely, from data integration platforms to data analytics software and machine learning algorithms.

Consider you're a data scientist working on a healthcare project. Selecting the appropriate tools and algorithms is essential to automate the analysis of patient data and generate insights for medical research.

Data quality is paramount in automation. Ensure that the data you collect is accurate, complete, and up-to-date. Data cleaning and validation processes are often part of data automation workflows.

Imagine you're a financial analyst automating the collection of financial data from various sources. Data cleaning ensures that errors and inconsistencies are addressed before analysis begins.

Security and privacy are critical considerations in data automation. Protect sensitive data by implementing encryption, access controls, and compliance measures.

For instance, if you're a privacy officer automating data collection for a healthcare organization, you must ensure that patient data remains secure and complies with regulations like HIPAA.

Regular monitoring and maintenance are essential to ensure that automated data processes continue to function correctly. Monitor for errors, anomalies, or data drift, and make necessary adjustments.

Consider you're an IT manager overseeing a data automation system for inventory management. Ongoing monitoring ensures that the system operates smoothly, minimizing disruptions to business operations.

Collaboration is often key to successful data automation. Involve stakeholders from various departments to ensure that automated insights align with business goals and strategies.

Imagine you're a business analyst implementing an automated customer feedback analysis system. Collaboration with marketing, sales, and product development teams ensures that customer insights are integrated into decision-making processes.

Continuous improvement is essential in data automation. Regularly evaluate the effectiveness of your automated processes and seek opportunities for optimization.

For instance, if you're a manufacturing manager automating production data collection, continuous improvement efforts can lead to increased efficiency and reduced downtime.

In summary, automating data collection and analysis is like having a trusted ally that empowers you with timely, accurate, and actionable insights. It enhances efficiency, scalability, and the ability to make informed decisions in today's data-driven world.

By defining clear objectives, selecting the right tools, ensuring data quality, prioritizing security and privacy, and fostering collaboration and continuous improvement, organizations can harness the power of data automation to drive innovation, competitiveness, and success.

Imagine you're a digital artisan crafting intricate jewelry, and scripting tools are your precision instruments, enabling you to create exquisite designs efficiently and with meticulous detail.

Scripting tools and techniques are a powerhouse in the world of automation, streamlining repetitive tasks, and empowering you to achieve remarkable efficiency in various domains.

At their core, scripting tools are software programs or scripts that execute a series of predefined instructions to automate tasks, manipulate data, or perform specific actions.

Consider you're a data analyst working with vast datasets, and scripting tools are your trusted companions, automating data cleaning, transformation, and analysis, saving you time and reducing the risk of errors.

One of the primary benefits of scripting tools is time savings. They allow you to complete tasks that would take hours or even days manually in a matter of minutes or seconds.

Imagine you're an IT administrator managing a network of hundreds of computers. Scripting tools can automate software installations, system updates, and user account management, significantly reducing the time and effort required.

Scripting tools also promote consistency and accuracy. By automating repetitive tasks, you ensure that each task is performed precisely according to your defined parameters.

Consider you're a web developer creating a portfolio of websites. Scripting tools can generate consistent and error-free code, ensuring that each website meets your design and functionality standards.

Scripting languages, such as Python, JavaScript, and PowerShell, are versatile tools for automation. They provide a robust foundation for creating scripts tailored to your specific needs.

Imagine you're a cybersecurity specialist investigating security incidents. Scripting languages allow you to write custom scripts to analyze log files, identify security breaches, and automate incident response procedures.

Scripting tools are invaluable for data manipulation and transformation. They enable you to reformat, filter, or merge data from various sources, making it suitable for analysis or reporting.

For instance, if you're a financial analyst dealing with financial data from different sources, scripting tools can automate the process of consolidating and cleansing data for accurate financial modeling.

Batch processing is a common application of scripting tools. It involves executing a series of commands or tasks in a batch or sequence.

Consider you're a video editor working on a project with multiple video clips. Batch processing scripts can automate tasks like resizing, cropping, or applying filters to all clips, saving you hours of manual work.

Task scheduling is another strength of scripting tools. You can schedule scripts to run at specific times or intervals, automating routine maintenance or data backup tasks.

Imagine you're a system administrator responsible for server maintenance. Task scheduling scripts can automate tasks like disk cleanup, log file rotation, and system updates during non-business hours to minimize disruption.

Scripting tools can also interact with external APIs (Application Programming Interfaces), enabling you to automate interactions with web services, databases, or third-party applications.

For instance, if you're a social media manager, scripting tools can automate posts and responses on social media platforms, ensuring a consistent online presence and engagement with your audience.

Regular expressions, or regex, are powerful patterns that scripting tools use to search for and manipulate text. They are invaluable for tasks like data extraction and text processing.

Consider you're a content curator extracting specific information from a large document. Regular expressions can be employed in scripting tools to efficiently extract the desired content, saving you time and effort.

Error handling and logging are essential aspects of scripting tools. They allow you to anticipate and handle exceptions or errors that may occur during script execution.

Imagine you're a software developer creating an application. Error handling scripts can log errors, provide meaningful error messages, and take appropriate actions to ensure that the application continues to run smoothly.

Scripting tools can be integrated into larger automation workflows, orchestrating complex processes across multiple systems or applications.

For example, if you're an e-commerce business owner, scripting tools can automate the entire order processing workflow, from order placement to inventory management, and customer notifications.

Version control systems, such as Git, play a crucial role in managing scripts. They enable you to track changes, collaborate with team members, and roll back to previous versions if issues arise.

Consider you're a software development team lead overseeing the development of automation scripts. Version control ensures that changes to scripts are tracked and coordinated among team members for seamless collaboration.

Documentation is paramount in scripting. Well-documented scripts include comments and explanations that make them understandable and maintainable by you and others.

Imagine you're an IT support specialist. Well-documented scripts help you troubleshoot and maintain automation tasks efficiently, even if they were written by someone else.

Testing is a critical part of scripting. It involves thoroughly validating scripts to ensure they perform as intended and do not introduce unexpected errors.

For instance, if you're a quality assurance engineer automating software testing, rigorous testing of your scripts guarantees the accuracy and reliability of your automated test cases.

Security considerations are vital when working with scripting tools. Scripts can be vulnerable to exploitation if not properly secured, so implementing access controls and encryption is crucial.

Consider you're a network security expert automating vulnerability scanning. Security measures in your scripts protect sensitive data and prevent unauthorized access to your scanning tools.

In summary, scripting tools and techniques are like the skilled artisans in your toolbox, ready to craft efficiency and precision into your daily tasks and workflows.

By harnessing the power of scripting languages, batch processing, task scheduling, and external APIs, you can automate a wide range of tasks, from data manipulation to error handling.

Version control, documentation, testing, and security practices ensure that your scripts are robust and maintainable, supporting collaboration and protecting your organization's data and systems.

Scripting tools are the magic wands that empower you to automate the mundane, so you can focus your time and energy on more creative and strategic endeavors, ultimately enhancing your productivity and effectiveness.

Chapter 7: Ethical Hacking for Intelligence Gathering

Ethical hacking, often referred to as "white hat" hacking, is a field of cybersecurity where skilled professionals use their knowledge and expertise to uncover vulnerabilities in computer systems, networks, and applications.

Think of ethical hackers as digital detectives who work with organizations to identify and rectify security weaknesses, ultimately strengthening their defenses against malicious cyber threats.

The fundamental principle of ethical hacking is to act within legal and ethical boundaries, obtaining proper authorization before conducting any assessments or tests on systems and networks.

Imagine you're an ethical hacker tasked with assessing the security of a company's web application. Your first step is to obtain written permission from the organization, ensuring that your actions are sanctioned and lawful.

Ethical hackers operate under a code of ethics, which includes principles like integrity, confidentiality, and respect for privacy. They are committed to protecting the interests and data of their clients while responsibly disclosing vulnerabilities.

Consider you're an ethical hacker testing the security of a financial institution. Your ethical responsibilities require you to handle sensitive financial data with the utmost care and report any discovered vulnerabilities promptly and discreetly.

The scope of ethical hacking can vary widely, from targeted assessments of specific systems to comprehensive evaluations of an organization's entire cybersecurity posture.

Imagine you're an ethical hacker hired by a government agency to assess the security of critical infrastructure. Your assessment may encompass networks, control systems, and physical security measures to ensure comprehensive protection.

One of the primary goals of ethical hacking is to identify vulnerabilities before malicious hackers can exploit them. This proactive approach helps organizations preempt cyberattacks and safeguard their digital assets.

Consider you're an ethical hacker conducting a penetration test on a corporate network. Your findings may reveal weaknesses that, if left unaddressed, could have been exploited by cybercriminals to breach the organization's defenses. Ethical hackers employ various techniques and tools to assess the security of systems and networks. They may conduct vulnerability assessments, penetration tests, or social engineering exercises, depending on the scope of the engagement. Imagine you're an ethical hacker using penetration testing tools to simulate cyberattacks on a company's network. Your objective is to identify weaknesses in network defenses, such as unpatched software or misconfigured firewalls. A critical aspect of ethical hacking is the methodology used to conduct assessments. Ethical hackers follow a systematic approach, which typically includes reconnaissance, scanning, exploitation, and reporting. Consider you're an ethical hacker following the methodology to assess a cloud-based application. During the reconnaissance phase, you gather information about the application's architecture and potential attack vectors.

Scanning involves actively probing the target system for vulnerabilities. Ethical hackers use scanning tools and techniques to identify weaknesses that could be exploited. Imagine you're an ethical hacker conducting a vulnerability scan on a web server. Your goal is to identify open ports, services, and known vulnerabilities that could be leveraged by attackers.

Exploitation is the phase where ethical hackers attempt to exploit identified vulnerabilities to demonstrate their impact. This step is crucial in providing concrete evidence to the organization.

Consider you're an ethical hacker exploiting a security vulnerability in a mobile app to gain unauthorized access to user data. Your actions serve as proof of concept and underscore the importance of addressing the vulnerability.

Reporting is the final step, where ethical hackers document their findings, assess the risk associated with each vulnerability, and provide recommendations for remediation.

Imagine you're an ethical hacker compiling a detailed report for your client, outlining the vulnerabilities discovered, their potential impact, and specific steps to mitigate the risks effectively.

Continuous learning and staying up-to-date with the latest cybersecurity trends and threats are essential for ethical hackers. They must adapt their skills and techniques to counter evolving attack vectors.

Consider you're an ethical hacker attending cybersecurity conferences and training programs to learn about emerging threats like ransomware and zero-day vulnerabilities. Staying informed helps you stay one step ahead of cybercriminals.

Ethical hacking extends beyond technology; it includes assessing human factors such as employee awareness and susceptibility to social engineering attacks.

Imagine you're an ethical hacker conducting a social engineering test on a company's staff. Your goal is to assess their ability to recognize and resist phishing attempts, thereby enhancing the organization's security awareness.

Certifications play a significant role in the ethical hacking field, as they validate the knowledge and skills of professionals. Popular certifications include Certified Ethical Hacker (CEH) and Offensive Security Certified Professional (OSCP).

Consider you're an aspiring ethical hacker preparing for the CEH exam. Earning this certification demonstrates your competence in identifying and addressing cybersecurity vulnerabilities.

Legal and ethical considerations are paramount in ethical hacking. Ethical hackers must adhere to laws and regulations governing cybersecurity assessments in their respective regions.

Imagine you're an ethical hacker working internationally. You need to be aware of the cybersecurity laws and regulations in each country where you conduct assessments to ensure compliance and avoid legal issues.

Collaboration is essential in the world of ethical hacking. Ethical hackers often work closely with organizations' IT and security teams to implement effective security measures and remediate vulnerabilities.

Consider you're an ethical hacker collaborating with an organization's IT department to apply security patches and implement access controls. This collaborative approach strengthens the organization's cybersecurity defenses.

In summary, ethical hacking is a dynamic and vital component of the cybersecurity landscape, with professionals dedicated to securing digital assets and safeguarding organizations from cyber threats.

Operating within ethical boundaries and following a systematic approach, ethical hackers play a pivotal role in identifying vulnerabilities, providing evidence of risks, and guiding organizations toward stronger security postures.

Continuous learning, adherence to ethical codes, and legal compliance are the cornerstones of ethical hacking, ensuring that these digital detectives operate responsibly and effectively in the ever-evolving battle against cyber threats.

Penetration testing for Open Source Intelligence (OSINT) combines the art of ethical hacking with the power of open-source information gathering to assess the security of organizations and individuals.

Imagine you're a skilled penetration tester, armed with knowledge and tools to evaluate digital footprints and identify vulnerabilities that could be exploited by malicious actors.

The primary goal of OSINT penetration testing is to uncover weaknesses in an organization's online presence, including their websites, social media profiles, and publicly available information, before adversaries can exploit them.

Consider you're conducting an OSINT penetration test for a financial institution. Your mission is to identify potential security gaps in their online infrastructure, such as exposed credentials or sensitive data.

One of the key principles of OSINT penetration testing is thorough reconnaissance. You start by gathering as much publicly available information as possible about the target, just as a malicious attacker might.

Imagine you're collecting data on a target organization's employees, their roles, and their social media accounts. This information provides insight into potential attack vectors and social engineering opportunities.

Reconnaissance extends beyond individuals; it encompasses web applications, network infrastructure, and digital assets. You map out the organization's online presence and pinpoint potential entry points.

Consider you're identifying the organization's web applications and services, determining which are publicly accessible, and assessing their security configurations.

OSINT penetration testers often leverage search engines, social media platforms, and specialized OSINT tools to harvest information. They meticulously document their findings for analysis and reporting.

Imagine you're using advanced search operators to uncover sensitive documents or vulnerabilities related to the target organization. Your findings will be crucial in demonstrating the potential risks.

One of the primary challenges in OSINT penetration testing is distinguishing between what is publicly accessible information and what constitutes a security vulnerability.

Consider you've discovered a publicly accessible database containing customer information. While it's tempting to access the data, ethical guidelines dictate that you must report the finding to the organization rather than exploit it. The assessment phase involves probing the identified entry points for vulnerabilities. This can include testing for common web application vulnerabilities like SQL injection or cross-site scripting (XSS). Imagine you're conducting a thorough analysis of a target's website, checking for misconfigured security headers or known vulnerabilities in the underlying content management system.

Social engineering is often a component of OSINT penetration testing. Testers may attempt to manipulate individuals into revealing sensitive information or taking unauthorized actions. Consider you're simulating a phishing attack on employees to evaluate their susceptibility. This helps the organization assess its staff's security awareness and training needs. Exploitation, in the context of OSINT penetration testing, refers to the demonstration of the impact of vulnerabilities. Testers may exploit identified weaknesses to showcase their potential consequences. Imagine you've identified a security flaw in a target organization's email system that could lead to unauthorized access. You would demonstrate this vulnerability to highlight the risk.

Reporting is a critical phase of OSINT penetration testing. Testers compile their findings, including identified vulnerabilities and their potential impact, into a comprehensive report.

Consider you're preparing a detailed report for the organization, providing a clear overview of the vulnerabilities found, their risk level, and recommendations for mitigation.

The ultimate goal of OSINT penetration testing is to help organizations enhance their security posture.

Recommendations may include patching vulnerabilities, improving access controls, or enhancing security awareness training.

Imagine you're working closely with the organization to implement the recommended security measures and ensure that identified vulnerabilities are addressed promptly.

OSINT penetration testing is a dynamic field that requires continuous learning and adaptation to keep pace with evolving threats and attack techniques.

Consider you're regularly updating your toolkit and staying informed about new OSINT tools and techniques to remain effective in your role as a penetration tester.

Legal and ethical considerations are paramount in OSINT penetration testing. Testers must operate within the bounds of the law and adhere to ethical guidelines, ensuring that their actions are responsible and just.

Imagine you're conducting an engagement that involves cross-border assessments. You must be aware of the legal and regulatory differences between jurisdictions to avoid legal complications.

In summary, OSINT penetration testing is a valuable practice that combines the art of ethical hacking with open-source information gathering to assess the security of organizations and individuals.

Through meticulous reconnaissance, vulnerability assessment, and responsible reporting, OSINT penetration testers help organizations identify and mitigate potential risks in their online presence, ultimately strengthening their cybersecurity defenses against malicious actors.

Chapter 8: Advanced Analysis and Visualization Tools

Utilizing advanced analytics for Open Source Intelligence (OSINT) takes the practice of gathering and analyzing publicly available information to a higher level.

Imagine you're an OSINT practitioner with a wealth of data at your disposal, and you want to extract meaningful insights from this vast ocean of information.

The foundation of advanced OSINT analytics lies in the ability to collect, process, and analyze data from a wide range of sources.

Consider you're collecting data from social media platforms, websites, news articles, and other public sources. This diverse data landscape provides you with a comprehensive view of your subject.

One of the key challenges in OSINT is dealing with unstructured data. Advanced analytics techniques allow you to extract structure and meaning from this data.

Imagine you're analyzing a large set of social media posts related to a specific event. Advanced text analysis tools help you identify sentiment, key themes, and potentially relevant information.

Machine learning and artificial intelligence (AI) play a significant role in advanced OSINT analytics. These technologies can automatically categorize, classify, and even predict patterns in the data.

Consider you're using machine learning algorithms to categorize news articles into different topics. This automation streamlines the process of identifying relevant information.

Visualization is a powerful tool in advanced OSINT analytics. Creating visual representations of data helps you understand complex relationships and trends more easily.

Imagine you're using a graph database to visualize connections between individuals or organizations. This graphical representation provides insights that are challenging to glean from raw data.

Geospatial analysis is another dimension of advanced OSINT analytics. It involves mapping and analyzing data based on geographic locations.

Consider you're using geospatial analysis to track the movement of a social media user. By analyzing their location data over time, you can gain valuable insights into their habits and activities.

Time-series analysis is essential for understanding how information evolves over time. Advanced OSINT practitioners use this technique to track trends and changes.

Imagine you're monitoring a specific hashtag on social media. Time-series analysis allows you to see when and how the usage of this hashtag increases or decreases.

Network analysis is a critical component of advanced OSINT analytics. It involves examining connections and relationships between entities, such as people, organizations, or websites.

Consider you're conducting network analysis to identify influential individuals in a particular online community. Understanding these key players can help you uncover hidden dynamics.

Link analysis is a subset of network analysis that focuses on examining the links or relationships between data points. It's particularly useful for identifying connections between websites, online communities, or individuals.

Imagine you're conducting link analysis to trace the connections between a series of websites sharing misinformation. This analysis can help reveal the spread of false information.

Entity recognition and extraction are fundamental in advanced OSINT analytics. These techniques involve identifying and extracting specific entities, such as names, dates, or locations, from unstructured text.

Consider you're using entity recognition to extract mentions of individuals and organizations from a large collection of news articles. This process simplifies the task of tracking their appearances in the media.

Collaborative filtering is a technique often used in recommendation systems, but it can also be applied to OSINT analytics. It involves making predictions and recommendations based on the preferences and behavior of similar users or entities.

Imagine you're applying collaborative filtering to suggest related topics or individuals to an OSINT analyst based on their past interests and searches.

Sentiment analysis is crucial for understanding public opinion and attitudes. Advanced OSINT analytics can automatically analyze sentiment in large volumes of text data.

Consider you're using sentiment analysis to gauge public sentiment about a particular government policy by analyzing social media posts and news articles. This information can inform decision-makers.

Event detection is an advanced analytics technique used to identify significant events or incidents in real-time or near-real-time data streams.

Imagine you're monitoring social media for breaking news. Event detection algorithms can automatically flag and prioritize posts related to emerging events, enabling rapid response.

Pattern recognition involves identifying recurring patterns or anomalies in data. This technique is particularly useful for detecting trends or irregularities.

Consider you're using pattern recognition to identify spikes in online discussions related to a particular product. This insight can inform marketing strategies and inventory management.

Natural language processing (NLP) is a branch of AI that focuses on the interaction between computers and human language. Advanced OSINT analytics use NLP to understand and extract meaning from text data.

Imagine you're applying NLP techniques to analyze customer reviews of a product. This analysis can reveal common themes, issues, and areas for improvement.

Predictive analytics is about using historical data to make predictions about future events or trends. In the context of OSINT, it can be applied to anticipate emerging threats or identify potential opportunities.

Consider you're using predictive analytics to forecast the likelihood of a cybersecurity attack based on historical attack patterns and online chatter. This information allows organizations to take proactive measures.

Privacy and ethical considerations are essential in advanced OSINT analytics. Practitioners must ensure that data is collected and used responsibly, respecting individuals' rights and privacy.

Imagine you're conducting OSINT research that involves collecting and analyzing social media data. It's crucial to anonymize and aggregate the data to protect individuals' privacy and comply with regulations.

In summary, advanced OSINT analytics is a multidisciplinary field that leverages technology, data science, and analytical techniques to extract valuable insights from publicly available information.

By harnessing the power of machine learning, visualization, geospatial analysis, and other advanced methods, OSINT practitioners can uncover hidden patterns, trends, and connections that provide organizations with a competitive edge, enhance decision-making, and bolster security measures.

Data visualization is a powerful tool in intelligence analysis, allowing analysts to transform complex data into clear and actionable insights.

Imagine you're an intelligence analyst faced with a vast amount of information, including text documents, images, and numerical data, related to a potential security threat.

Data visualization helps you make sense of this information by presenting it in a visual format that is easier to understand and interpret.

Consider you're creating a graph that displays the connections between individuals involved in a criminal network. This visual representation can reveal patterns and relationships that might not be apparent in raw data.

One of the key benefits of data visualization is its ability to condense large datasets into concise and informative graphics.

Imagine you're summarizing a year's worth of financial transactions for a fraud investigation. Instead of sifting through thousands of records, you can create a bar chart that highlights unusual spending patterns.

Charts and graphs are common forms of data visualization that provide analysts with a quick overview of trends, comparisons, and anomalies.

Consider you're using a line chart to track the fluctuations in stock prices over time. This visual representation allows you to identify trends and potential investment opportunities.

Maps are another powerful tool in intelligence analysis, especially when dealing with geospatial data.

Imagine you're plotting the locations of reported incidents in a city to identify crime hotspots. A heatmap or a cluster map can help law enforcement allocate resources effectively.

Network diagrams are valuable for understanding relationships and connections between individuals or entities.

Consider you're analyzing communications between terrorist organizations. A network diagram can illustrate the hierarchy and communication patterns, aiding in the identification of key figures.

Heatmaps are a form of data visualization that uses color gradients to represent the density or distribution of data points.

Imagine you're analyzing customer demographics for a retail business. A heatmap can show you which areas have the highest concentration of potential customers.

Pie charts are useful for displaying the composition of a whole, showing how a set of data is divided into different categories or segments.

Consider you're visualizing the distribution of expenses in a budget. A pie chart can provide a clear breakdown of where the money is being allocated.

Time-series graphs are essential for tracking data over time and identifying patterns or trends.

Imagine you're monitoring the spread of a disease outbreak. A time-series graph can help you see how the number of cases evolves over days or weeks.

Scatter plots allow analysts to explore the relationship between two variables and identify correlations or outliers.

Consider you're studying the correlation between temperature and ice cream sales. A scatter plot can reveal whether warmer weather leads to increased sales.

Word clouds are a unique form of data visualization that visually represent the frequency of words in a text document.

Imagine you're analyzing public sentiment in social media comments. A word cloud can highlight the most frequently used words, providing insights into popular topics or opinions.

Dashboard-style visualizations are valuable for aggregating multiple data visualizations into a single, interactive interface.

Consider you're monitoring various key performance indicators (KPIs) for a business. A dashboard can display real-time data on sales, customer satisfaction, and website traffic in one place.

Data visualization tools and software make it easier for analysts to create, customize, and share visualizations.

Imagine you're using a data visualization platform that allows you to import data from multiple sources and choose from a variety of chart types and customization options.

Color coding is a fundamental aspect of data visualization, helping to differentiate categories, highlight important information, and convey meaning.

Consider you're creating a bar chart that compares revenue across different product categories. Using different colors for each category makes it easy to distinguish between them.

Effective data visualization considers the target audience and tailors the visuals to their needs and preferences.

Imagine you're presenting intelligence findings to a group of policymakers. Your data visualization should be clear, concise, and relevant to their decision-making process.

Accessibility is a critical aspect of data visualization, ensuring that the visual representations are understandable and usable by individuals with disabilities.

Consider you're designing a data visualization for a government agency. It's essential to follow accessibility guidelines to ensure that all stakeholders can access and interpret the information.

Interactive data visualizations allow users to explore the data, drill down into specific details, and gain a deeper understanding of the information presented.

Imagine you're creating an interactive map that displays crime data. Users can click on specific areas to view more detailed information about individual incidents.

Data visualization can enhance situational awareness in intelligence analysis by providing a real-time, visual overview of ongoing events.

Consider you're monitoring social media for potential security threats during a major event. A live dashboard displaying relevant keywords and sentiment analysis can help intelligence analysts stay informed.

Storytelling through data visualization is a powerful way to convey complex narratives and insights to a broader audience.

Imagine you're creating a data visualization that tells the story of a cyberattack. By combining visuals with explanatory text, you can help stakeholders understand the incident's timeline and impact.

Advanced data visualization techniques, such as 3D modeling and virtual reality, offer new dimensions for exploring and analyzing data.

Consider you're visualizing a complex urban environment for urban planning. 3D modeling and virtual reality can provide city planners with an immersive experience to assess potential changes.

Ethical considerations in data visualization include ensuring that visualizations do not mislead or manipulate information to support a specific agenda.

Imagine you're working on a data visualization for a controversial political issue. It's essential to present the data objectively and transparently, without bias.

In summary, data visualization is a valuable tool in intelligence analysis, helping analysts make sense of complex information, identify patterns, and communicate findings effectively. Whether using traditional charts and graphs or advanced techniques like interactive dashboards and storytelling, data visualization enhances the analytical process and supports informed decision-making in various fields, from security and law enforcement to business and public policy.

Chapter 9: Threat Intelligence and Cybersecurity

Understanding threat intelligence frameworks is crucial in today's digital landscape, where organizations face a myriad of cybersecurity threats.

Imagine you're responsible for the cybersecurity of a large financial institution, and you need to stay ahead of potential threats that could compromise sensitive customer data.

A threat intelligence framework is like a structured roadmap that helps organizations collect, analyze, and act on threat intelligence effectively.

Consider it as your guiding compass in the complex world of cybersecurity, providing a structured approach to identifying, assessing, and mitigating threats.

One of the fundamental aspects of a threat intelligence framework is the collection of data from various sources.

Imagine you're gathering information from internal logs, external threat feeds, and open-source intelligence to create a comprehensive view of potential threats.

Once you have collected data, the next step is to process and analyze it to identify patterns, trends, and potential threats.

Consider you're using machine learning algorithms to detect anomalous activities in your network traffic, which could indicate a cyberattack in progress.

A crucial component of threat intelligence is the dissemination of actionable information to relevant stakeholders.

Imagine you've detected a new malware strain targeting your industry. Sharing this information promptly with your security team and partners can help them prepare defenses.

In the context of threat intelligence, a structured framework helps organizations prioritize threats based on their potential impact and likelihood.

Consider you're using a risk assessment matrix to categorize threats as low, medium, or high risk, allowing you to focus resources on the most critical issues.

A threat intelligence framework also encompasses the concept of threat feeds, which are sources of information about known threats and vulnerabilities.

Imagine subscribing to threat feeds that provide real-time updates on emerging threats, enabling your organization to proactively defend against them.

Threat actors, such as hackers and cybercriminals, continually evolve their tactics and techniques. A threat intelligence framework helps organizations stay one step ahead.

Consider you're monitoring the dark web for discussions related to your industry. Early detection of threats can enable you to adapt your defenses accordingly.

Intelligence sharing is a crucial aspect of threat intelligence frameworks. Organizations often collaborate to share threat information and bolster collective defenses.

Imagine you're part of an industry-specific Information Sharing and Analysis Center (ISAC). Sharing intelligence with peers can help all members improve their security posture.

Threat intelligence frameworks also address the importance of integrating threat intelligence into an organization's existing cybersecurity infrastructure.

Consider you're using threat intelligence feeds to automatically update your intrusion detection system's rules, enhancing its ability to detect and block threats.

Automation plays a significant role in threat intelligence frameworks, as it allows organizations to respond rapidly to threats.

Imagine a scenario where an automated system detects a phishing campaign targeting your employees and immediately blocks malicious emails.

A critical element of threat intelligence is the analysis of tactics, techniques, and procedures (TTPs) employed by threat actors.

Consider you're studying the TTPs of a known nation-state-sponsored hacking group. Understanding their methods can help you defend against future attacks.

Another important aspect is the attribution of threats, which involves identifying the individuals, groups, or nations behind attacks.

Imagine you're collaborating with law enforcement agencies to trace the origins of a cyberattack. Attribution can lead to legal action against threat actors.

Threat intelligence frameworks also emphasize the importance of threat hunting, a proactive approach to identifying hidden threats within an organization's environment.

Consider you're using advanced analytics and forensics tools to search for signs of compromise that may have eluded automated detection.

Incident response planning is a key component of threat intelligence frameworks, helping organizations prepare for and respond to cybersecurity incidents effectively.

Imagine your organization experiences a data breach. An incident response plan developed with threat intelligence can guide your team's actions.

Threat intelligence frameworks recognize the need for continuous monitoring and adaptation to evolving threats.

Consider that cybersecurity is an ongoing battle, and your organization must continually update its threat intelligence practices to stay resilient.

A threat intelligence framework often includes a threat intelligence lifecycle, which consists of stages like planning, collection, analysis, dissemination, and feedback.

Imagine your organization follows this lifecycle to systematically address threats, ensuring that intelligence informs decision-making at each step.

In addition to external threats, organizations must also consider insider threats and incorporate them into their threat intelligence frameworks.

Consider you're monitoring user activity to detect any suspicious behavior by employees or contractors who may pose an internal threat.

Ethical considerations are vital in threat intelligence, as organizations must ensure that their intelligence-gathering activities adhere to legal and ethical standards.

Imagine your organization respects individuals' privacy rights and complies with relevant laws while conducting threat intelligence operations.

The adoption of threat intelligence frameworks is not limited to large organizations. Small and medium-sized enterprises (SMEs) can also benefit from structured threat intelligence practices.

Consider you're the owner of an SME that relies on online sales. Implementing a threat intelligence framework can help protect your e-commerce platform from fraud and cyberattacks.

Threat intelligence frameworks are not static; they evolve along with the threat landscape.

Imagine you're updating your framework to address emerging threats such as ransomware-as-a-service or supply chain attacks.

Education and training play a significant role in effective threat intelligence. Organizations must invest in the development of skilled analysts and security professionals.

Consider your organization providing regular training sessions to your security team, keeping them up-to-date on the latest threat intelligence techniques and tools.

International collaboration is vital in addressing global threats. Threat intelligence frameworks often involve partnerships with other countries and international organizations.

Imagine your government collaborating with international agencies to combat cybercrime that transcends national borders, such as coordinated cyberattacks.

In summary, understanding threat intelligence frameworks is essential for organizations of all sizes to navigate the complex landscape of cybersecurity threats. These frameworks provide a structured approach to collecting, analyzing, and acting on threat intelligence, enabling organizations to proactively defend against evolving threats. By incorporating ethical considerations, collaboration, and continuous learning, organizations can strengthen their security posture and protect their digital assets effectively.

In today's interconnected digital world, OSINT plays a vital role in strengthening cybersecurity defenses. Imagine you're responsible for the cybersecurity of a medium-sized company that relies on digital operations. You know that cyber threats are constantly evolving, and attackers are becoming more sophisticated. That's where OSINT, or Open Source Intelligence, comes into play as a valuable asset in your cybersecurity arsenal. At its core, OSINT involves collecting and analyzing publicly available information from a wide range of sources. These sources include websites, social media, news articles, public records, and more. By harnessing the power of OSINT, organizations can gather valuable insights into potential threats and vulnerabilities. Consider a scenario where your organization's website experiences a sudden increase in traffic. OSINT tools can help you analyze the source of this traffic and determine if it's legitimate or a distributed denial-of-service (DDoS) attack in progress. One of the key benefits of OSINT is its ability to provide early warning signs of cyber threats. Imagine you're monitoring discussions on underground forums related to your industry. OSINT can alert you to chatter about new malware strains or vulnerabilities that could impact your organization. Furthermore, OSINT can assist in the identification of potential threat actors. For instance, if you discover that a particular hacker group is discussing your industry on social media, it may indicate a heightened risk. OSINT tools and techniques can also aid in understanding the tactics and techniques employed by cybercriminals. Consider the case of a phishing campaign targeting your organization's employees. OSINT can help you analyze the phishing emails, uncovering patterns and indicators that assist in threat mitigation. In the realm of cybersecurity defense, OSINT is not limited to external threats alone. It can also be a valuable resource for monitoring internal threats. Imagine you're concerned about a disgruntled employee leaking sensitive information. OSINT can help you keep an eye on that individual's online activities for any signs of potential data exfiltration. Another aspect of OSINT's role in cybersecurity defense is vulnerability assessment. By regularly monitoring OSINT sources, organizations can stay informed about newly discovered vulnerabilities in software and systems. Consider the importance of promptly patching known vulnerabilities to prevent exploitation by malicious actors. OSINT can also play a role in threat intelligence sharing and collaboration. Imagine you're part of an industry-specific Information Sharing and Analysis Center (ISAC). Sharing OSINT-derived threat intelligence with peers can enhance collective defenses against common adversaries. In addition to proactive defense, OSINT can be a valuable tool in incident response. Consider a situation where your organization experiences a data breach. OSINT can assist in identifying the extent of the breach and tracing the source of the attack. Furthermore, OSINT can aid in the recovery process by monitoring for leaked company data on the dark web. It's worth noting that OSINT is not a standalone solution but rather a complementary component of a robust cybersecurity strategy. Imagine your organization employs a multi-layered security approach, including firewalls, intrusion detection systems, and employee training. OSINT serves as an additional layer, providing insights that help fine-tune existing security measures. In the context of OSINT, automation can significantly enhance cybersecurity defense. Consider the vast amount of data available on the internet. Automation tools can help collect and analyze this data at scale, identifying potential threats more efficiently than manual methods. For example, OSINT automation can continuously scan for mentions of your organization on social media platforms, alerting you to any suspicious activity. Ethical considerations are paramount in OSINT practices. Imagine you're conducting OSINT research on a competitor. It's crucial to ensure that your methods adhere to legal and ethical standards, respecting privacy and intellectual property rights. Furthermore, OSINT practitioners must exercise discretion when sharing sensitive information. Consider a situation where you uncover a critical security flaw in a third-party vendor's software. While responsible disclosure is essential, publicly exposing the vulnerability could lead to exploitation before a patch is available. OSINT is not a one-size-fits-all approach, and organizations should tailor their OSINT efforts to their specific needs and industry. Imagine you're in charge of cybersecurity for a healthcare institution. Your OSINT focus may include monitoring for discussions related to medical device vulnerabilities or patient data breaches. In contrast, a financial institution's OSINT priorities may revolve around tracking discussions on financial fraud and regulatory compliance. Education and training are critical aspects of effective OSINT utilization in cybersecurity defense. Imagine your cybersecurity team undergoing regular training sessions to stay updated on the latest OSINT tools, techniques, and best practices. Moreover, staying informed about evolving threats is essential, as cyber adversaries continually adapt their tactics. Consider the ever-changing landscape of ransomware attacks and the need to adapt OSINT strategies accordingly. In summary, OSINT's role in cybersecurity defense is indispensable in today's digital age. It empowers organizations to proactively identify threats, assess vulnerabilities, and respond effectively to cyber incidents. By integrating OSINT into their broader cybersecurity strategies and adhering to ethical standards, organizations can bolster their defenses and safeguard their digital assets.

Chapter 10: Case Studies in Advanced OSINT Operations

Let's dive into the real-world applications of advanced OSINT, where the rubber meets the road in harnessing open-source intelligence techniques for a wide range of purposes.

Imagine you're a cybersecurity professional tasked with identifying vulnerabilities in your organization's digital infrastructure.

Advanced OSINT can be a game-changer in this scenario, helping you gather information from publicly available sources to pinpoint potential weaknesses before malicious actors do.

Consider a scenario where you're conducting a red team exercise, simulating a cyberattack on your organization.

Advanced OSINT allows the red team to gather extensive data on the organization, from employee names and email addresses to server configurations and software versions, creating a realistic and effective attack simulation.

Now, shift your focus to the world of law enforcement and investigations.

Imagine you're working on a missing persons case, and you need to track down a person who disappeared under mysterious circumstances.

Advanced OSINT techniques enable investigators to scour the internet for digital footprints left behind by the missing individual, such as social media activity, online purchases, or forum posts, which could provide crucial leads.

Consider a different scenario within law enforcement, where you're investigating a potential threat made against a public figure.

Advanced OSINT allows investigators to monitor social media platforms and online forums in real-time to gauge the credibility of the threat and take preventive action if necessary.

Advanced OSINT is also a valuable tool in the field of competitive intelligence.

Imagine you're a market researcher trying to gain insights into a rival company's strategies.

By delving into publicly available information about the competitor's product launches, executive movements, and financial reports, you can formulate a more informed strategy to stay ahead in the market.

Consider a different perspective within competitive intelligence, where you're a journalist investigating a major corporate scandal.

Advanced OSINT techniques can help you uncover hidden connections, track offshore financial transactions, and piece together a comprehensive narrative that sheds light on the scandal's intricacies.

Let's switch gears to the realm of online reputation management.

Imagine you're a brand or individual dealing with a smear campaign or negative online publicity.

Advanced OSINT allows you to monitor the internet for mentions, reviews, or articles that could harm your reputation and take timely actions to mitigate the damage.

Consider a scenario where you're a security analyst responsible for protecting a high-profile executive or public figure.

Advanced OSINT serves as a critical tool in threat assessment, helping you identify potential risks, detect early signs of targeted attacks, and proactively safeguard the individual.

Now, let's explore the role of advanced OSINT in the domain of geopolitical analysis.

Imagine you're an intelligence analyst tracking developments in a volatile region.

Advanced OSINT can help you collect data from various sources, including social media, satellite imagery, and news articles, to gain a comprehensive understanding of the situation on the ground.

Consider a different perspective within geopolitical analysis, where you're a researcher studying the activities of non-state actors or terrorist organizations.

Advanced OSINT provides access to online forums, encrypted messaging platforms, and dark web communities, allowing you to monitor their activities and assess potential threats.

In the field of cybersecurity, imagine you're a threat hunter tasked with identifying and neutralizing advanced persistent threats (APTs).

Advanced OSINT tools and techniques enable you to monitor underground forums and hacker communities, where APT actors often communicate and share their tactics, techniques, and procedures (TTPs).

Consider a scenario within cybersecurity where you're a penetration tester evaluating an organization's security posture.

Advanced OSINT assists you in gathering intelligence about the target, including employee information, network configurations, and potential attack vectors, to conduct a thorough and realistic assessment.

Advanced OSINT also plays a crucial role in digital forensics.

Imagine you're a digital forensic analyst examining a compromised system.

Advanced OSINT sources can provide you with insights into the attacker's methods, motivations, and potential accomplices, aiding in the reconstruction of digital crime scenes.

Now, shift your perspective to the world of academia.

Imagine you're a researcher investigating the spread of misinformation and fake news on social media.

Advanced OSINT tools enable you to collect and analyze vast datasets from platforms like Twitter and Facebook, helping you uncover trends, sources of disinformation, and the impact on public opinion.

Consider a different research angle, where you're studying the influence of foreign actors on domestic politics.

Advanced OSINT techniques can assist in identifying covert online campaigns, tracking their origins, and assessing their impact on electoral processes or policy debates.

In the domain of financial intelligence, imagine you're a compliance officer at a financial institution tasked with identifying money laundering activities.

Advanced OSINT can help you monitor cryptocurrency transactions, track illicit financial flows, and identify suspicious entities by analyzing publicly available blockchain data.

Consider a different perspective within financial intelligence, where you're an investigator working on a fraud case.

Advanced OSINT allows you to uncover hidden assets, trace financial connections, and gather evidence of fraudulent activities by examining publicly accessible financial records and online transactions.

Switching gears to the humanitarian sector, imagine you're part of an organization responding to a natural disaster.

Advanced OSINT sources, such as satellite imagery and social media data, enable you to assess the extent of the disaster, identify affected areas, and coordinate relief efforts more effectively.

Consider a different scenario within humanitarian aid, where you're monitoring human rights abuses in conflict zones.

Advanced OSINT techniques help you collect evidence, including photos, videos, and witness testimonies, from open sources to document violations and raise awareness on a global scale.

Advanced OSINT is also a valuable asset in the world of academia and research.

Imagine you're a social scientist studying the impact of urban development on local communities.

Advanced OSINT sources provide access to geospatial data, social media conversations, and municipal records, helping you analyze trends, identify disparities, and inform policy recommendations.

Consider a different research perspective, where you're investigating the influence of social media on political polarization.

Advanced OSINT tools and methodologies allow you to analyze vast datasets of user-generated content, discern echo chambers, and understand the dynamics of online discourse.

In the realm of legal investigations, imagine you're a lawyer representing a client in a complex litigation case.

Advanced OSINT techniques can help you uncover critical information about opposing parties, including their online activities, affiliations, and potential conflicts of interest.

Consider a different legal scenario, where you're a criminal defense attorney defending a client against cybercrime charges.

Advanced OSINT sources provide access to digital evidence, enabling you to scrutinize online communications, trace IP addresses, and build a robust defense strategy.

In the context of advanced OSINT, ethical considerations remain paramount.

Imagine you're conducting OSINT research that involves gathering data from social media platforms.

It's crucial to respect privacy settings, adhere to platform terms of service, and ensure that your actions comply with legal and ethical standards.

Furthermore, advanced OSINT practitioners should exercise caution when handling sensitive information and be mindful of the potential consequences of their actions.

Consider a scenario where you're researching a controversial topic that could impact individuals or organizations negatively.

Ethical responsibility dictates that you use OSINT methods judiciously, avoiding harm and adhering to principles of fairness and transparency.

In summary, the real-world applications of advanced OSINT are vast and multifaceted.

From cybersecurity defense to investigations, competitive intelligence to geopolitical analysis, and academia to humanitarian aid, advanced OSINT techniques offer valuable insights and capabilities across diverse domains. However, practitioners must always prioritize ethical considerations and responsible use of OSINT methods to ensure positive outcomes and respect for privacy and legal standards. Exploring expert-level OSINT operations can provide valuable insights and knowledge that go beyond the fundamentals. Imagine embarking on a journey to understand the advanced techniques and strategies employed by seasoned OSINT professionals. These experts have honed their skills through years of experience and have developed a deep understanding of the intricacies of open-source intelligence. By delving into their practices and methods, you can gain a deeper appreciation for the power of OSINT in various contexts. Consider the scenario where an expert OSINT analyst is tasked with investigating a cyberattack on a critical Infrastructure facility. They rely on a combination of advanced search queries, data analysis, and digital forensics to trace the attack's origin and the techniques used by the threat actors. These experts possess the ability to uncover hidden online personas and track their activities across the internet. Imagine the case of a corporate espionage investigation where an expert OSINT practitioner is called upon to identify the individuals behind a data breach. They meticulously analyze social media profiles, online forums, and publicly available data to piece together a comprehensive picture of the culprits and their motives. In the world of threat intelligence, expert OSINT analysts play a crucial role in monitoring emerging cyber threats. They continuously scan the dark web, hacker forums, and underground communities to identify new malware variants, vulnerabilities, and potential attack vectors. Consider a scenario where a security company relies on expert OSINT analysts to provide real-time threat intelligence feeds to their clients, helping them stay ahead of evolving cyber threats. Expert OSINT practitioners are also instrumental in conducting digital reconnaissance for penetration testing and ethical hacking. Imagine a situation where they are tasked with simulating a targeted cyberattack on a financial institution. They use advanced OSINT tools and techniques to gather information about the organization's employees, network infrastructure, and potential vulnerabilities. These experts excel in crafting complex search queries that yield precise results, enabling them to uncover critical data hidden within the vast expanse of the internet. Consider the case of a legal firm preparing for a high-stakes litigation case. Expert OSINT analysts play a pivotal role in gathering evidence, monitoring online discussions related to the case, and uncovering digital trails that may influence the outcome. Their ability to sift through massive amounts of information efficiently is a testament to their expertise. In the realm of competitive intelligence, expert OSINT practitioners are sought after by businesses seeking to gain a competitive edge. Imagine a market research firm relying on their skills to analyze competitors' strategies, product launches, and customer sentiment. These experts excel in analyzing social media networks and trends, identifying patterns that can inform marketing and product development decisions. Consider a scenario where an expert OSINT analyst is hired by a political campaign to assess the online sentiment surrounding a candidate. They use advanced sentiment analysis techniques to gauge public opinion, helping the campaign tailor its messaging and strategy accordingly. Expert OSINT practitioners also play a crucial role in ensuring online reputation management. Imagine a prominent public figure facing a smear campaign or negative online publicity. These experts employ advanced monitoring tools to track mentions, reviews, and articles that could harm the individual's reputation. Their ability to respond swiftly and effectively is a testament to their expertise in managing online narratives. In the field of geospatial analysis, expert OSINT analysts harness the power of advanced mapping tools and GIS integration. They can identify geolocation-based threats, analyze satellite imagery, and assess the impact of geopolitical events on a region. Consider a scenario where an expert OSINT practitioner is part of a humanitarian organization responding to a natural disaster. They leverage geospatial data to assess the extent of damage, plan relief efforts, and coordinate resources effectively. Expert OSINT analysts also excel in the field of cybersecurity. Imagine a cybersecurity company relying on their expertise to identify vulnerabilities and potential threats. These experts have a keen understanding of the tactics and techniques employed by cybercriminals, allowing them to provide actionable threat intelligence. Consider a situation where an expert OSINT analyst is monitoring a dark web marketplace known for selling stolen data. They gather intelligence on new listings, compromised accounts, and potential data breaches, enabling organizations to proactively protect their assets. In the realm of digital forensics, expert OSINT practitioners excel in analyzing digital artifacts and metadata. They can reconstruct digital crime scenes, trace the source of cyberattacks, and provide critical evidence in legal cases. Imagine a law enforcement agency relying on their expertise to solve a complex cybercrime involving financial fraud and identity theft. These experts painstakingly examine digital footprints, uncovering the trail of the perpetrators. Expert OSINT practitioners are also instrumental in conducting OSINT-driven investigations. Consider a scenario where they are tasked with uncovering corporate espionage activities targeting a technology company. They employ advanced analytical tools to connect the dots between seemingly unrelated events, revealing a sophisticated espionage network. In the world of financial intelligence, expert OSINT analysts are essential in identifying money laundering and financial crimes. Imagine a financial institution relying on their expertise to detect suspicious transactions and comply with anti-money laundering regulations. These experts meticulously analyze cryptocurrency transactions, financial records, and blockchain data to uncover illicit activities. Expert OSINT practitioners are also at the forefront of research and academia. Imagine a social scientist using their expertise to study the impact of social media on political polarization. These experts collect and analyze vast datasets, providing valuable insights into the dynamics of online discourse. Consider a scenario where an expert OSINT analyst contributes to academic research by uncovering patterns in online misinformation and propaganda campaigns. Their findings inform discussions on disinformation's impact on society and democracy. In the legal field, expert OSINT analysts assist in building strong cases for litigation. Imagine a legal team relying on their expertise to uncover digital evidence that supports their client's claims. These experts leave no digital stone unturned, ensuring that all relevant information is brought to light. Expert OSINT practitioners also contribute to humanitarian efforts. Consider an international organization using their expertise to monitor human rights abuses in conflict zones. These experts gather evidence, document violations, and raise awareness on a global scale, advocating for justice and accountability. In summary, learning from expert-level OSINT operations offers a wealth of knowledge and practical insights across diverse fields and industries. Expert OSINT practitioners demonstrate the power of advanced techniques, precision, and the ability to uncover hidden information within the vast realm of open-source intelligence. Their expertise is invaluable in addressing cybersecurity threats, conducting investigations, informing decision-making, and advancing research in an ever-evolving digital landscape.

BOOK 3
DIGITAL FOOTPRINT ANALYSIS
HARNESSING OSINT FOR PROFILING AND
INVESTIGATIONS

ROB BOTWRIGHT

Chapter 1: Understanding the Digital Footprint

Understanding the concept of a digital footprint is essential in today's interconnected world. Think of your digital footprint as the trail of digital breadcrumbs you leave behind while using the internet. It's a comprehensive record of your online activities, interactions, and information. Imagine every website you visit, every social media post you make, every email you send, and every online transaction you engage in. All of these actions contribute to your digital footprint. Your digital footprint can be vast, comprising a wide range of data, from your social media profiles to your online shopping habits. This data is scattered across various platforms, websites, and servers, forming a digital representation of your online presence. Your digital footprint is not just about what you share intentionally; it also includes data generated passively, such as your IP address, device information, and browsing history. Consider the websites you visit regularly, the photos you upload, the comments you leave on forums, and the searches you perform on search engines. All of these actions create data points that collectively make up your digital footprint. Your digital footprint can have far-reaching implications, both positive and negative. Imagine a scenario where you're applying for a job, and your potential employer conducts an online background check. They may review your social media profiles, online posts, and any publicly available information to assess your suitability for the position. Your digital footprint can influence their perception of you and impact your chances of being hired. Consider the importance of managing your digital footprint to present a professional and positive image to potential employers. On the flip side, your digital footprint can also be a valuable asset when used strategically. Imagine you're a small business owner looking to expand your customer base. You can leverage your online presence, including your website, social media accounts, and customer reviews, to attract new clients and build trust. Your digital footprint serves as a digital storefront, allowing potential customers to learn about your products or services. Consider the power of online marketing and reputation management in growing your business. In today's digital age, privacy and security are paramount when it comes to managing your digital footprint. Imagine the importance of safeguarding your personal information, financial details, and sensitive data from cyber threats. You need to be vigilant about protecting your online accounts with strong passwords, enabling two-factor authentication, and being cautious about sharing personal information online. Consider the potential consequences of a data breach or identity theft, highlighting the need for digital security measures. Your digital footprint extends beyond your personal life; it can also impact your online identity and reputation. Imagine a scenario where false information or negative content about you is posted online. This can harm your reputation and affect your personal and professional life. You must be proactive in monitoring your digital presence and addressing any inaccuracies or damaging content. Consider the importance of online reputation management tools and strategies. Your digital footprint is not static; it evolves as you continue to engage with the digital world. Imagine the changes that occur as you create new social media accounts, update your LinkedIn profile, or change your online habits. These actions contribute to the ongoing development of your digital footprint. Consider the need for periodic reviews and updates to ensure that your online presence accurately reflects your goals and values. In summary, understanding the basics of your digital footprint is crucial in today's digital landscape. It encompasses the data and traces you leave behind while navigating the internet, impacting various aspects of your life. Managing and protecting your digital footprint is essential for personal and professional success, privacy, and security in the digital age. The impact of digital footprints on open-source intelligence (OSINT) is profound and far-reaching. Imagine the wealth of information that individuals and organizations unwittingly expose through their digital activities. Every online interaction, whether it's posting on social media, conducting online transactions, or simply browsing the web, contributes to the creation of digital footprints. Consider the implications of this constant data generation in the context of OSINT. OSINT practitioners rely on digital footprints as a valuable source of information for various purposes. Imagine a scenario where a cybersecurity analyst is investigating a cyberattack on a company's network. They begin by examining the digital footprints left behind by the attackers. These footprints can include traces of malicious code, IP addresses used for command and control servers, and patterns of behavior. Consider the importance of digital footprints in identifying the attack's origin, techniques employed, and potential vulnerabilities exploited. In the realm of threat intelligence, digital footprints play a pivotal role in monitoring and detecting emerging cyber threats. Imagine a threat analyst tracking the activities of a hacker group known for launching advanced persistent threats (APTs). They rely on the digital footprints left by the group's members, such as their online personas, communication patterns, and malware signatures. Consider how the analysis of these footprints can provide insights into the APT group's tactics, techniques, and procedures (TTPs). In the field of investigative journalism, digital footprints are a goldmine of information. Imagine an investigative reporter working on a story about corporate corruption. They use OSINT techniques to trace the digital footprints of individuals involved, such as their social media posts, email communications, and financial transactions. Consider the role of digital footprints in uncovering evidence and connecting the dots in investigative reporting. Law enforcement agencies also rely on digital footprints in criminal investigations. Imagine a detective investigating a missing persons case. They analyze the digital footprints of the missing individual, including their last online activity, location data, and social media interactions. Consider the value of digital footprints in narrowing down search areas and generating leads in such cases. Digital footprints extend beyond individuals to encompass organizations and entities. Imagine a competitive intelligence analyst researching a rival company. They scrutinize the company's online presence, examining its website, press releases, and social media posts. Consider the insights gained from the digital footprints of competing businesses, informing strategic decisions. The impact of digital footprints on OSINT is not limited to cybersecurity, threat intelligence, journalism, law enforcement, or competitive intelligence. Consider the broader societal implications of the vast amounts of digital footprints generated daily. Individuals and organizations are increasingly aware of the potential consequences of their digital actions. Imagine the shift towards more cautious online behavior and increased privacy measures as people seek to minimize their digital footprints. The notion of "digital hygiene" has gained prominence, emphasizing responsible online behavior and data protection. Consider the role of education and awareness campaigns in promoting digital hygiene practices. In the age of social media, the impact of digital footprints on reputation management cannot be overstated. Imagine a public figure who faces a crisis due to negative online publicity. They engage in online reputation management to mitigate the damage caused by harmful digital footprints. Consider the strategies employed to suppress negative search results and promote positive content. The business world is also acutely aware of the impact of digital footprints. Imagine a company that closely monitors its online reputation and customer sentiment. They use OSINT techniques to gather data from customer reviews, social media mentions, and online forums. Consider the insights gained from analyzing this data, leading to improvements in products and services. Digital footprints are valuable not only in OSINT but also in marketing and customer engagement. Imagine a marketing team using digital footprints to understand customer preferences and tailor personalized advertising campaigns. Consider the benefits of delivering relevant content to consumers based on their online behavior. The impact of digital footprints on OSINT is further amplified by advancements in technology. Imagine the role of artificial intelligence (AI) and machine learning in analyzing massive datasets of digital footprints. These technologies can identify patterns, anomalies, and trends that human analysts might overlook. Consider the potential for AI-driven OSINT tools to enhance the efficiency and effectiveness of investigations. However, it's crucial to balance the benefits of digital footprints with privacy concerns. Imagine a debate over the ethical use of OSINT data and the need to protect individuals' privacy rights. Consider the importance of regulations and guidelines to ensure responsible OSINT practices. The impact of digital footprints on OSINT continues to evolve as technology advances and society adapts. Imagine the future of OSINT, where augmented reality, the Internet of Things (IoT), and quantum computing create new sources of digital footprints. Consider the challenges and opportunities that these developments present for OSINT practitioners. In summary, the impact of digital footprints on OSINT is profound and multifaceted. These digital traces provide a wealth of information for cybersecurity, threat intelligence, investigative journalism, law enforcement, competitive intelligence, and reputation management. As technology and awareness grow, the role of digital footprints in OSINT will continue to shape our digital landscape.

Chapter 2: Establishing a Comprehensive OSINT Workflow

Designing an effective open-source intelligence (OSINT) workflow is essential for efficiently gathering and analyzing information from various sources. Imagine embarking on an OSINT investigation without a structured workflow, and you may find yourself overwhelmed by data. An organized workflow not only streamlines the process but also ensures that you don't miss crucial details. Consider the OSINT workflow as a roadmap that guides you from the initial data collection to the final analysis and reporting. The first step in designing an effective OSINT workflow is defining your objectives and scope. Imagine you're conducting OSINT for a cybersecurity threat assessment. Your objective might be to identify potential vulnerabilities and threats to your organization's network. Consider the importance of having a clear goal to focus your efforts and resources effectively. Once you've established your objectives, the next step is to identify the sources of information you'll need. Imagine you're interested in monitoring a specific social media platform for mentions of your brand. You'll need to determine which social media channels to monitor and which keywords or hashtags to track. Consider the significance of selecting the right sources to gather relevant data. With your objectives and sources identified, it's time to plan your data collection strategy. Imagine you're gathering data from websites, social media, and online forums. You'll need to decide how frequently you'll collect data, whether it's in real-time or periodically. Consider the trade-offs between real-time data collection and periodic updates based on your goals. Implementing effective data collection tools and techniques is crucial in the OSINT workflow. Imagine you're using web scraping tools to extract information from websites. You'll need to select the appropriate scraping tools, set up the parameters, and schedule data retrieval. Consider the importance of automating data collection to save time and ensure consistency. As data begins to flow into your OSINT pipeline, it's essential to preprocess and clean the information. Imagine you're collecting social media posts mentioning your brand. You'll need to remove duplicates, filter out irrelevant content, and standardize the data for analysis. Consider the role of data cleaning in ensuring the quality and accuracy of your OSINT dataset. The analysis phase of the OSINT workflow is where you extract insights and intelligence from the collected data. Imagine you're analyzing social media sentiment to gauge public opinion about a product launch. You'll need to apply sentiment analysis techniques to categorize posts as positive, negative, or neutral. Consider the value of turning raw data into actionable intelligence through analysis. Visualization tools play a vital role in conveying your findings effectively. Imagine you've identified trends in social media sentiment data. You can create charts and graphs to visualize these trends, making them more accessible to stakeholders. Consider the power of data visualization in communicating complex information. Throughout the OSINT workflow, it's essential to maintain a secure and organized data repository. Imagine you're working on a long-term OSINT project that spans months. You'll need a system to store and archive the collected data securely. Consider the importance of data security and management in maintaining the integrity of your OSINT efforts. Documentation is a critical aspect of the OSINT workflow. Imagine a scenario where you've uncovered significant insights during your investigation. You need to document your findings, methodology, and sources for reference and reporting. Consider the role of documentation in ensuring transparency and accountability in your work. Communication is key in sharing the results of your OSINT efforts with stakeholders. Imagine you've discovered a potential security threat to your organization. You'll need to present your findings to the cybersecurity team and provide recommendations. Consider the importance of effective communication in driving action based on your OSINT findings. Feedback and continuous improvement are essential in refining your OSINT workflow. Imagine receiving feedback from stakeholders about the usefulness of your intelligence reports. You can use this feedback to make adjustments and enhancements to your workflow. Consider the value of a dynamic and evolving OSINT process. Collaboration can enhance the effectiveness of your OSINT workflow. Imagine you're working on a complex OSINT investigation that requires expertise in various domains. Collaborating with subject matter experts can provide valuable insights and perspectives. Consider the benefits of teamwork in tackling multifaceted OSINT challenges. Ethical considerations are paramount throughout the OSINT workflow. Imagine you come across sensitive or personal information during your data collection. You'll need to adhere to ethical guidelines and legal regulations to protect individuals' privacy. Consider the importance of ethical conduct in maintaining trust and credibility in OSINT. Adaptability is a crucial trait in the world of OSINT. Imagine a situation where your initial data sources are no longer yielding relevant information. You'll need to adapt your strategy and explore alternative sources or methods. Consider the agility required to navigate the ever-changing landscape of OSINT. In summary, designing an effective OSINT workflow is essential for successfully harnessing open-source intelligence. By defining objectives, selecting sources, planning data collection, implementing tools and techniques, preprocessing data, conducting analysis, visualizing findings, maintaining data security, documenting, communicating, seeking feedback, collaborating, upholding ethics, and staying adaptable, you can navigate the complex world of OSINT with confidence and competence. Workflow automation and optimization are critical components of any efficient and productive operation. Imagine you're managing a large-scale OSINT project that involves monitoring multiple online sources. Automation can significantly streamline your workflow by automating repetitive tasks. Consider the time and effort saved by using automated data collection tools that can gather information round the clock. Automation can also enhance data preprocessing, making it faster and more accurate. Imagine you're dealing with vast amounts of unstructured data from various sources. Automation tools can help standardize, clean, and organize this data for analysis. Consider the benefits of consistent and error-free data preprocessing achieved through automation. One of the key aspects of workflow automation is the use of scripts and custom programs. Imagine you're tasked with extracting specific information from websites on a regular basis. You can create custom web scraping scripts to automate this process, reducing manual effort. Consider the flexibility and precision that custom scripts offer in data collection and manipulation. Workflow optimization goes hand in hand with automation, aiming to make every step of the process more efficient. Imagine you're analyzing social media data to track a marketing campaign's performance. Optimizing your analysis workflow can help you identify trends and insights more quickly. Consider the advantage of timely decision-making based on optimized data analysis. Workflow optimization often involves fine-tuning the order of tasks and resource allocation. Imagine you're managing a team of OSINT analysts working on different aspects of a project. Optimizing task assignments and resource allocation can ensure that each team member's skills are maximized. Consider the improved productivity and utilization of human resources achieved through optimization. Feedback loops are integral to workflow optimization. Imagine you've implemented a new automation tool in your OSINT workflow. Collecting feedback from team members about its usability and effectiveness can lead to refinements. Consider the iterative nature of workflow optimization, where feedback drives continuous improvement. Automation and optimization can also enhance the documentation and reporting aspects of OSINT. Imagine you're preparing an intelligence report for a client or senior management. Automation tools can generate standardized reports, while optimization ensures clarity and relevance. Consider the time saved in report generation and the increased impact of well-organized reports. Data integration is a vital component of workflow optimization. Imagine you're gathering data from various sources, such as social media, news websites, and public records. Integrating these diverse datasets into a unified format simplifies analysis and enhances insights. Consider the advantages of a holistic view of information achieved through data integration. Workflow automation and optimization extend beyond data collection and analysis. Imagine you're coordinating OSINT efforts across multiple teams or departments. Automation can facilitate communication and task assignment, while optimization ensures alignment with goals. Consider the enhanced collaboration and coordination that automation and optimization can bring. The scalability of an OSINT operation benefits significantly from automation and optimization. Imagine your OSINT needs grow as you take on more projects and clients. An optimized and automated workflow can handle increased data volumes and complexity. Consider the adaptability of your OSINT processes to meet growing demands. Cybersecurity and threat intelligence are domains where workflow automation is particularly crucial. Imagine you're a cybersecurity analyst monitoring network logs for suspicious activity. Automation can swiftly identify and flag potential threats, allowing rapid response. Consider the proactive defense capabilities offered by automated threat detection. Workflow optimization in threat intelligence can improve the prioritization of threats. Imagine you're managing a list of potential vulnerabilities and their associated risks. Optimizing your threat assessment process ensures that the most critical threats are addressed first. Consider the reduced exposure to high-risk threats achieved through optimization. In the context of competitive intelligence, automation and optimization enable real-time monitoring. Imagine you're tracking your competitors' product launches and marketing campaigns. Automation tools can deliver alerts when significant events occur, while optimization ensures relevancy. Consider the strategic advantage of timely insights gained through real-time monitoring. Social media analysis benefits greatly from workflow automation and optimization. Imagine you're monitoring brand mentions on multiple social platforms. Automation can consolidate data, and optimization can uncover sentiment trends and customer preferences. Consider the improved customer engagement and brand management enabled by these processes. Ethical considerations remain paramount in OSINT, even when employing automation. Imagine you're using automated data collection tools to gather information about individuals. Ethical guidelines and privacy regulations must be adhered to, and optimization can include ethical checks. Consider the importance of ethical conduct and responsible automation in OSINT. The future of OSINT will likely see further advancements in automation and optimization. Imagine the possibilities of machine learning and AI-driven OSINT tools that adapt and self-optimize. The role of OSINT professionals may evolve to focus on overseeing and refining automated processes. Consider the exciting prospects and challenges that automation and optimization present in the future of OSINT. In summary, workflow automation and optimization are essential elements in the world of OSINT. They improve efficiency, accuracy, scalability, and responsiveness across various domains, from cybersecurity to competitive intelligence. By embracing automation and continually optimizing workflows, OSINT practitioners can stay at the forefront of intelligence gathering and analysis.

Chapter 3: Tracing Online Identities and Personas

In the digital age, where much of our lives are lived online, identifying and understanding online identities has become a crucial aspect of open-source intelligence (OSINT). Imagine you're tasked with investigating a social media account with potentially malicious activity. Identifying the person or entity behind that account can provide valuable insights. Consider the significance of techniques for unmasking online personas and their potential impact. Online identities come in various forms, from social media profiles to email addresses and pseudonyms. Imagine you need to determine if two seemingly unrelated online identities belong to the same individual. Linking these identities can reveal hidden connections and patterns. Consider the implications of accurately identifying individuals across multiple online platforms. One common technique for identifying online identities is through data triangulation. Imagine you're investigating a user who has used different aliases across various websites. By collecting and cross-referencing data from these platforms, you can build a more comprehensive profile. Consider the power of data triangulation in connecting the dots of online personas. Metadata analysis is another valuable tool for identifying online identities. Imagine you have a photo posted online with no accompanying information about the uploader. Examining the photo's metadata can provide clues, such as location and device details. Consider the potential insights gained from metadata analysis in identifying users. Social network analysis is a technique often employed in identifying online identities. Imagine you're investigating a group of individuals involved in an online community. Mapping their connections and interactions can help uncover the central figures and their roles. Consider the significance of social network analysis in understanding the dynamics of online groups. Username analysis can also be instrumental in identifying online identities. Imagine you come across a username on a forum or social media platform. Analyzing the username for patterns, references, or associations can lead to valuable insights. Consider the role of username analysis in deciphering the meaning and context behind online aliases. Behavioral analysis is a technique that delves into the online behavior of individuals. Imagine you're trying to determine if a particular user is the same person behind multiple accounts. Studying their posting habits, writing style, and interests can provide clues. Consider the depth of insights gained from behavioral analysis in linking online identities. Advanced search techniques can aid in identifying online identities. Imagine you have limited information about an individual but want to find their online presence. Using specialized search engines and operators can narrow down the search results effectively. Consider the precision and efficiency offered by advanced search techniques in online identity discovery. Language analysis can be a powerful tool for identifying online identities. Imagine you're investigating a series of threatening messages posted anonymously. Analyzing the language used may help identify the author based on their unique writing style. Consider the role of linguistic analysis in unmasking individuals hiding behind online anonymity. Geolocation data can assist in identifying online identities with a physical component. Imagine you're tracking the movements of an individual through their online check-ins. Geolocating their activities can help pinpoint their real-world identity and location. Consider the potential value of geolocation data in connecting online personas to the offline world. Sentiment analysis can be applied to identify online identities based on emotional cues. Imagine you're trying to determine if a user is connected to a particular cause or group. Analyzing their posts for sentiment and affiliations can reveal hidden connections. Consider the insights gained from sentiment analysis in uncovering the motivations behind online identities. Anonymity networks and privacy tools can complicate the process of identifying online identities. Imagine you're investigating a user who uses Tor or a VPN to conceal their IP address. These technologies make tracing back to a specific individual more challenging. Consider the complexities involved in identifying online identities when anonymity is a factor. Machine learning and AI are increasingly employed in identifying online identities. Imagine you have a large dataset of online conversations to analyze. Machine learning algorithms can help identify patterns and anomalies to unmask hidden identities. Consider the potential of AI-driven techniques in streamlining the identification process. Ethical considerations are paramount when identifying online identities. Imagine you have discovered information about an individual's online activities. Respecting their privacy and adhering to legal and ethical guidelines is essential. Consider the importance of ethical conduct in online identity investigations. False positives and errors can occur when identifying online identities. Imagine you misidentify an individual based on incomplete or inaccurate information. Verifying the accuracy of your findings is crucial to avoid harm or misinformation. Consider the need for diligence and validation in the identification process. In summary, techniques for identifying online identities are critical tools in the realm of open-source intelligence. From data triangulation and metadata analysis to social network analysis and username examination, these techniques provide a comprehensive toolkit for OSINT practitioners. When applied ethically and thoughtfully, these techniques enable the unveiling of hidden online personas and the understanding of the individuals behind them. Profiling online personas is a fundamental aspect of intelligence gathering in the digital age. Imagine you're tasked with understanding the motives and activities of an individual operating under a pseudonym. Creating a profile of their online persona can provide valuable insights. Consider the significance of online persona profiling in uncovering hidden information. Online personas come in various forms, from social media profiles to forum avatars and blog authors. Imagine you're investigating a person of interest who maintains multiple online identities across different platforms. Building a comprehensive profile that connects these personas is essential. Consider the advantages of linking diverse online identities for a holistic understanding. One key element of profiling online personas is information aggregation. Imagine you're collecting data from various online sources, such as social media posts, forum discussions, and blog comments. Aggregating this information into a unified dataset forms the foundation for analysis. Consider the importance of comprehensive data collection in building accurate online persona profiles. Data normalization and cleaning are essential steps in the profiling process. Imagine you're dealing with unstructured data containing misspellings, abbreviations, and variations in writing style. Normalizing and cleaning this data ensure consistency and accuracy in your analysis. Consider the benefits of error-free and standardized data in persona profiling. Profile enrichment involves augmenting your dataset with additional context. Imagine you have information about a user's online activity, but it lacks details about their offline life. Enriching the profile with data like real-world events and affiliations can provide a broader perspective. Consider the depth of insights gained from enriched online persona profiles. Social network analysis plays a vital role in profiling online personas. Imagine you're investigating an individual who participates in various online communities. Mapping their connections, interactions, and influence within these networks can reveal their role. Consider the significance of social network analysis in understanding the dynamics of online personas. Behavioral analysis delves into the online behavior of individuals behind personas. Imagine you're trying to determine the motives of a user who frequently posts on a political forum. Analyzing their posting habits, sentiment, and engagement with specific topics can provide clues. Consider the depth of insights gained from behavioral analysis in profiling online personas. Language analysis can be instrumental in understanding the nuances of online personas. Imagine you're studying a user who uses different communication styles on various platforms. Analyzing their language use can reveal patterns, preferences, and potential indicators. Consider the power of linguistic analysis in deciphering the traits of online personas. Geolocation data can add a spatial dimension to online persona profiles. Imagine you're tracing the movements of an individual who shares location-tagged photos. Geolocating these activities can help connect online personas to real-world locations. Consider the insights gained from geolocation data in persona profiling. Sentiment analysis offers a window into the emotional aspects of online personas. Imagine you're investigating a user who frequently expresses strong opinions. Analyzing their posts for sentiment can reveal their emotional disposition and affiliations. Consider the role of sentiment analysis in understanding the motivations behind online personas. Timeline construction helps create a chronological view of online persona activities. Imagine you're building a timeline of an individual's online interactions and postings. This timeline can highlight key events, trends, and shifts in their behavior. Consider the value of timeline construction in tracing the evolution of online personas. Profile visualization tools enable you to present complex persona data intuitively. Imagine you're preparing a report for your intelligence agency or client. Visualizing the connections, networks, and activities of online personas can enhance understanding. Consider the impact of clear and concise persona visualizations in conveying insights. Machine learning and AI are increasingly used in online persona profiling. Imagine you have a large dataset of online activities to analyze. Machine learning algorithms can help identify patterns and anomalies, streamlining the profiling process. Consider the potential of AI-driven techniques in enhancing the accuracy and efficiency of persona profiling. Ethical considerations remain paramount when profiling online personas. Imagine you've uncovered personal information about an individual's online activities. Respecting their privacy and adhering to legal and ethical guidelines is essential. Consider the importance of ethical conduct in online persona profiling. False positives and errors can occur during persona profiling. Imagine you misinterpret an individual's online behavior or misattribute posts to them. Vigilance in verification and validation is crucial to avoid harm or misinformation. Consider the need for diligence and accuracy in online persona profiling. In summary, profiling online personas is a multifaceted and dynamic field within open-source intelligence. From data aggregation and behavioral analysis to language and sentiment analysis, these techniques provide a comprehensive toolkit for understanding individuals operating in the digital realm. When applied ethically and rigorously, online persona profiling can uncover valuable insights that inform intelligence gathering and decision-making processes.

Chapter 4: Analyzing Social Media Trails

Extracting insights from social media activity is a crucial aspect of open-source intelligence in the digital age. Imagine you're tasked with understanding the sentiment and trends related to a specific topic on social media. Analyzing social media data can provide valuable insights into public opinions and behaviors. Consider the significance of social media as a vast source of real-time information. Social media platforms, such as Twitter, Facebook, Instagram, and LinkedIn, are rich sources of user-generated content. Imagine you need to monitor conversations related to a product launch or a political event. These platforms offer a wealth of data in the form of posts, comments, likes, shares, and hashtags. Consider the depth of information available within social media ecosystems. One key aspect of extracting insights from social media is data collection. Imagine you're using specialized tools to gather data from various social media platforms. This data collection process involves accessing APIs (Application Programming Interfaces) provided by these platforms. Consider the importance of ethical and responsible data collection practices. Data preprocessing is an essential step in preparing social media data for analysis. Imagine you're dealing with a large dataset containing text, images, and videos. Cleaning, filtering, and structuring this data ensure its suitability for analysis. Consider the benefits of organized and error-free data for extracting meaningful insights. Sentiment analysis plays a vital role in understanding public sentiment from social media activity. Imagine you want to gauge public reactions to a recent news event. Sentiment analysis algorithms can classify posts as positive, negative, or neutral based on the language used. Consider the power of sentiment analysis in identifying public sentiment trends. Topic modeling is another technique used to extract insights from social media data. Imagine you're interested in identifying prevalent topics within a specific online community. Topic modeling algorithms can uncover underlying themes and trends in conversations. Consider the value of topic modeling in uncovering hidden patterns in social media discussions. Network analysis enables the exploration of connections between social media users. Imagine you want to understand the influence and interactions of individuals in a particular network. Network analysis can help identify key players, opinion leaders, and communities. Consider the insights gained from visualizing social media networks and their connections. Temporal analysis focuses on the evolution of topics and trends over time. Imagine you're tracking the popularity of a hashtag related to a social movement. Temporal analysis can reveal when and how certain topics gain traction or lose relevance. Consider the importance of understanding the dynamics of time in social media insights. Geospatial analysis adds a spatial dimension to social media data. Imagine you're interested in the geographical distribution of social media posts. Geospatial analysis can map out the locations associated with user-generated content. Consider the insights gained from connecting social media activity to real-world locations. User profiling involves creating profiles of social media users based on their activities. Imagine you want to understand the characteristics and preferences of a target audience. User profiling can help identify demographic information, interests, and behavior patterns. Consider the relevance of user profiling in tailoring content and marketing strategies. Natural language processing (NLP) techniques are essential for text analysis. Imagine you're analyzing thousands of social media posts for key insights. NLP algorithms can extract keywords, sentiments, and entities from textual data. Consider the efficiency of NLP in processing and understanding large volumes of text. Image and video analysis expand the scope of social media insights. Imagine you want to detect visual content related to a specific event or brand. Image and video analysis tools can identify and classify multimedia content. Consider the value of multimedia analysis in capturing diverse forms of user-generated content. Machine learning and AI algorithms are increasingly used in social media insights. Imagine you have a vast dataset of social media posts to analyze. Machine learning models can automatically identify patterns and trends. Consider the potential of AI-driven techniques in automating social media analysis. Ethical considerations are paramount when extracting insights from social media. Imagine you're working with sensitive user data and personal information. Respecting privacy, consent, and adhering to ethical guidelines is crucial. Consider the importance of ethical conduct in handling social media data. False positives and misinterpretations can occur when analyzing social media data. Imagine you misclassify a sentiment or misunderstand the context of a post. Validation and cross-referencing of results are essential to ensure accuracy. Consider the need for diligence and critical thinking in social media insights. In summary, extracting insights from social media activity is a dynamic and evolving field within open-source intelligence. From data collection and preprocessing to sentiment analysis and machine learning, these techniques offer a comprehensive toolkit for understanding the digital landscape. When applied ethically and responsibly, social media insights can inform decision-making, marketing strategies, and public sentiment analysis. Behavioral analysis and predictive profiling are essential techniques in the realm of open-source intelligence. Imagine you're trying to anticipate the actions and intentions of individuals or groups. Behavioral analysis involves studying patterns of behavior to gain insights into future actions. Consider the importance of understanding behavioral cues in various contexts. Predictive profiling, on the other hand, aims to create profiles that predict future behaviors and actions. Imagine you want to identify potential threats or opportunities based on historical data. Predictive profiling can help in assessing risks and making informed decisions. Consider the power of predictive profiling in a wide range of applications. Both behavioral analysis and predictive profiling require a multidisciplinary approach. Imagine you're dealing with diverse data sources, including online behavior, financial transactions, and social interactions. Integrating data from different domains can provide a more comprehensive understanding of individuals or groups. Consider the benefits of a holistic view in behavioral analysis and predictive profiling. Behavioral analysis begins with data collection and monitoring. Imagine you're tracking online activities, such as website visits, social media interactions, and communication patterns. These digital footprints can reveal valuable information about preferences, interests, and affiliations.

Consider the wealth of data available for behavioral analysis in the digital age. Pattern recognition is a key component of behavioral analysis. Imagine you're using machine learning algorithms to identify recurring patterns. These patterns may include specific keywords in communications, time-based activities, or changes in behavior. Consider the potential of pattern recognition in detecting anomalies and predicting future actions. Behavioral analysis can be applied in various domains, including cybersecurity. Imagine you're responsible for identifying potential insider threats within an organization. Analyzing employee behavior patterns can help in early detection and risk mitigation. Consider the role of behavioral analysis in enhancing security measures. Psychological profiling is often used in criminal investigations. Imagine you're a law enforcement officer trying to understand the mindset of a suspect. Psychological profiling can provide insights into motives, traits, and potential actions. Consider the relevance of psychological profiling in criminal justice. In the context of financial markets, behavioral analysis plays a significant role. Imagine you're an investor trying to predict market trends. Studying the behavior of traders and investors can offer clues about market sentiment. Consider the importance of behavioral analysis in financial decision-making. Predictive profiling takes behavioral analysis a step further. Imagine you're a security analyst aiming to identify potential threats to a company. Predictive profiling can help in creating risk profiles that anticipate future actions. Consider the value of proactive measures in threat assessment. Machine learning and artificial intelligence are pivotal in predictive profiling. Imagine you have vast datasets and need to identify high-risk individuals or events. Machine learning models can analyze historical data to make predictions. Consider the power of machine learning in automating predictive profiling. In the context of counterterrorism, predictive profiling is crucial. Imagine you're a national security agency trying to prevent acts of terrorism. Predictive profiling can assist in identifying individuals or groups with extremist tendencies. Consider the role of predictive profiling in national security efforts. Privacy concerns are paramount in behavioral analysis and predictive profiling. Imagine you're collecting and analyzing personal data for profiling purposes. Respecting privacy rights and ethical considerations is essential. Consider the need for responsible data handling and consent. False positives and misinterpretations are risks in predictive profiling. Imagine you misclassify an individual as a high-risk threat when they are not. Validation and continuous refinement of profiling models are essential. Consider the importance of accuracy and minimizing false alarms. In summary, behavioral analysis and predictive profiling are powerful tools in open-source intelligence. From understanding online behaviors to predicting future actions, these techniques have a wide range of applications. When used responsibly and ethically, they can enhance security, decision-making, and risk assessment in various domains. The evolving field of behavioral analysis and predictive profiling continues to shape the way we gather and utilize information for the greater good.

Chapter 5: Uncovering Digital Artifacts and Metadata

Metadata plays a pivotal role in the world of open-source intelligence. Imagine you're exploring the digital footprints left behind by individuals or organizations. Metadata encompasses a variety of data that accompanies digital files and online content. Consider the significance of metadata in uncovering hidden information. When you take a photo with your smartphone, for example, metadata is embedded within the image file. Imagine you're investigating an incident, and you come across a photo posted online. Metadata in that photo could reveal the date, time, and even the GPS coordinates of where it was taken. Consider the wealth of information hidden within metadata. Metadata can exist in various forms, including EXIF data in images, ID3 tags in music files, and PDF document properties. Imagine you're analyzing a collection of documents related to a corporate merger. Document metadata may contain details about the author, creation date, and revision history. Consider the potential of metadata in providing context and provenance. Social media platforms also generate metadata associated with posts, tweets, and user profiles. Imagine you're tracking social media activity to understand an individual's online presence. Metadata can reveal when a post was made, the device used, and the location if enabled. Consider the role of social media metadata in profiling and investigations. Metadata is not limited to text and images; it extends to other digital assets, such as videos and audio recordings. Imagine you're reviewing a video clip shared on a video-sharing platform. Video metadata can include information about the camera used, recording date, and even location data. Consider the value of video metadata in verifying authenticity and context. Geolocation metadata is particularly relevant in OSINT, providing information about the physical location where content was created. Imagine you're analyzing geotagged photos shared on a social network. Geolocation metadata can pinpoint the exact coordinates of where the photo was taken. Consider the utility of geolocation metadata in mapping and tracking. Metadata is not always visible to the naked eye, making it a valuable source of hidden information. Imagine you're inspecting a document to understand its origins. Hidden metadata may reveal details about the author's identity or the software used to create it. Consider the advantage of uncovering concealed metadata in investigations. Metadata can be manually edited or stripped from files, but it often remains intact. Imagine you're dealing with an image that has been altered to remove metadata. Advanced forensic tools can sometimes recover deleted or altered metadata. Consider the persistence of metadata and its potential recoverability. Metadata analysis is an integral part of OSINT investigations. Imagine you're conducting research on an organization's online activities. Analyzing metadata can help you piece together a timeline and track changes over time. Consider the role of metadata in establishing a digital trail. Metadata can also be leveraged for geospatial intelligence (GEOINT). Imagine you're analyzing satellite imagery for a disaster response operation. Geospatial metadata can provide critical information about the location and timestamp of imagery. Consider the applications of geospatial metadata in emergency situations. Metadata analysis tools are available to assist OSINT practitioners in extracting and interpreting metadata. Imagine you're working on a digital forensics case. Specialized software can help automate the extraction and analysis of metadata. Consider the efficiency gained through metadata analysis tools. Metadata has ethical implications when used in OSINT. Imagine you're handling personal information contained within metadata. Respecting privacy and adhering to legal and ethical standards is paramount. Consider the need for responsible metadata handling and data protection. False or misleading metadata can be used to obfuscate information. Imagine you're encountering fabricated metadata intended to mislead investigators. Verification and cross-referencing are essential to ensure the accuracy of metadata. Consider the challenges posed by deceptive metadata practices. In summary, metadata is a hidden treasure trove of information in the world of open-source intelligence. From geolocation data in photos to hidden details in documents, metadata can provide crucial context and insights. As OSINT practitioners, understanding how to extract, analyze, and interpret metadata is a valuable skill. But it's essential to do so responsibly, respecting privacy and ethical boundaries while maximizing the potential of this valuable source of information. Tracing digital artifacts to their sources is a fundamental aspect of open-source intelligence. Imagine you come across a piece of digital information, like an image or a document, during your investigation. Digital artifacts can contain valuable clues and insights, but to fully understand their significance, you need to trace them back to their origins. Consider the process of tracing digital artifacts as akin to following a breadcrumb trail in the digital landscape. Digital artifacts are traces of digital activities or creations left behind in the online world. Imagine these artifacts as footprints in the sand, each with the potential to lead you to a source of information or an individual. Examples of digital artifacts include files, emails, images, videos, and more. Consider the vast array of digital artifacts that exist, waiting to be analyzed and traced. Metadata, as discussed earlier, is one of the essential digital artifacts. Imagine you're examining an image, and you notice the metadata contains information about the camera used and the location where the photo was taken. Tracing this metadata back to its source can help you uncover who took the photo and where. Consider the role of metadata as a foundational digital artifact in tracing origins. URLs and hyperlinks are another set of digital artifacts that offer pathways to trace. Imagine you're investigating a suspicious website mentioned in a forum post. Following the URL can lead you to the source of the content and potentially reveal the author or organization behind it. Consider URLs as digital signposts guiding you to the original sources of information. Digital artifacts often leave behind digital fingerprints. Imagine you're examining a document, and you notice certain formatting styles or language patterns. These can be like fingerprints, unique to the software or author who created the document. Tracing these fingerprints can help you identify the source or authorship of the document. Consider the significance of digital fingerprints in source attribution. Emails are rich sources of digital artifacts. Imagine you receive an anonymous email containing sensitive information. Tracing the email headers and analyzing its content can provide insights into the sender's identity and motives. Consider the value of email analysis in uncovering hidden sources. IP addresses are essential digital artifacts for tracing the origins of online activities. Imagine you're investigating a cyberattack on a company's server. Tracing the IP address responsible for the attack can lead you to the source, whether it's an individual or an organization. Consider the critical role of IP addresses in cyber investigations. Digital artifacts can also be found in social media interactions. Imagine you're examining a tweet that contains potentially harmful information. Tracing the tweet's origin can help you understand who posted it and why. Consider the power of social media analysis in tracing digital artifacts. Keyword analysis is a valuable technique for tracing digital artifacts. Imagine you're searching for information related to a particular topic. By analyzing the keywords used in documents or online discussions, you can trace relevant sources. Consider how keyword analysis can streamline the process of source tracing. Digital artifacts can be deceptive, requiring careful analysis and verification. Imagine you come across a forged document intended to mislead investigators. Tracing the artifact's true source may involve forensic analysis and cross-referencing with other evidence. Consider the challenges posed by deceptive digital artifacts. Collaboration and information sharing among OSINT practitioners are essential in tracing digital artifacts. Imagine you're part of a team working on a complex investigation. Sharing insights and findings with colleagues can help collectively trace digital artifacts. Consider the benefits of a collaborative approach in source attribution. Legal and ethical considerations must guide the tracing of digital artifacts. Imagine you have access to a potentially valuable digital artifact, but it may involve privacy concerns. Respecting privacy and adhering to legal boundaries is crucial when tracing digital sources. Consider the need for responsible and ethical conduct in OSINT. False leads and dead ends are common in the process of tracing digital artifacts. Imagine you invest significant effort into tracing an artifact, only to find it leads to a dead end. Persistence and adaptability are essential qualities for OSINT practitioners. Consider the importance of resilience in the face of challenges. In summary, tracing digital artifacts to their sources is a core skill in open-source intelligence. Whether you're analyzing metadata, following URLs, or examining digital fingerprints, the ability to trace digital artifacts can uncover hidden information and shed light on the origins of digital content. It's a process that requires a keen eye, critical thinking, and a commitment to ethical and responsible conduct in the digital realm. As you delve deeper into the world of OSINT, mastering the art of tracing digital artifacts will become an invaluable tool In your investigative toolkit.

Chapter 6: Profiling Individuals and Organizations

Creating comprehensive profiles is a fundamental skill in open-source intelligence (OSINT). Imagine you're investigating an individual, a company, or an organization. A comprehensive profile provides a holistic view, offering valuable insights for various purposes, from security assessments to business research. Consider this process as akin to piecing together a puzzle, where each element contributes to the bigger picture. Profiles can be built for a wide range of subjects, including individuals, businesses, government agencies, and more. Imagine you're tasked with creating a profile for a potential business partner. A thorough profile can help you assess their reliability, credibility, and potential risks. Consider the versatility of profile-building in different contexts. Profiles typically include a range of information, from basic demographics to in-depth behavioral patterns. Imagine you're creating a profile for a person of interest in a security investigation. You'll need to gather data on their personal details, online presence, affiliations, and activities. Consider the depth of information required for a comprehensive profile. A vital starting point in profile creation is data collection. Imagine you're gathering information from various sources, such as social media, public records, news articles, and more. The more diverse your data sources, the richer and more accurate your profile can be. Consider the importance of casting a wide net in your data collection efforts. Keyword analysis plays a significant role in profile creation. Imagine you're searching for online mentions and discussions related to your subject. By using specific keywords and search operators, you can uncover valuable information.

Consider keyword analysis as a precision tool for targeted data collection. Social media is a goldmine for profile-building. Imagine you're investigating an individual's online persona. Their social media profiles can reveal interests, connections, and behaviors. Consider the wealth of information hidden within social media platforms. Metadata analysis is another powerful technique for profile creation. Imagine you're examining the metadata of digital artifacts associated with your subject. Metadata can include timestamps, geolocation data, and authorship information. Consider the potential insights metadata analysis can provide. Building comprehensive profiles often involves analyzing digital footprints. Imagine you're tracing the subject's online activities, from forum posts to blog comments. These digital footprints can help you understand their online behavior and interests. Consider digital footprints as clues that paint a picture of your subject. Open-source information can reveal affiliations and associations. Imagine you're researching an organization's leadership team. By examining public records, press releases, and news articles, you can identify key figures. Consider how affiliations and associations contribute to a profile's completeness. Visual content can be a valuable source of information. Imagine you come across images or videos related to your subject. Analyzing visual content can yield insights about their activities and surroundings. Consider the significance of visual content in profile-building. Network analysis is a technique that uncovers connections between individuals and entities. Imagine you're investigating a network of individuals involved in a particular industry. By mapping out relationships, you can understand influence and collaboration. Consider network analysis as a way to uncover hidden dynamics. Language analysis is a tool for profiling based on written or spoken content. Imagine you're analyzing text or speech samples to identify linguistic patterns. These patterns can provide clues about a subject's background or origin. Consider the role of language analysis in understanding communication styles. Time and activity analysis can reveal behavioral patterns. Imagine you're studying an individual's online presence over a specific period. By tracking their activities, you can identify routines and trends. Consider how time and activity analysis contribute to behavioral profiles. Geospatial analysis adds a spatial dimension to profiles. Imagine you're creating a profile for a company's physical locations. Geospatial data can help you understand the distribution and reach of the business. Consider the value of geospatial analysis in business intelligence. Psychological profiling delves into personality traits and motivations. Imagine you're working on a security assessment. Psychological profiling can help you anticipate behavior and assess potential threats. Consider the relevance of psychological insights in profiling. In-depth interviews and surveys can provide firsthand information. Imagine you have the opportunity to interview a key informant. Their insights can add depth and accuracy to your profiles. Consider the importance of direct engagement in certain cases. Ethical considerations are paramount in profile creation. Imagine you're handling sensitive information or conducting research on private individuals. Respecting privacy and adhering to legal boundaries is essential. Consider the need for ethical conduct in OSINT practices. Verification is a critical step in profile-building. Imagine you've collected a wealth of information about your subject. Before finalizing the profile, it's crucial to verify the accuracy of the data. Consider verification as a safeguard against misinformation. Profile maintenance is an ongoing process. Imagine you've created a profile for a competitor in the business world. Market dynamics change, and maintaining an up-to-date profile is essential. Consider the importance of keeping profiles current. Collaboration and information sharing enhance profile quality. Imagine you're part of a team working on a complex investigation. Sharing insights and findings with colleagues can lead to more comprehensive profiles. Consider the benefits of collaborative profiling efforts. In summary, creating comprehensive profiles is both an art and a science in the world of open-source intelligence. Whether you're investigating individuals, organizations, or entities, the techniques discussed here can help you build profiles that provide valuable insights. These profiles are not static documents but dynamic representations that evolve with time and new information. Mastering the art of profile creation is a key skill for any OSINT practitioner, and it's a skill that continues to grow and adapt alongside the ever-changing landscape of open-source information. Profiling corporate entities and associations is a complex but essential aspect of open-source intelligence (OSINT). Imagine you're tasked with researching a multinational corporation. This endeavor requires a different approach than profiling individuals. Consider the diversity and depth of information needed for corporate profiles. Corporate entities encompass a wide range of subjects, from businesses to government agencies. Imagine you're profiling a government agency involved in international trade. Such entities have distinct structures, goals, and areas of influence. Consider the complexity of corporate entities and their multifaceted nature. Corporate profiling involves gathering information from various sources. Imagine you're collecting data from financial reports, press releases, websites, and industry publications. These sources provide valuable insights into a corporation's activities and strategies. Consider the importance of data diversity in corporate profiling. Keyword analysis plays a pivotal role in uncovering relevant information. Imagine you're using targeted keywords to search for news articles and reports related to a company. Keyword analysis narrows down search results, ensuring relevance. Consider the precision offered by keyword analysis in corporate profiling. Financial data is a cornerstone of corporate profiling. Imagine you're examining a company's financial statements, including revenue, expenses, and assets. This data helps assess financial health and performance. Consider the significance of financial analysis in corporate profiling. Company websites are rich sources of information. Imagine you're exploring a corporation's website to gather details about its products, services, and mission. Company websites often contain valuable insights into their operations and priorities. Consider the convenience of company websites as primary data sources. Social media presence is a key aspect of corporate profiling. Imagine you're analyzing a company's social media accounts to gauge its online engagement and reputation. Social media activity reflects a corporation's interaction with its audience. Consider the role of social media analysis in corporate profiling. Market research reports provide industry context. Imagine you're studying market reports to understand a corporation's competitive landscape. These reports offer insights into market trends and competitors. Consider the value of market research in corporate profiling. Regulatory filings and compliance records are crucial. Imagine you're reviewing regulatory filings to assess a corporation's adherence to legal requirements. These records reveal information about governance and compliance practices. Consider the importance of regulatory analysis in corporate profiling. Stakeholder analysis helps identify influential parties. Imagine you're mapping out a corporation's stakeholders, from shareholders to partners. Understanding stakeholder dynamics is essential for strategic insights. Consider stakeholder analysis as a tool for assessing corporate influence. Competitive intelligence uncovers rival strategies. Imagine you're researching a company's competitors to evaluate their strengths and weaknesses. Competitive intelligence aids in benchmarking and strategy development. Consider the role of competitive analysis in corporate profiling. Corporate culture assessment provides a glimpse into organizational values. Imagine you're exploring employee reviews and testimonials to understand a corporation's culture. Corporate culture can impact decision-making and public perception. Consider the relevance of culture assessment in corporate profiling. Geospatial analysis adds location-based context. Imagine you're mapping a corporation's physical presence across different regions. Geospatial data helps assess market reach and distribution. Consider the spatial dimension of corporate profiling. Financial modeling can forecast performance. Imagine you're using financial models to predict a corporation's future financial health. These models rely on historical data and industry trends. Consider the potential of financial modeling in corporate profiling. Network analysis uncovers affiliations and collaborations. Imagine you're mapping out a corporation's network of partnerships and alliances. Network analysis reveals strategic connections and influence. Consider the insights gained through network analysis in corporate profiling. Environmental, social, and governance (ESG) criteria matter. Imagine you're evaluating a corporation's ESG practices, from environmental sustainability to social responsibility. ESG factors are increasingly important to stakeholders and investors. Consider the growing significance of ESG analysis in corporate profiling. Ethical considerations are paramount in corporate profiling. Imagine you're handling sensitive corporate information and trade secrets. Respecting ethical boundaries and legal constraints is essential. Consider the need for ethical conduct in OSINT practices. Verification is crucial in corporate profiling. Imagine you've gathered extensive data about a corporation. Before finalizing the profile, it's essential to verify the accuracy of the information. Consider verification as a safeguard against misinformation. Profile maintenance is an ongoing process. Imagine you've created a corporate profile for an investment analysis. Economic conditions change, and maintaining an up-to-date profile is essential. Consider the importance of keeping corporate profiles current. Collaboration and information sharing enhance profile quality. Imagine you're part of a team researching a corporation's global subsidiaries. Sharing insights and findings with colleagues can lead to more comprehensive profiles. Consider the benefits of collaborative profiling efforts. In summary, profiling corporate entities and associations is a dynamic and multifaceted task within the realm of open-source intelligence. Whether you're examining businesses, government agencies, or nonprofit organizations, the techniques discussed here are crucial for creating comprehensive and insightful corporate profiles. These profiles serve as invaluable resources for decision-making, risk assessment, due diligence, and strategic planning in various fields, from finance to cybersecurity.

Chapter 7: Investigative Techniques with Digital Footprints

In the realm of open-source intelligence (OSINT), advanced investigative approaches take center stage, offering powerful tools for professionals seeking to delve deeper into the information landscape. These approaches are designed to uncover hidden insights, relationships, and patterns that may not be immediately apparent through standard OSINT techniques. Imagine you're investigating a complex cybersecurity breach, and the initial OSINT data reveals several IP addresses and domain names associated with the attack. Standard OSINT techniques may provide basic information about these entities, but advanced investigative approaches can take you much further. Consider the value of passive DNS analysis, a technique that allows you to trace the historical changes and associations of domain names. By analyzing DNS records over time, you can uncover patterns of behavior, identify related infrastructure, and gain a more comprehensive view of the attacker's operations. This level of detail can be crucial in understanding the scope and sophistication of the cyber threat. Another advanced investigative approach involves the use of historical WHOIS data. Imagine you're dealing with a case where a malicious actor registered multiple domains to launch phishing campaigns. Standard WHOIS data may only provide current registration information, but historical WHOIS data can reveal the registrant's previous actions, including past domain registrations and changes in ownership. By examining the historical record, you can build a timeline of the attacker's activities and potentially identify recurring patterns or tactics. Such insights can be instrumental in threat intelligence and attribution efforts. Advanced investigative approaches also extend to social media analysis. Imagine you're tasked with profiling an individual whose online presence spans multiple platforms, from Facebook to Twitter and LinkedIn. Standard OSINT techniques may help you gather basic information, but advanced approaches involve deep social media analysis. This includes sentiment analysis, which assesses the emotional tone of a person's posts and interactions. By analyzing sentiment, you can gain insights into the individual's state of mind, potential affiliations, and even detect indicators of malicious intent or radicalization. Such nuanced analysis is valuable in profiling and threat assessment. Geospatial analysis is another advanced approach that plays a vital role in OSINT investigations. Imagine you're investigating an incident with geospatial relevance, such as a protest or a disaster response operation. Standard OSINT methods may provide location data, but advanced geospatial analysis can offer a deeper understanding. This involves overlaying multiple layers of geospatial information, including satellite imagery, social media posts with location tags, and geotagged photos. By integrating these diverse sources, you can create a comprehensive geospatial picture, enabling you to track movements, assess crowd dynamics, and identify critical points of interest. Advanced investigative approaches also encompass the analysis of online communities and forums. Imagine you're researching a specific threat actor or extremist group operating in the dark corners of the internet. Standard OSINT techniques may provide limited access to public forums, but advanced approaches involve infiltrating closed or private online communities. This requires a deep understanding of the target group's behaviors, communication methods, and access points. Through covert infiltration and participation, you can gather critical intelligence, monitor activities, and gain insights into planned actions. Such clandestine operations demand a high level of expertise and discretion. Advanced investigative approaches also extend to linguistic analysis. Imagine you're dealing with a case involving threats or harassment online, and the language used is highly coded or cryptic. Standard OSINT methods may struggle to decipher the meaning behind such messages, but linguistic analysis can decode hidden messages or threats. This approach involves examining language patterns, slang, and context to uncover the true intent behind the communication. Linguistic analysis can be an invaluable tool in threat assessment and cybersecurity. Consider the importance of combining advanced investigative approaches with ethical considerations. These techniques often require a deeper level of intrusion and surveillance, raising ethical questions about privacy and consent. It's crucial for OSINT practitioners to adhere to strict ethical guidelines and legal boundaries when employing these approaches. Privacy and civil liberties must always be respected, and any information collected must be handled with care and sensitivity. In summary, advanced investigative approaches in open-source intelligence offer a formidable arsenal of techniques for professionals seeking to uncover hidden insights and patterns. These methods, which include passive DNS analysis, historical WHOIS data examination, sentiment analysis, geospatial analysis, online community infiltration, linguistic analysis, and others, allow investigators to go beyond the surface and gain a deeper understanding of complex situations. However, it's essential to balance the power of these approaches with ethical considerations to ensure responsible and lawful use in OSINT investigations. In the world of open-source intelligence (OSINT), one of the most challenging and rewarding endeavors is linking digital footprints to real-world identities. This process involves uncovering the individuals behind the online personas, social media accounts, and digital trails left across the internet. Imagine you have a collection of data points, such as usernames, email addresses, and online aliases associated with a specific individual. The goal is to piece together this digital puzzle and connect it to the person's true identity. The process often begins with gathering all available information related to the target, no matter how fragmented or seemingly insignificant. This could include social media profiles, forum posts, blog comments, and any online activity associated with the individual. Think of it as assembling a jigsaw puzzle; each piece, no matter how small, contributes to the overall picture. One of the key challenges in linking digital footprints to real-world identities is dealing with the vast amount of data available. The internet is a treasure trove of information, and sifting through it can be overwhelming. To manage this, OSINT practitioners use specialized tools and techniques to automate data collection and analysis. For example, web scraping bots can gather data from websites and social media platforms, while data analysis software can help identify patterns and connections. Imagine you're investigating a person who uses the pseudonym "TechGeek123" on various online forums. You might start by collecting all instances of this username across different platforms, noting the content and context of each post. Next, you can examine any publicly available information associated with "TechGeek123," such as email addresses or profile details. This information can serve as valuable starting points for further investigation. Social media analysis is a crucial aspect of linking digital footprints to real-world identities. Imagine you're trying to identify the owner of a Twitter account with the handle "@CryptoExpert." By examining the account's followers, who they follow, and the content they engage with, you can gain insights into the individual's interests and potential affiliations. Additionally, geolocation data from social media posts or photos can provide clues about the person's whereabouts. Imagine a situation where you're investigating an individual who frequently shares photos taken at a specific coffee shop in New York City. This information can narrow down the geographical scope of your search and help you focus on potential leads in that area. Email addresses play a significant role in linking digital footprints to real-world identities. An individual's email address often serves as a central point for online activities. Through email analysis, you can uncover connections between different online personas and services. Consider a scenario where you've discovered that the email address "john.doe@email.com" is associated with the username "JD1985" on a gaming forum. Further research might reveal that the same email address is used to register accounts on various e-commerce websites and social media platforms. This pattern suggests that "JD1985" and "john.doe@email.com" likely belong to the same individual. Linking digital footprints to real-world identities may also involve analyzing linguistic patterns and writing styles. Imagine you're investigating an individual who operates multiple online accounts under different aliases. By comparing the writing style, vocabulary, and grammar across these accounts, you can identify commonalities that point to a single author. This linguistic analysis can be a powerful tool for establishing connections between digital personas. However, it's essential to exercise caution when drawing conclusions based on writing style, as it's not always definitive proof of identity. In some cases, OSINT practitioners turn to legal and public records to confirm real-world identities. This may involve searching for information such as phone numbers, addresses, and professional affiliations. Consider a situation where you've linked an online persona to the name "John Smith." You can use publicly available records, such as property records or business registrations, to verify whether there is a real-world individual named John Smith associated with the digital footprint. Linking digital footprints to real-world identities often requires creativity and persistence. Imagine you're investigating a target who uses a combination of pseudonyms, VPNs, and encrypted communication tools to protect their anonymity. In such cases, OSINT practitioners must employ advanced techniques, such as tracing IP addresses, monitoring online behavior over an extended period, and even employing social engineering tactics. The process may also involve collaborating with other experts, such as forensic analysts or law enforcement agencies, to access additional resources and expertise. Maintaining a clear and organized investigative workflow is crucial in this endeavor. Imagine you've collected a vast amount of data related to the target's digital footprints. To make sense of it all, you can create a structured timeline or visual map that connects the dots between online activities and potential real-world actions. This visualization can help you identify gaps in your knowledge and prioritize areas for further investigation. Ultimately, successfully linking digital footprints to real-world identities requires a combination of technical skills, analytical thinking, and persistence. It's a complex process that can yield valuable insights for various purposes, from cybersecurity and law enforcement to corporate investigations and threat assessment. As the digital landscape continues to evolve, OSINT practitioners must adapt and develop new techniques to stay ahead of those who seek to remain anonymous in the online world.

Chapter 8: Legal and Ethical Considerations in Footprint Analysis

Navigating the legal landscape in the field of open-source intelligence (OSINT) is essential for ethical and lawful data collection and analysis. Understanding the legal frameworks and privacy regulations that apply to OSINT activities is crucial for practitioners. The first step in this journey is recognizing that OSINT operates within the broader context of privacy and data protection laws. Privacy laws vary significantly from one country to another, and even within regions, such as the European Union, where the General Data Protection Regulation (GDPR) sets a comprehensive standard. Before embarking on an OSINT investigation, it's essential to familiarize yourself with the legal requirements in your jurisdiction. In many cases, OSINT activities that involve collecting publicly available information are not subject to stringent legal restrictions. However, certain boundaries must be respected to avoid infringing on individuals' privacy rights. For instance, in the United States, the First Amendment protects the freedom of speech and the press, allowing for the collection of public information without constraints. However, this protection does not extend to activities that involve hacking, unauthorized access to protected systems, or harassment. Even in jurisdictions with more permissive regulations, ethical considerations should guide OSINT practitioners. Respecting individuals' privacy and consent is a fundamental principle. Imagine you're conducting OSINT research on a particular individual, and you come across their social media profiles, which contain personal information and photos. It's essential to remember that even though this information is publicly accessible, it doesn't grant you the right to misuse it or invade their privacy. In some cases, OSINT practitioners may encounter legal gray areas, especially when dealing with emerging technologies and digital platforms. Consider the use of web scraping tools to collect data from websites. While scraping publicly available information may not necessarily violate the law, automated scraping that overwhelms a site's server or violates its terms of service could lead to legal issues. Navigating these gray areas requires careful consideration of both legal and ethical factors. Ethical guidelines often complement legal frameworks and help OSINT practitioners make informed decisions. It's essential to abide by a code of ethics that promotes responsible and lawful OSINT practices. A foundational ethical principle in OSINT is transparency. Imagine you're conducting OSINT for a corporate investigation, and you plan to gather information from publicly available sources. You should be transparent about your intentions and conduct your research openly, without attempting to conceal your identity or motives. This transparency helps maintain trust and credibility in the field. Another critical ethical principle is proportionality. It's crucial to ensure that your OSINT activities are proportionate to the goals of your investigation. For example, if you're conducting OSINT for a background check on a potential employee, the level of scrutiny should be commensurate with the position they're applying for. Excessive or invasive investigations can raise ethical concerns. When dealing with personal information, such as email addresses, phone numbers, or social media profiles, it's essential to obtain data through lawful means and with the individual's consent whenever possible. Imagine you're researching an individual who has a public LinkedIn profile. You can reach out to them through the platform, introduce yourself, and explain your research purpose. Seeking consent demonstrates respect for their privacy and builds a more ethical and responsible OSINT practice. Responsible data handling is another core aspect of ethical OSINT. This means safeguarding the information you collect, minimizing data exposure, and ensuring secure storage and transmission. Imagine you've compiled a comprehensive report based on your OSINT findings. It's your responsibility to protect this sensitive information and share it only with authorized individuals or entities. Incorporating data protection measures is not only ethical but also helps mitigate legal risks. Transparency and accountability are key principles in ethical OSINT. Imagine you're conducting OSINT for a cybersecurity assessment of a company's online vulnerabilities. It's essential to keep clear records of your activities, sources, and methodologies. This transparency allows for peer review, quality assurance, and compliance with legal requirements. Being accountable for your actions and decisions is crucial in maintaining ethical integrity. As the digital landscape continues to evolve, so do legal and privacy considerations in OSINT. New regulations and court decisions may impact how OSINT practitioners operate. For example, the interpretation of data protection laws, such as the GDPR, may evolve over time, affecting the collection and processing of personal data. To stay compliant and ethical, OSINT practitioners must stay informed about legal developments and adapt their practices accordingly. Imagine you're working on an OSINT project, and you discover a potential legal or ethical dilemma. Seeking legal counsel or consulting with colleagues who specialize in privacy and data protection can provide guidance and help you make informed decisions. In some cases, organizations may establish their own internal policies and guidelines for ethical OSINT practices. These guidelines can provide clarity and direction for practitioners while aligning with the organization's values and compliance requirements. Ultimately, a strong foundation in both legal frameworks and ethical principles is essential for anyone engaged in OSINT activities. By balancing legal compliance with ethical considerations, OSINT practitioners can conduct responsible and lawful investigations that respect individuals' privacy rights and maintain the integrity of the field. Ethical practices in digital footprint analysis are of paramount importance, ensuring that individuals' privacy rights and data protection are upheld. As we delve into the world of uncovering and examining digital footprints, it's crucial to maintain the highest ethical standards throughout our investigative journey. Digital footprint analysis involves scrutinizing the traces individuals leave behind as they navigate the online realm. These traces encompass a vast array of data, including online behaviors, interactions, and personal information. Ethical considerations in this field are multifaceted, encompassing respect for privacy, informed consent, responsible data handling, and transparency. Imagine you're tasked with conducting digital footprint analysis on an individual to gather insights for a corporate investigation. Before embarking on this journey, you must first seek a clear understanding of the ethical guidelines that should govern your actions. Respecting privacy is a foundational ethical principle in digital footprint analysis. Individuals have a right to privacy, even in the digital realm, and this right should be upheld at all times. Consider a scenario where you stumble upon an individual's private blog, sharing personal thoughts and experiences. Ethical practice dictates that you should respect the boundaries of their online space and avoid intruding into their personal life without a legitimate reason. Moreover, obtaining informed consent is essential in digital footprint analysis. This means that if you plan to collect and analyze someone's online data, you should seek their permission whenever possible. Imagine you're investigating a potential job candidate, and you want to review their public social media profiles for insights. Seeking their consent before accessing this information is not only ethical but also respectful of their autonomy. Responsible data handling is another critical aspect of ethical digital footprint analysis. This involves safeguarding the information you collect, ensuring it's used only for the intended purpose and maintaining strict security measures. Imagine you've compiled a comprehensive report based on your digital footprint analysis. It's crucial to protect this sensitive information from unauthorized access and use. Adhering to data protection principles helps prevent potential data breaches and privacy violations. Transparency is a key tenet of ethical digital footprint analysis. Imagine you're conducting digital footprint analysis on an individual for a legal case. It's vital to be transparent about your intentions and inform them of the nature and scope of your investigation. This transparency builds trust and ensures that individuals are aware of how their online data is being used. While these ethical principles provide a solid foundation for digital footprint analysis, practitioners must also navigate the complexities of the digital landscape. One of these challenges is tracing online identities and personas. In the age of social media, individuals often create multiple online identities and personas, each serving a specific purpose. These identities may vary in the information shared, the tone used, and the communities engaged with. Imagine you're tasked with analyzing an individual's digital footprint, and you discover that they maintain several social media profiles, each projecting a different image. Ethical practice in this context involves distinguishing between public and private personas and respecting the individual's intentions. It's essential not to make assumptions or draw conclusions based solely on one aspect of their online presence. Another ethical consideration is the analysis of social media trails. Social media platforms are treasure troves of information, offering insights into an individual's thoughts, interests, and connections. However, ethical practitioners must be cautious not to misuse or misinterpret this data. Consider a scenario where you're analyzing an individual's Twitter feed, and you come across tweets expressing personal challenges and vulnerabilities. Ethical practice dictates that you handle this information with sensitivity and empathy, refraining from exploiting their vulnerabilities. Ethical digital footprint analysis extends to the uncovering of digital artifacts and metadata. Imagine you're conducting research on a subject and come across a set of photos shared on a public forum. While these photos may appear benign, it's essential to consider the ethical implications of using them without permission. Respecting copyright and intellectual property rights is an integral part of ethical practice in digital footprint analysis. Additionally, practitioners should be mindful of the potential consequences of their actions. In some cases, the information uncovered through digital footprint analysis may have far-reaching effects on individuals' lives. Imagine you're analyzing the online activities of a political activist, and your findings lead to their identification and subsequent harassment. Ethical practitioners should consider the potential harm that may result from their actions and weigh it against the public interest. In some cases, responsible disclosure may be necessary to minimize harm and ensure ethical conduct. Lastly, ethical digital footprint analysis includes ongoing self-reflection and accountability. Practitioners should regularly evaluate their methods, practices, and ethical considerations. Imagine you're part of a team conducting digital footprint analysis, and you encounter a challenging ethical dilemma. Seeking guidance from peers, mentors, or ethical committees can help navigate these complex situations. Ethical practice in digital footprint analysis is not a one-size-fits-all approach; it requires adaptability and a commitment to upholding individuals' rights and dignity. As technology continues to evolve, ethical considerations in digital footprint analysis will remain at the forefront of responsible and respectful data analysis. By adhering to these ethical principles, practitioners can maintain the integrity of their work and ensure that digital footprint analysis serves as a valuable tool for insights without compromising ethical standards.

Chapter 9: Cybersecurity Implications and Threat Assessment

Assessing digital footprint-related threats is a critical aspect of modern cybersecurity and personal privacy protection. As individuals and organizations continue to engage with the digital world, they inadvertently leave behind traces of their online activities. These traces, collectively known as the digital footprint, encompass a wide range of data, including social media interactions, online purchases, and website visits. While digital footprints can be valuable for personalization and convenience, they also pose potential threats to individuals' privacy and security. In this chapter, we'll explore the various threats associated with digital footprints and discuss strategies for assessing and mitigating these risks. One of the most significant threats related to digital footprints is the risk of personal information exposure. As individuals navigate the internet, they often share personal details, such as their name, address, phone number, and even financial information, on various online platforms. This information, if not adequately protected, can be exploited by cybercriminals for identity theft, fraud, or harassment. Assessing the potential exposure of personal information within one's digital footprint is a crucial step in mitigating this threat. Imagine you're a cybersecurity professional tasked with evaluating an individual's online presence for potential vulnerabilities. You would start by conducting a comprehensive analysis of their digital footprint to identify any instances where personal information has been shared or leaked. Social media platforms, in particular, are fertile ground for personal information exposure. Individuals often share a wealth of personal data on social networks, from their birthdate to their current location. To assess the risk of personal information exposure, you would examine their privacy settings on these platforms and evaluate their posting habits. Are they sharing sensitive information publicly, or have they implemented strong privacy controls to limit access to trusted contacts only? Another significant threat linked to digital footprints is online reputation damage. In the digital age, one's online presence plays a crucial role in shaping their reputation, both personally and professionally. Negative content, whether true or false, can tarnish an individual's image and impact their relationships, career, or even their safety. To assess the risk of online reputation damage, you would need to conduct a reputation audit. This involves searching for mentions of the individual's name or online handles across various online platforms. Are there negative reviews, comments, or posts that could harm their reputation? If so, you would then evaluate the source and credibility of this content to determine its potential impact. Online harassment and cyberbullying are pressing threats associated with digital footprints, especially in the realm of social media. Individuals may face online abuse, threats, or cyberbullying from anonymous or known individuals. To assess the risk of online harassment, you would analyze the individual's social media profiles and interactions. Have they been the target of harassment campaigns or received threatening messages? Understanding the scope and severity of such threats is crucial for implementing protective measures. Additionally, the risk of data breaches and unauthorized access to accounts is a significant concern tied to digital footprints. If an individual's online accounts are compromised, malicious actors can gain access to their personal and financial information. Assessing this threat involves examining the security measures in place for their online accounts. Are they using strong, unique passwords and enabling two-factor authentication? Have there been any signs of unauthorized access or suspicious activity? A thorough assessment can help identify vulnerabilities and prevent potential breaches. Privacy invasion is another serious threat that individuals may face due to their digital footprints. Imagine you're a privacy advocate helping individuals protect their online privacy. You would work with them to assess the extent to which their digital footprint allows third parties, such as advertisers or data brokers, to track their online behavior. Understanding the data collection practices of websites and online services is essential in mitigating this threat. One approach is to use browser extensions or privacy-focused search engines that limit data tracking and profiling. Moreover, the risk of phishing attacks and social engineering attempts can be associated with digital footprints. Malicious actors may exploit the information available in an individual's online presence to craft convincing phishing emails or messages. Assessing this threat involves educating individuals about phishing risks and teaching them to recognize and report suspicious communications. Cybersecurity awareness and training are valuable tools in mitigating these risks. In summary, assessing digital footprint-related threats is a multifaceted process that requires a thorough examination of an individual's online presence. This assessment involves evaluating the exposure of personal information, the risk of online reputation damage, the potential for online harassment, the vulnerability to data breaches, the invasion of privacy, and the susceptibility to phishing attacks. By understanding these threats and implementing appropriate safeguards, individuals can better protect their digital footprints and reduce their risk of online harm. In the following chapters, we will delve deeper into strategies and tools for mitigating these threats and enhancing digital footprint security. Incorporating footprint analysis into cybersecurity strategies is a proactive approach to enhancing an organization's security posture. In today's digital landscape, where data breaches and cyberattacks are prevalent, understanding the potential risks associated with digital footprints is crucial. Footprint analysis involves a comprehensive examination of an organization's online presence, identifying vulnerabilities and potential attack vectors. To effectively incorporate footprint analysis into cybersecurity strategies, organizations need to follow a structured approach. First, they should establish clear objectives and goals for the analysis, defining what they aim to achieve through this process. These objectives could include assessing the visibility of sensitive information, identifying potential attack surfaces, and evaluating the organization's online reputation. Once the objectives are defined, organizations can proceed to collect and analyze relevant data. This data can include information about the organization's web applications, domain names, IP addresses, and employee online profiles. By gathering this information, organizations can create a comprehensive inventory of their digital assets, which is essential for footprint analysis. With the data in hand, the next step is to conduct a thorough analysis of the digital footprint. This analysis should include an assessment of the organization's web presence, including websites, subdomains, and associated third-party services. Additionally, it should evaluate the organization's social media profiles, employee online activities, and mentions of the organization on external websites and forums. By conducting this analysis, organizations can identify potential security gaps and areas of vulnerability. One critical aspect of incorporating footprint analysis into cybersecurity strategies is the identification of information exposure. Organizations must assess whether sensitive information, such as proprietary data or personally identifiable information (PII), is exposed online. If such information is discovered, immediate steps should be taken to secure it and limit access to authorized personnel only. Furthermore, organizations should assess their online reputation as part of footprint analysis. Negative mentions, reviews, or comments about the organization can be exploited by threat actors to tarnish its image or launch targeted attacks. Understanding and managing online reputation is a vital aspect of cybersecurity. Footprint analysis also extends to assessing the security of an organization's web applications and systems. This involves evaluating the security configurations of web servers, databases, and other digital assets. Common security misconfigurations, such as open ports or weak access controls, can be identified and rectified through this analysis. Moreover, organizations should be vigilant about potential attack surfaces created by third-party services or integrations. Cyber attackers often exploit these weak points to gain unauthorized access. Therefore, footprint analysis should include a review of third-party relationships and their security practices. Additionally, assessing the online presence and behaviors of employees is crucial. Employees may unintentionally expose sensitive information or fall victim to social engineering attacks. Educating employees about cybersecurity best practices and monitoring their online activities can help mitigate these risks. Incorporating footprint analysis into cybersecurity strategies also involves continuous monitoring. Digital footprints are not static; they evolve as organizations expand their online presence and cyber threats evolve. Therefore, organizations should establish regular monitoring processes to detect changes in their footprint and identify emerging threats. This ongoing vigilance allows for proactive threat mitigation.

Furthermore, organizations should implement measures to protect their digital assets and data. This can include strengthening access controls, implementing web application firewalls, and employing threat intelligence solutions. The goal is to bolster the organization's cybersecurity posture based on the insights gained from footprint analysis. It's also essential to have an incident response plan in place. Even with proactive measures, security incidents can occur. Having a well-defined plan for responding to incidents, including those related to digital footprints, can minimize damage and facilitate a swift recovery. Finally, organizations should invest in employee training and awareness programs. Human error remains a significant factor in cybersecurity incidents. By educating employees about the importance of cybersecurity and the risks associated with digital footprints, organizations can create a culture of security. Incorporating footprint analysis into cybersecurity strategies is not a one-time effort but an ongoing practice. Cyber threats constantly evolve, and organizations must adapt their strategies accordingly. By regularly assessing their digital footprint, identifying vulnerabilities, and taking proactive measures, organizations can significantly enhance their cybersecurity defenses. In the ever-changing digital landscape, a comprehensive understanding of an organization's digital presence is a valuable asset in safeguarding against cyber threats.

Chapter 10: Real-World Case Studies in Digital Footprint Analysis

Learning from notable footprint analysis cases provides invaluable insights into the real-world applications and implications of this essential cybersecurity practice. These cases offer practical lessons that can help organizations enhance their security postures and mitigate potential risks associated with their digital footprints. One such notable case is the data breach suffered by Equifax, one of the major credit reporting agencies in the United States. In 2017, Equifax experienced a massive data breach that exposed the personal information of approximately 147 million individuals. This breach was a stark reminder of the importance of footprint analysis in identifying and securing vulnerabilities. The attackers exploited a known vulnerability in Equifax's web application, which could have been detected and remediated through proactive footprint analysis. The Equifax case underscores the critical need for organizations to continuously monitor their web applications and digital assets for security flaws. Another instructive case is the cyberattack on the Democratic National Committee (DNC) during the 2016 U.S. presidential election. In this case, threat actors believed to be affiliated with a nation-state conducted a sophisticated phishing campaign that led to the compromise of DNC email accounts. Footprint analysis plays a pivotal role in such cases by tracing the attackers' activities and identifying the entry points they used. By examining their digital footprints, organizations can gain insights into the tactics, techniques, and procedures (TTPs) employed by threat actors, enabling better defense strategies. Furthermore, the Facebook-Cambridge Analytica scandal serves as a significant example of the implications of data exposure within an organization's digital footprint. Cambridge Analytica, a political consulting firm, obtained and exploited the personal data of millions of Facebook users without their consent. This case highlights the importance of not only securing an organization's own data but also being vigilant about the third-party relationships and integrations that can create security risks. Organizations must conduct comprehensive footprint analysis to identify and assess potential third-party vulnerabilities. The incident involving SolarWinds, a leading provider of IT management software, is another case that emphasizes the significance of footprint analysis in identifying supply chain attacks. In this case, threat actors compromised the SolarWinds software update mechanism to distribute malware to thousands of organizations, including government agencies and major corporations. Effective footprint analysis could have helped detect the suspicious activities and anomalies associated with the compromised updates. The SolarWinds incident underscores the importance of monitoring an organization's digital footprint beyond its own assets and extending into its supply chain. Moreover, the case of Marriott International's data breach illustrates the far-reaching consequences of insufficient footprint analysis. Marriott suffered a breach in 2018 that exposed the personal information of approximately 500 million guests. The breach went undetected for several years, allowing threat actors to access and exfiltrate sensitive data. Had Marriott conducted thorough and continuous footprint analysis, it might have detected the unauthorized access and data exfiltration earlier, minimizing the impact of the breach. These notable cases demonstrate that effective footprint analysis is not merely a technical task but a strategic imperative for organizations. It involves a holistic approach that encompasses not only an organization's own digital assets but also its third-party relationships, supply chain, and potential attack vectors. By learning from these cases, organizations can better appreciate the importance of proactive footprint analysis in safeguarding their digital presence. They can also glean valuable lessons on incident response and the necessity of having a robust cybersecurity strategy in place. Footprint analysis is not a static process; it requires continuous monitoring and adaptation to evolving cyber threats. By staying vigilant and learning from both successful and unsuccessful cases, organizations can fortify their cybersecurity defenses and reduce the risk of data breaches and cyberattacks.

These cases serve as real-world reminders that digital footprints are not static but dynamic, requiring ongoing attention and diligence to protect an organization's digital assets and reputation. Applying footprint analysis principles to complex scenarios is a crucial aspect of modern cybersecurity and intelligence operations. In these intricate situations, understanding and leveraging the power of digital footprints can be the difference between success and failure. Complex scenarios often involve multifaceted networks, diverse data sources, and elusive adversaries. Traditional cybersecurity measures may not suffice in such cases, making footprint analysis an indispensable tool.

One of the key challenges in complex scenarios is dealing with the vast amount of data generated by digital footprints. As organizations and individuals engage with online platforms, they leave traces in the form of digital footprints. These footprints include a wide range of information, from social media posts and emails to log files and metadata. Analyzing this extensive and diverse data requires specialized techniques and tools.

Furthermore, complex scenarios often involve dynamic and evolving threats. Adversaries can change their tactics, techniques, and procedures (TTPs) rapidly. To counter these threats effectively, analysts must continuously adapt their footprint analysis methods. This adaptability is essential to stay ahead of malicious actors who seek to exploit vulnerabilities in an organization's digital footprint.

In complex scenarios, digital footprints extend beyond traditional boundaries. They encompass not only an organization's internal systems and data but also its connections with external entities, such as partners, suppliers, and customers. Understanding the interdependencies and potential risks within this extended digital footprint is critical. It requires a comprehensive approach to footprint analysis that considers the broader ecosystem in which an organization operates.

Moreover, complex scenarios often involve advanced persistent threats (APTs) and nation-state actors. These adversaries are highly skilled and motivated, making them formidable opponents. Footprint analysis becomes a strategic tool in identifying and countering APTs. By tracing their digital footprints, analysts can uncover patterns of behavior, infiltration attempts, and potential vulnerabilities.

In addition to external threats, complex scenarios may involve insider threats. Employees or contractors with access to sensitive information can misuse their privileges or inadvertently expose critical data. Footprint analysis plays a pivotal role in detecting and mitigating insider threats. It helps organizations monitor user activities, identify unusual behavior, and prevent data breaches.

One of the fundamental principles of applying footprint analysis in complex scenarios is intelligence-driven cybersecurity. This approach involves gathering actionable intelligence from digital footprints and using it to inform security decisions. It goes beyond traditional perimeter-based defenses and focuses on understanding the motivations, capabilities, and intentions of adversaries.

In intelligence-driven cybersecurity, analysts gather and analyze data from various sources, including open source intelligence (OSINT), human intelligence (HUMINT), and technical intelligence (TECHINT). They combine these sources to build a comprehensive picture of the threat landscape. This intelligence-driven approach allows organizations to proactively detect and respond to threats, even in complex scenarios.

Furthermore, complex scenarios often require collaborative efforts among organizations, government agencies, and cybersecurity experts. Information sharing and threat intelligence sharing become essential components of combating sophisticated threats. Digital footprints can serve as a common language for sharing insights and identifying common attack patterns.

The application of footprint analysis principles in complex scenarios also involves strategic planning. Organizations must define their risk tolerance, establish incident response protocols, and allocate resources effectively. Footprint analysis supports these strategic initiatives by providing insights into potential risks and vulnerabilities.

In summary, applying footprint analysis principles to complex scenarios is an essential aspect of modern cybersecurity and intelligence operations. It involves dealing with vast amounts of data, adapting to dynamic threats, considering extended digital footprints, countering advanced adversaries, and adopting an intelligence-driven approach. By mastering these principles, organizations can enhance their cybersecurity posture and effectively navigate the complexities of the digital age.

Complex scenarios require advanced techniques and tools for footprint analysis, as well as a strategic, intelligence-driven approach. Digital footprints extend beyond traditional boundaries and encompass both internal and external ecosystems. Understanding the motivations and tactics of adversaries is crucial in countering advanced persistent threats (APTs) and nation-state actors. Insider threats also need to be addressed through footprint analysis. Intelligence-driven cybersecurity, based on actionable intelligence gathered from various sources, is essential in complex scenarios. Collaboration and information sharing among organizations and cybersecurity experts are vital components of tackling sophisticated threats. Strategic planning, risk assessment, and resource allocation are essential to effective footprint analysis in complex scenarios. In summary, mastering the principles of footprint analysis is paramount for organizations seeking to enhance their cybersecurity posture in today's complex digital landscape.

BOOK 4
EXPERT OSINT
CYBER RECONNAISSANCE AND THREAT INTELLIGENCE

ROB BOTWRIGHT

Chapter 1: Advanced OSINT Recap

Reviewing key concepts and techniques is a fundamental step in any learning journey, especially in a field as dynamic and complex as open-source intelligence (OSINT). It allows practitioners to consolidate their knowledge, identify areas for improvement, and stay updated with the latest developments. Whether you're new to OSINT or a seasoned professional, periodic reviews are essential for maintaining proficiency and adapting to evolving challenges.

One of the foundational concepts in OSINT is the idea that a wealth of valuable information is publicly available on the internet. This information includes data from websites, social media platforms, forums, and other online sources. OSINT practitioners leverage this publicly accessible data to gather intelligence, investigate individuals or entities, and assess potential threats or vulnerabilities.

To effectively conduct OSINT operations, it's crucial to understand the principles of information discovery. This involves employing various search techniques, including search engines, advanced search operators, and specialized OSINT tools. Proficiency in crafting precise search queries is a valuable skill, as it enables practitioners to uncover specific pieces of information within the vast sea of online data.

Targeted information gathering is another vital aspect of OSINT. This technique involves focusing on specific individuals, organizations, or topics to gather relevant intelligence. Practitioners use a combination of tools and methods, such as social media analysis, domain name research, and email tracking, to acquire actionable insights. These insights can be used for purposes ranging from background checks to threat assessments.

Advanced social media analysis is a specialized skill that OSINT professionals often develop. Social media platforms are treasure troves of information, but sifting through the vast amount of content can be daunting. Proficient analysts can extract meaningful data from social media posts, profiles, and interactions to build comprehensive profiles of individuals or entities.

Delving into the dark web is another aspect of OSINT that requires specific techniques and precautions. The dark web is a hidden part of the internet that is not indexed by conventional search engines. It's often associated with illegal activities, making it a subject of interest for law enforcement and security professionals. OSINT practitioners exploring the dark web must employ specialized tools and follow strict ethical guidelines to navigate this clandestine environment safely.

OSINT automation and scripting are critical skills for streamlining information gathering processes. By automating repetitive tasks and leveraging scripts, practitioners can save time and ensure consistent results. Automation tools can help monitor websites for changes, track social media trends, and aggregate data from multiple sources, enhancing the efficiency of OSINT operations.

Ethical hacking techniques can be applied to OSINT for intelligence gathering. Ethical hackers use their expertise to identify vulnerabilities and weaknesses in systems, networks, and applications. In an OSINT context, ethical hacking can involve scanning for open ports, analyzing network configurations, and identifying potential security risks that may expose sensitive information.

OSINT professionals also rely on advanced analysis and visualization tools to make sense of the data they collect. These tools allow practitioners to analyze patterns, detect anomalies, and visualize complex information in a way that is easy to understand. Visualization tools can be particularly helpful in identifying trends, relationships, and potential threats within large datasets.

Threat intelligence and cybersecurity are closely intertwined with OSINT. Understanding the current threat landscape, including emerging threats and attack vectors, is essential for protecting organizations and individuals. OSINT provides valuable insights into the tactics, techniques, and procedures (TTPs) employed by malicious actors, enabling proactive threat mitigation.

Case studies are invaluable resources for OSINT practitioners to hone their skills and learn from real-world scenarios. By examining successful OSINT operations and analyzing the strategies employed, practitioners can gain a deeper understanding of effective techniques and approaches. Case studies also offer an opportunity to reflect on challenges faced and lessons learned.

In the ever-evolving landscape of OSINT, staying updated with the latest trends and advancements is crucial. Future trends in OSINT may include advancements in artificial intelligence (AI) and machine learning, which can enhance data analysis and automation capabilities. Additionally, increased emphasis on privacy and data protection regulations may influence how OSINT is conducted in the future.

In summary, reviewing key concepts and techniques in OSINT is a continuous process that empowers practitioners to navigate the dynamic world of online intelligence effectively. Whether you're a novice or an experienced professional, maintaining proficiency in search strategies, targeted information gathering, social media analysis, dark web exploration, automation, ethical hacking, analysis tools, threat intelligence, and case studies is essential for success in this field. As OSINT continues to evolve, staying informed about emerging trends and adapting to new challenges will be paramount for practitioners dedicated to harnessing the power of publicly available information for intelligence purposes.

Building on foundational OSINT knowledge is a natural progression for practitioners looking to advance their skills and capabilities in the field of open-source intelligence. As with any discipline, OSINT is built on a solid foundation of fundamental principles and techniques that provide a starting point for learning and exploration. However, the field of OSINT is dynamic and constantly evolving, requiring practitioners to continually expand their knowledge and adapt to new challenges and opportunities.

One of the key aspects of building on foundational OSINT knowledge is the development of advanced search techniques. While basic search engine queries are a fundamental skill, practitioners can take their search capabilities to the next level by learning to use specialized search operators and advanced search engines. These operators and engines enable users to perform more precise and targeted searches, which is often crucial when gathering specific information from the vast ocean of online data.

Advanced search operators, such as Boolean operators, wildcards, and proximity operators, provide the means to refine search queries and retrieve highly relevant results. Boolean operators like AND, OR, and NOT allow practitioners to combine keywords and phrases to narrow down search results or expand their scope. Wildcards, such as asterisks (*) and question marks (?), can be used to replace characters in search terms, making it easier to find variations of a keyword. Proximity operators like NEAR and AROUND enable users to specify the proximity of keywords within a document, helping to identify connections between pieces of information.

In addition to mastering these search operators, practitioners can benefit from exploring specialized search engines that are tailored to specific types of data or sources. For example, there are search engines designed for searching academic publications, patents, government documents, and even social media posts. Learning to navigate and leverage these specialized search engines can greatly enhance the efficiency and effectiveness of OSINT operations.

Another area of growth in OSINT involves expanding one's understanding of the dark web. The dark web is a part of the internet that is intentionally hidden and not indexed by traditional search engines. It is often associated with illegal activities, making it a subject of interest for OSINT practitioners and law enforcement agencies. Building on foundational knowledge, individuals can explore the dark web safely and ethically by using specialized tools like Tor and understanding the importance of maintaining privacy and security while doing so.

Moreover, building on foundational OSINT knowledge includes mastering advanced social media analysis techniques. Social media platforms are rich sources of information, but analyzing the vast amount of content can be challenging. Advanced practitioners can delve deeper into social media analysis by learning to identify patterns, trends, and anomalies in user behavior. They can also become proficient in using tools and techniques for sentiment analysis, which involves assessing the emotional tone of social media posts and comments.

Ethical considerations remain a crucial aspect of OSINT, and practitioners should build on their foundational knowledge by staying current with ethical guidelines and best practices. As the field evolves, new ethical dilemmas and issues may arise, such as the responsible use of automation and artificial intelligence in OSINT. Practitioners should continually educate themselves on these matters and strive to uphold the highest ethical standards in their work.

Expanding one's OSINT toolkit is another important aspect of building on foundational knowledge. This includes exploring and mastering a wider range of OSINT tools and software applications. Some tools may be specifically designed for data collection and analysis, while others may focus on visualization or automation. Practitioners can benefit from building expertise in using these tools to enhance their OSINT capabilities.

Furthermore, developing expertise in geospatial analysis is a valuable skill that builds on foundational OSINT knowledge. Geospatial analysis involves using geographic information system (GIS) technologies to analyze and visualize data in a spatial context. This can be particularly useful for OSINT practitioners when mapping the locations of individuals, events, or activities mentioned in online sources. It adds another layer of context to the information being gathered.

Incorporating OSINT into broader intelligence and security frameworks is an advanced approach that practitioners can explore. OSINT can complement other sources of intelligence, such as human intelligence (HUMINT) and signals intelligence (SIGINT), to provide a more comprehensive understanding of a situation or threat. Integrating OSINT into intelligence analysis workflows and decision-making processes requires a deep understanding of both OSINT techniques and the broader intelligence landscape.

Additionally, staying informed about emerging technologies and trends in OSINT is crucial for building on foundational knowledge. As technology evolves, new tools, techniques, and data sources become available. Practitioners should actively seek out training, conferences, and publications related to OSINT to stay up to date with the latest developments.

In summary, building on foundational OSINT knowledge is a dynamic and ongoing process that involves mastering advanced search techniques, exploring specialized search engines, delving into the dark web safely and ethically, advancing social media analysis skills, staying current with ethical guidelines, expanding the OSINT toolkit, developing geospatial analysis expertise, incorporating OSINT into broader intelligence frameworks, and staying informed about emerging technologies and trends. By continually honing their skills and knowledge, OSINT practitioners can remain effective and adaptable in the ever-changing landscape of open-source intelligence.

Chapter 2: Cyber Reconnaissance Fundamentals

Understanding the basics of cyber reconnaissance is essential in the realm of cybersecurity and intelligence gathering, as it serves as the foundation for identifying, collecting, and analyzing digital information for various purposes.

Cyber reconnaissance, often referred to as cyber recce or cyber intel, encompasses a wide range of activities aimed at acquiring information about an adversary's digital infrastructure, vulnerabilities, intentions, and capabilities.

At its core, cyber reconnaissance is the process of actively seeking and passively monitoring digital footprints left by individuals, organizations, or entities in the online realm.

It involves gathering data from publicly accessible sources, analyzing network traffic, and utilizing various tools and techniques to gain insights into potential threats or vulnerabilities.

One fundamental aspect of cyber reconnaissance is understanding the importance of OSINT, or Open-Source Intelligence, which involves collecting information from publicly available sources, such as websites, social media platforms, forums, and databases.

OSINT serves as a valuable starting point for cyber reconnaissance, as it provides a wealth of information that can be used to identify targets, assess vulnerabilities, and understand potential adversaries.

As part of cyber reconnaissance, practitioners often utilize search engines and specialized OSINT tools to conduct targeted searches and gather relevant data.

These searches can range from basic keyword searches to more advanced queries using Boolean operators and other search modifiers to narrow down results.

Another key element of cyber reconnaissance is passive data collection, which involves monitoring and analyzing information that is openly available without direct interaction with the target.

Passive data collection techniques include examining DNS records, WHOIS information, and publicly available metadata from files and documents.

This approach is often used to gather information about an organization's domain names, IP addresses, and network infrastructure.

Active data collection, on the other hand, involves direct interaction with the target to obtain information.

This can include scanning network ports, conducting vulnerability assessments, and probing for weaknesses in a target's digital defenses.

While active data collection may yield valuable insights, it can also be riskier and potentially trigger security alerts, making it important for practitioners to exercise caution and adhere to ethical guidelines.

Understanding the importance of attribution is another fundamental concept in cyber reconnaissance. Attribution involves identifying the source or origin of a cyber threat or attack. In the world of cyber warfare and intelligence, determining attribution is often a complex and challenging task, as threat actors can go to great lengths to conceal their identities and locations. However, attribution is crucial for responding to cyber threats, developing effective countermeasures, and holding threat actors accountable. Advanced cyber reconnaissance techniques may involve analyzing digital signatures, examining malware characteristics, and tracing network traffic back to its source in an effort to attribute cyber attacks accurately. Furthermore, the basics of cyber reconnaissance include an understanding of the cyber threat landscape. Practitioners need to stay informed about the latest cyber threats, attack vectors, and trends in the cybersecurity landscape to effectively assess and respond to potential risks. This knowledge helps in identifying emerging threats and vulnerabilities that may not be widely known or addressed in existing security measures.

Additionally, threat intelligence feeds and sharing forums play a critical role in providing up-to-date information on cyber threats, allowing organizations and individuals to enhance their cyber reconnaissance efforts.

An essential component of cyber reconnaissance is the consideration of legal and ethical boundaries.

Practitioners must operate within the confines of applicable laws and regulations, respecting individuals' privacy and adhering to ethical guidelines.

Unauthorized access, hacking, or any other unlawful activities are strictly prohibited and can have severe legal consequences.

Ethical considerations are paramount, and practitioners should conduct cyber reconnaissance with integrity and responsibility, ensuring that their actions do not harm individuals or organizations.

Moreover, cyber reconnaissance is a continually evolving field, driven by advances in technology and the ever-changing tactics of threat actors.

As new digital platforms, communication methods, and technologies emerge, practitioners must adapt their strategies and techniques to remain effective in the face of evolving cyber threats.

This adaptability and willingness to stay current with industry developments are essential traits for successful cyber reconnaissance professionals.

In summary, understanding the basics of cyber reconnaissance is foundational for individuals and organizations seeking to protect their digital assets, identify potential threats, and gather intelligence in the ever-expanding digital landscape.

It involves leveraging OSINT, passive and active data collection, attribution, awareness of the cyber threat landscape, legal and ethical considerations, and adaptability to stay ahead in the world of cybersecurity and intelligence gathering.

By mastering these fundamentals, practitioners can embark on a journey of becoming proficient in cyber reconnaissance and contributing to the defense of digital assets and information.

Reconnaissance tools and methodologies are essential components of cyber intelligence gathering, aiding practitioners in acquiring valuable information about potential adversaries, vulnerabilities, and digital landscapes.

These tools and methods encompass a wide range of techniques designed to gather data and assess the digital environment effectively.

One crucial aspect of reconnaissance is the use of network scanning tools. These tools enable practitioners to discover devices, open ports, and services running on target systems, providing insights into potential entry points for further investigation.

Network scanners, such as Nmap, can conduct comprehensive scans to identify hosts and services, along with their associated vulnerabilities.

Similarly, vulnerability scanning tools, like Nessus and OpenVAS, help pinpoint weaknesses in the target's network or systems by analyzing known vulnerabilities and misconfigurations.

These tools assist in assessing the security posture of the target and prioritizing remediation efforts.

Web reconnaissance tools are vital for gathering information from publicly accessible web pages and databases. Web scrapers, like Scrapy and Beautiful Soup, can extract data from websites and forums, aiding in the collection of OSINT.

Additionally, search engine scraping tools, such as Google Dorks, help practitioners refine searches and find specific information efficiently.

Social media reconnaissance tools play a crucial role in analyzing online personas and trends. Tools like Maltego enable practitioners to visualize connections between individuals, organizations, and digital artifacts, helping identify potential threats and threat actors.

Similarly, sentiment analysis tools, like Python's NLTK library, analyze text data from social media to gauge public sentiment and detect trends or emerging issues.

Passive DNS and WHOIS lookup tools provide valuable insights into domain names, IP addresses, and their associated information.

These tools, such as PassiveTotal and DNSdumpster, can help practitioners identify infrastructure related to threat actors and track the movement of malicious domains.

Another method of reconnaissance involves exploiting public repositories, such as GitHub, to find sensitive information inadvertently exposed by developers.

GitHub dorks and search queries can reveal code repositories containing credentials, keys, or configurations that may pose security risks if left unsecured.

Furthermore, data leakage reconnaissance tools like Shodan and Censys scan the internet for exposed devices, services, and databases.

These tools can uncover vulnerabilities and open ports in Internet of Things (IoT) devices, industrial control systems, and other connected assets.

Reconnaissance methodologies also extend to deep and dark web investigations. Practitioners use specialized search engines like Tor and I2P to access hidden services and forums.

These environments may host discussions related to cybercrime, hacking, and other illicit activities, making them critical areas for threat intelligence gathering.

Moreover, digital forensics tools aid in analyzing digital artifacts, logs, and system traces. Tools like Autopsy and The Sleuth Kit enable practitioners to recover, analyze, and preserve digital evidence from compromised systems.

Email reconnaissance tools assist in identifying potential threats through the analysis of email headers, sender information, and the detection of phishing attempts.

Tools like MXToolBox and Email Header Analyzer help verify the legitimacy of email communications and prevent email-based attacks.

Geospatial reconnaissance tools leverage geographic information systems (GIS) for mapping and analyzing digital data in the physical world.

These tools allow practitioners to visualize the geographic distribution of threats, assets, and vulnerabilities, aiding in threat assessment and risk mitigation.

Mobile device reconnaissance tools, such as ADB (Android Debug Bridge), help analyze mobile applications and devices for vulnerabilities and potential risks.

They assist in uncovering data leakage, insecure permissions, and other security issues in mobile apps.

Furthermore, open-source threat intelligence feeds and sharing platforms provide practitioners with access to up-to-date information about emerging threats and indicators of compromise.

These platforms enable collaboration within the cybersecurity community and facilitate the sharing of actionable threat intelligence.

Understanding the methodologies of cyber reconnaissance is essential for conducting effective intelligence gathering and threat analysis.

The reconnaissance process involves multiple stages, including planning, data collection, analysis, and reporting, each requiring a tailored approach and the use of appropriate tools.

The use of reconnaissance tools and methodologies is not limited to cybersecurity professionals but extends to law enforcement agencies, intelligence agencies, and organizations seeking to protect their digital assets.

It is crucial to recognize that while reconnaissance tools provide valuable insights, practitioners must operate within legal and ethical boundaries, respecting privacy and adhering to applicable regulations.

Additionally, reconnaissance is an ongoing process, as the digital landscape is constantly evolving, and new threats and vulnerabilities emerge regularly.

In summary, reconnaissance tools and methodologies are indispensable components of cyber intelligence gathering, aiding practitioners in acquiring, analyzing, and visualizing data critical for threat assessment and mitigation.

These tools encompass network scanning, vulnerability assessment, web scraping, social media analysis, passive DNS lookup, dark web investigation, geospatial analysis, mobile device analysis, and email reconnaissance.

Understanding and mastering these reconnaissance techniques are essential for cybersecurity professionals and organizations seeking to bolster their security posture and effectively respond to emerging threats.

Chapter 3: Mapping the Digital Battlefield

Geospatial analysis plays a pivotal role in cyber reconnaissance by combining geographical data with digital information to gain a deeper understanding of the digital landscape.

This approach involves the integration of geographic information systems (GIS) and cyber threat intelligence to visualize and analyze the geographical aspects of cyber threats.

In a world where cyberattacks can have physical implications, geospatial analysis provides valuable insights into the location, distribution, and potential impact of cyber threats.

One of the key benefits of geospatial analysis is its ability to map the physical locations of IP addresses, domain names, and other digital artifacts.

This process allows cyber threat analysts to identify the geographical origins of cyberattacks or malicious activities.

For example, by mapping the locations of IP addresses associated with a phishing campaign, analysts can pinpoint the regions or countries that are most targeted.

Geospatial analysis also aids in identifying emerging trends and patterns in cyber threats. By visualizing the geographical distribution of cyberattacks over time, analysts can detect shifts in attack patterns.

For instance, an increase in cyberattacks originating from a specific region may indicate the emergence of a new threat actor or the deployment of a botnet in that area.

Furthermore, geospatial analysis helps organizations assess their exposure to cyber threats based on their physical location.

By overlaying threat data with organizational data, businesses can evaluate their cyber risk in different geographic regions.

This information is invaluable for making informed decisions about cybersecurity investments and resource allocation.

Geospatial analysis also supports incident response and mitigation efforts. In the event of a cyberattack, knowing the physical location of affected assets can expedite response actions.

For example, if a distributed denial-of-service (DDoS) attack targets a company's data center, geospatial analysis can help pinpoint the data center's location and facilitate the deployment of protective measures.

Moreover, geospatial analysis aids in threat attribution, which is the process of identifying the individuals or groups responsible for cyberattacks.

By combining digital evidence with geographical information, analysts can build a more comprehensive profile of threat actors.

For instance, if a cybercriminal's online activities lead to the discovery of their physical location, law enforcement agencies can use this information to apprehend them.

In the realm of threat intelligence, geospatial analysis contributes to the creation of geospatial threat indicators.

These indicators are designed to alert organizations about potential threats based on their geographical relevance.

For example, if a new malware strain is detected in a specific country, organizations operating in that region can receive targeted alerts and guidance on how to mitigate the threat.

Additionally, geospatial analysis enhances the understanding of threat landscapes in critical infrastructure sectors.

For industries like energy, transportation, and telecommunications, knowing the geographical distribution of vulnerabilities and potential threats is vital for ensuring the resilience of critical systems.

Government agencies also leverage geospatial analysis to protect national security interests and critical infrastructure.

This approach enables them to monitor and respond to cyber threats that may have physical or geopolitical implications.

In summary, geospatial analysis is a valuable tool in cyber reconnaissance, providing insights into the geographical aspects of cyber threats.

It helps in threat attribution, incident response, risk assessment, and the creation of geospatial threat indicators.

Moreover, geospatial analysis plays a crucial role in safeguarding critical infrastructure and supporting national security efforts.

As the cyber threat landscape continues to evolve, the integration of geographical data with cyber threat intelligence remains essential for a comprehensive understanding of the digital battlefield.

Mapping digital assets and vulnerabilities is a critical aspect of cybersecurity, allowing organizations to gain a comprehensive view of their information technology landscape.

This process involves identifying, cataloging, and assessing all digital assets and potential weaknesses within an organization's infrastructure.

Digital assets encompass a wide range of components, including hardware devices, software applications, data repositories, and network resources.

Mapping these assets is the first step in understanding the attack surface, which is the sum of all potential points where an attacker could exploit vulnerabilities to breach an organization's security.

To effectively map digital assets, organizations need to conduct asset discovery and inventory management.

Asset discovery involves actively scanning the network to identify all devices and systems connected to it.

This includes servers, workstations, routers, switches, IoT devices, and any other equipment that could be part of the IT ecosystem.

Asset inventory management involves maintaining a comprehensive database that records details about each digital asset, such as its name, type, location, owner, and the software and data it contains.

Vulnerabilities, on the other hand, are weaknesses or flaws in digital assets or configurations that could be exploited by attackers.

Common vulnerabilities include unpatched software, misconfigured devices, weak passwords, and known security issues within applications.

Mapping vulnerabilities is essential because it helps organizations prioritize their security efforts by identifying areas of highest risk.

One widely used approach for mapping vulnerabilities is vulnerability scanning.

Vulnerability scanning tools systematically check digital assets for known vulnerabilities, providing a list of issues that need to be addressed.

The data collected during vulnerability scanning can then be integrated into the asset inventory, creating a comprehensive view of the organization's digital assets and their associated vulnerabilities.

Asset and vulnerability mapping go hand in hand because understanding the relationship between assets and vulnerabilities is crucial for risk assessment and mitigation.

By correlating which vulnerabilities are present on which assets, organizations can determine the potential impact of a security breach and the likelihood of exploitation.

This information is invaluable for prioritizing remediation efforts and allocating resources effectively.

Asset and vulnerability mapping also help organizations comply with regulatory requirements and industry standards.

Many regulations, such as the General Data Protection Regulation (GDPR) and the Health Insurance Portability and Accountability Act (HIPAA), require organizations to maintain an inventory of their digital assets and regularly assess and address vulnerabilities.

Furthermore, mapping digital assets and vulnerabilities plays a crucial role in incident response and recovery.

In the event of a security incident, knowing the organization's assets and their vulnerabilities is essential for containing the breach and minimizing damage.

Security teams can quickly identify the affected assets and take appropriate action to mitigate the impact.

Continuous monitoring of digital assets and vulnerabilities is essential in today's dynamic and evolving threat landscape.

New vulnerabilities are discovered regularly, and the IT environment within organizations is constantly changing with the addition or retirement of assets.

To address these challenges, organizations should implement automated solutions for asset and vulnerability management.

These tools can perform continuous asset discovery, inventory management, and vulnerability scanning, providing real-time insights into the security posture.

Additionally, organizations should establish a structured process for remediating vulnerabilities, including patch management, configuration management, and vulnerability assessment.

Regularly reviewing and updating the asset and vulnerability mapping is crucial to maintaining a strong security posture.

Collaboration between IT and security teams is essential for effective asset and vulnerability mapping.

IT teams are responsible for managing digital assets, while security teams focus on assessing and mitigating vulnerabilities.

Close cooperation ensures that both teams have the necessary information to protect the organization's digital assets effectively.

In summary, mapping digital assets and vulnerabilities is a fundamental cybersecurity practice that enables organizations to understand their IT landscape, prioritize security efforts, and comply with regulations.

It is a continuous and collaborative process that helps organizations stay resilient in the face of evolving cyber threats.

By maintaining an up-to-date and comprehensive view of their assets and vulnerabilities, organizations can reduce their risk exposure and respond effectively to security incidents.

Chapter 4: Advanced Dark Web Investigations

Exploring the deep and dark web requires a unique set of strategies and precautions, as it is a realm shrouded in anonymity and often associated with illicit activities.

The deep web refers to parts of the internet that are not indexed by traditional search engines like Google, and they include databases, password-protected websites, and other unindexed content.

On the other hand, the dark web is a subset of the deep web, accessible only through specialized software like Tor, and it is intentionally hidden to provide anonymity to its users.

To navigate and explore these hidden corners of the internet, individuals and organizations need to adopt a thoughtful approach.

The first step in deep and dark web exploration is understanding the technology that enables access.

Tor, short for "The Onion Router," is the most well-known tool for accessing the dark web.

It routes internet traffic through a network of volunteer-run servers, encrypting data at each step to provide anonymity.

To access the dark web, users typically need to download and install the Tor browser, which allows them to access websites with the ".onion" domain.

It's essential to download Tor from the official website to avoid downloading compromised versions that may contain malware.

Once the Tor browser is set up, users can begin exploring the dark web, but they should be cautious and informed about the risks involved.

Anonymity is a double-edged sword in dark web exploration. While it provides privacy, it also attracts cybercriminals and malicious actors.

Therefore, individuals and organizations should take precautions to protect their identity and data.

One fundamental practice is never using personal information or identifiable usernames when engaging with dark web content.

Additionally, users should consider using a Virtual Private Network (VPN) in conjunction with Tor to add an extra layer of security.

A VPN masks the user's IP address, making it even more challenging for anyone to trace their online activities back to them.

Another critical aspect of deep and dark web exploration is information gathering.

This involves using specialized search engines and directories that are designed to index and catalog dark web websites.

Popular search engines for the dark web include DuckDuckGo and NotEvil.

These search engines provide access to a wide range of websites on the dark web, allowing users to find information on various topics.

It's important to note that while exploring the dark web, individuals may come across illegal and unethical content.

This could include marketplaces for illegal drugs, stolen data, or other illicit goods and services.

Engaging with such content is not only illegal but also exposes individuals to significant risks.

Therefore, it's crucial to approach dark web exploration with ethical and legal boundaries in mind.

For researchers and cybersecurity professionals, dark web exploration can be a valuable source of threat intelligence.

Monitoring underground forums and marketplaces can provide insights into emerging cyber threats and vulnerabilities.

However, even in a professional context, it's vital to adhere to ethical guidelines and legal restrictions.

When conducting research on the dark web, individuals should use pseudonyms and avoid sharing any personally identifiable information.

Furthermore, it's essential to respect the privacy and security of others and not engage in any illegal activities.

Dark web marketplaces can be a hub for illegal goods and services, and some may offer sensitive data for sale.

To stay safe and within legal boundaries, researchers should never purchase or interact with stolen or illegal content.

Instead, they can focus on analyzing trends, understanding threat actors, and identifying potential vulnerabilities.

As with any online activity, maintaining digital hygiene is crucial when exploring the deep and dark web.

This includes keeping software and security tools up to date, using strong and unique passwords, and regularly scanning for malware.

Phishing attacks are also prevalent on the dark web, so users should be vigilant about clicking on links or downloading files from untrusted sources.

Moreover, individuals should be cautious about sharing any personal or financial information, even on seemingly legitimate websites.

Another important consideration is the potential psychological impact of dark web exploration.

Exposure to disturbing or illegal content can be emotionally taxing, so users should be prepared for the possibility of encountering such material.

Having a support network and seeking professional help if necessary is essential for maintaining mental well-being.

In summary, deep and dark web exploration is a complex and potentially risky endeavor.

While it can offer valuable insights and research opportunities, it also poses significant challenges related to privacy, security, and ethical considerations.

Adopting a cautious and informed approach, using anonymity tools like Tor and VPNs, and adhering to legal and ethical boundaries are essential for a safe and responsible exploration of the deep and dark web.

Investigating illicit activities and underground markets is a complex and crucial aspect of cybersecurity and law enforcement efforts in the digital age.

The term "underground markets" refers to online platforms where illegal goods and services are bought and sold, often with a degree of anonymity.

These markets operate on the dark web, a hidden part of the internet accessible only through specialized tools like the Tor browser, which conceals users' identities.

Illicit activities and underground markets encompass a wide range of illegal transactions, including the sale of drugs, stolen data, counterfeit documents, hacking services, and more.

Cybersecurity professionals, law enforcement agencies, and ethical hackers often engage in investigating these activities to protect individuals and organizations from cyber threats.

One of the key challenges in investigating underground markets is the anonymity provided by the dark web and cryptocurrency transactions.

Many transactions in these markets use cryptocurrencies like Bitcoin to facilitate payments, making it difficult to trace the flow of money.

To address this challenge, investigators employ various techniques, including blockchain analysis, to trace cryptocurrency transactions and identify individuals involved in illegal activities.

Moreover, investigators often collaborate with international law enforcement agencies to gather intelligence and build cases against cybercriminals operating in different jurisdictions.

While the dark web and underground markets pose significant challenges, they also offer opportunities for investigators to gather valuable threat intelligence.

By monitoring these platforms, investigators can identify emerging cyber threats, vulnerabilities, and trends in criminal activities.

However, it's crucial to approach these investigations with a clear understanding of ethical and legal boundaries.

Respecting individuals' privacy, even in the context of criminal investigations, is essential.

Investigations into underground markets require a combination of technical skills and domain expertise.

Investigators often pose as buyers or sellers to gain access to these markets, assess their operations, and collect evidence.

However, doing so necessitates a deep understanding of the terminology, culture, and norms prevalent in these online communities.

Moreover, investigators must be cautious not to inadvertently engage in illegal activities themselves, as law enforcement agencies adhere to strict legal standards in their operations.

One of the most significant challenges in investigating underground markets is the constant evolution of these platforms.

As law enforcement agencies shut down one marketplace, others quickly emerge, often with improved security features and new methods to evade detection.

This cat-and-mouse game between investigators and cybercriminals highlights the need for continuous adaptation and innovation in investigative techniques.

Another important aspect of investigating illicit activities and underground markets is the role of threat intelligence.

Cybersecurity professionals and law enforcement agencies leverage threat intelligence to proactively identify potential threats and vulnerabilities.

Threat intelligence involves collecting, analyzing, and disseminating information about cyber threats and threat actors.

In the context of underground markets, threat intelligence can help investigators understand the tactics, techniques, and procedures used by cybercriminals.

It can also provide insights into the infrastructure and tools employed in these illicit activities.

The sharing of threat intelligence among cybersecurity professionals and law enforcement agencies is critical in building a comprehensive picture of the cyber threat landscape.

Open-source intelligence (OSINT) plays a significant role in investigating underground markets.

OSINT involves collecting information from publicly available sources, and it can provide valuable insights into the activities of threat actors.

Investigators use OSINT tools and techniques to monitor social media, forums, and websites frequented by cybercriminals.

By analyzing the information gathered through OSINT, investigators can identify connections between individuals, track the dissemination of stolen data, and uncover new leads in their investigations.

Ethical considerations are paramount when investigating illicit activities and underground markets.

Maintaining the rule of law and respecting individuals' rights, even those engaged in criminal activities, is a fundamental principle of any ethical investigation.

Ethical hackers, for example, adhere to strict codes of conduct and legal frameworks when conducting penetration tests or participating in investigations.

Moreover, investigators must consider the potential harm that may come from disclosing vulnerabilities or exposing sensitive data.

In some cases, responsible disclosure to affected parties or vendors is necessary to mitigate risks.

As the digital landscape continues to evolve, investigators face new challenges in uncovering and combatting illicit activities and underground markets.

The rise of cryptocurrencies, anonymous communication tools, and sophisticated encryption methods pose significant hurdles.

However, with collaboration, innovative techniques, and a commitment to ethical practices, cybersecurity professionals and law enforcement agencies can make meaningful progress in disrupting and deterring cybercriminal activities.

In summary, investigating illicit activities and underground markets is a complex and vital endeavor in the field of cybersecurity and law enforcement.

It requires a deep understanding of technology, legal frameworks, ethical considerations, and threat intelligence.

By staying ahead of cybercriminals and adapting to the evolving landscape, investigators can play a crucial role in safeguarding individuals and organizations from cyber threats.

Chapter 5: Deep Dive into Attribution and Deception

Advanced attribution techniques are a critical component of cybersecurity and digital forensics, aimed at identifying the individuals or groups responsible for cyberattacks and illicit activities in the digital realm. These techniques go beyond surface-level investigations and involve sophisticated methodologies to unmask cybercriminals.

In the world of cybersecurity, attribution refers to the process of attributing a cyberattack or malicious activity to a specific actor or group. It's akin to solving a digital mystery where skilled investigators use various clues and digital breadcrumbs to unveil the identities of threat actors.

Attribution is essential because it enables organizations and law enforcement agencies to take appropriate action against cybercriminals, whether through legal means or by bolstering their cybersecurity defenses.

Advanced attribution techniques often begin with the collection of digital artifacts, which are traces of activities left behind by threat actors during their operations. These artifacts can include IP addresses, domain names, email addresses, malware samples, and more.

One key aspect of attribution is the analysis of malware used in cyberattacks. Malware often contains clues, such as code signatures, encryption methods, or unique features, that can lead investigators to the authors or distributors of the malware.

Advanced attribution techniques also involve the examination of infrastructure used by threat actors. This includes scrutinizing the servers, hosting providers, and network paths utilized in cyberattacks. By tracing the infrastructure, investigators can identify patterns and connections that may link back to specific threat actors or groups.

A crucial component of advanced attribution is the analysis of cybercriminals' tactics, techniques, and procedures (TTPs). Threat actors often have distinct modus operandi that can provide insights into their identities or affiliations. For instance, certain hacking groups may favor specific attack methods or tools, which can become distinctive signatures.

Another critical aspect of advanced attribution is the study of threat intelligence. Threat intelligence involves collecting and analyzing information about cyber threats and threat actors. By aggregating data from various sources, such as open-source intelligence (OSINT), malware analysis, and dark web monitoring, investigators can build a comprehensive profile of threat actors.

Behavioral analysis plays a significant role in advanced attribution techniques. By examining the behavior of threat actors during an attack, investigators can gain insights into their motivations, capabilities, and potentially even their geographic locations. Behavioral analysis may involve studying patterns of communication, timing of attacks, or the choice of targets.

Advanced attribution often requires collaboration among cybersecurity professionals, law enforcement agencies, and international organizations. Threat actors can operate from different parts of the world, making it necessary to coordinate efforts across borders to identify and apprehend them.

One challenge in advanced attribution is the use of false flags by threat actors. Cybercriminals sometimes employ deception techniques to mislead investigators. They may plant false clues, use virtual private networks (VPNs) or anonymizing tools to hide their true locations, or employ tactics that mimic the behavior of other threat groups.

To counter these challenges, advanced attribution techniques must rely on a combination of technical expertise, domain knowledge, and access to cutting-edge tools and technologies. Investigators must constantly adapt and refine their methods to keep pace with the evolving tactics of cybercriminals.

Ethical considerations are crucial in the practice of advanced attribution techniques. Investigators must adhere to legal and ethical standards when conducting their investigations. Respecting individuals' rights and privacy, even in the context of cybercrime, is paramount.

Moreover, there's an ethical responsibility to ensure that attribution is accurate and evidence-based. Misattribution can have severe consequences, potentially harming innocent parties or escalating geopolitical tensions.

In recent years, state-sponsored cyberattacks have gained significant attention, with nation-states engaging in cyber espionage, sabotage, and disinformation campaigns. Advanced attribution techniques are often employed to trace these attacks back to specific nation-states.

In such cases, indicators like the use of custom-built malware, known as advanced persistent threats (APTs), or the presence of specific language artifacts in code or metadata can help attribute cyberattacks to particular countries or state-sponsored groups.

Advanced attribution techniques are not limited to government agencies or large organizations. Small and medium-sized enterprises (SMEs) also benefit from these techniques as they face cyber threats, including ransomware attacks and data breaches.

SMEs can leverage the expertise of cybersecurity professionals and managed security service providers (MSSPs) to conduct advanced attribution investigations. These investigations can help SMEs understand the motivations and tactics of threat actors targeting their organizations.

In summary, advanced attribution techniques are a critical component of modern cybersecurity and digital forensics. They involve a multidisciplinary approach that combines technical analysis, behavioral profiling, and threat intelligence.

These techniques are essential for identifying cybercriminals, nation-states, or threat groups responsible for cyberattacks and illicit activities. However, ethical considerations and accuracy in attribution are paramount, as misattribution can have severe consequences.

As the cyber threat landscape continues to evolve, the practice of advanced attribution will remain essential for protecting organizations and individuals from cyber threats and holding threat actors accountable for their actions.

Detecting and analyzing deceptive tactics is a critical skill in the realm of cybersecurity and digital forensics, as cybercriminals often employ various forms of deception to mask their activities and evade detection. Understanding these tactics and being able to uncover them is essential for identifying threats and protecting digital assets.

Deception in the digital world can take many forms, ranging from simple obfuscation techniques to more sophisticated strategies aimed at misdirecting investigators and concealing malicious actions. To effectively detect and analyze these tactics, cybersecurity professionals need a combination of technical expertise, creativity, and a deep understanding of cyber threats.

One common form of deception used by cybercriminals is the use of fake or malicious websites designed to mimic legitimate ones. These fake websites often have URLs that closely resemble the real ones, making it challenging for users to distinguish between them. Cybercriminals may use these deceptive sites to steal login credentials, distribute malware, or carry out phishing attacks.

To detect and analyze these deceptive websites, cybersecurity professionals can use techniques such as analyzing the domain name, checking for SSL certificates, and examining the website's content for inconsistencies or suspicious elements. These methods can help identify fraudulent websites and protect users from falling victim to cyberattacks.

Another deceptive tactic employed by cybercriminals is the use of social engineering techniques to manipulate individuals into revealing sensitive information or performing actions that benefit the attacker. This can include tactics like pretexting, where an attacker impersonates a trusted entity to gain access to confidential data, or baiting, where malicious files or links are disguised as enticing offers or downloads.

To detect and analyze social engineering tactics, cybersecurity professionals must remain vigilant and educate users about the dangers of sharing sensitive information or clicking on suspicious links. Additionally, monitoring network traffic and analyzing email communications can help identify signs of social engineering attempts.

In the realm of malware analysis, cybercriminals often use deception to evade detection by security tools and researchers. They may employ techniques such as polymorphism, where the code of a malware variant changes with each infection, making it challenging for signature-based antivirus solutions to identify and block the malware.

To detect and analyze deceptive malware tactics, cybersecurity professionals can use behavior-based analysis methods that focus on the actions of the malware rather than static signatures. This approach allows for the identification of malicious behavior patterns, even in the presence of polymorphic or evasive malware.

Deceptive tactics can also be used in the context of cyber espionage and advanced persistent threats (APTs). APT actors often employ sophisticated techniques to maintain a low profile and avoid detection for extended periods. They may use decoy documents, false flags, and other obfuscation methods to mislead investigators.

To detect and analyze APT-related deceptive tactics, cybersecurity professionals need to look for anomalies and inconsistencies in network traffic and system logs. Advanced threat hunting techniques, such as anomaly detection and baselining, can help identify unusual behavior that may indicate the presence of APT actors.

In addition to deceptive tactics used by cybercriminals, cybersecurity professionals must also be vigilant about disinformation campaigns and fake news in the digital realm. Disinformation is the deliberate spreading of false or misleading information with the intent to deceive or manipulate public opinion.

Detecting and analyzing disinformation campaigns involves examining the source of information, verifying facts, and cross-referencing information with trusted sources. It requires critical thinking skills and a healthy skepticism towards online content.

Deceptive tactics are not limited to cybercriminals; they can also be employed by nation-states for various purposes, including influence operations and information warfare. Nation-state actors may create fake personas, disseminate propaganda, and engage in covert activities to achieve their objectives.

To detect and analyze nation-state-sponsored deceptive tactics, cybersecurity professionals often work closely with government agencies and international organizations. These efforts may involve threat intelligence sharing, attribution analysis, and diplomatic efforts to address state-sponsored cyber threats.

Ethical considerations are paramount when detecting and analyzing deceptive tactics. Investigators and cybersecurity professionals must ensure that their actions are within legal and ethical boundaries, respecting individuals' rights and privacy. Misuse of deception-detection techniques can have serious consequences, including legal repercussions.

In summary, detecting and analyzing deceptive tactics in the digital realm is a crucial aspect of cybersecurity and digital forensics. Cybercriminals, nation-states, and threat actors employ a wide range of deceptive techniques to mask their activities and achieve their objectives.

Cybersecurity professionals must remain vigilant, continuously update their knowledge, and leverage a combination of technical expertise and critical thinking to uncover deceptive tactics. Additionally, ethical considerations and compliance with legal standards are essential to ensure that deception-detection efforts are conducted responsibly and within the bounds of the law.

Chapter 6: Threat Intelligence Frameworks and Models

Threat intelligence frameworks play a crucial role in modern cybersecurity strategies, helping organizations identify, analyze, and respond to emerging threats effectively. These frameworks provide a structured approach to collecting, processing, and disseminating information about potential threats and vulnerabilities.

One of the fundamental aspects of threat intelligence frameworks is the collection of data from various sources. This data can include indicators of compromise (IoCs), such as malware signatures, IP addresses, and domain names associated with known threats. It can also encompass contextual information, such as threat actor profiles, tactics, techniques, and procedures (TTPs), and historical attack data.

The first step in building a threat intelligence framework is to define the objectives and scope of the intelligence program. Organizations need to determine what specific threats they are concerned about and what assets or data they want to protect. This helps in tailoring the framework to meet their unique needs and priorities.

Next, organizations must establish a process for collecting threat intelligence data. This process involves identifying relevant data sources, such as open-source threat feeds, commercial threat intelligence providers, government agencies, and internal logs and reports. The goal is to gather a wide range of data to paint a comprehensive picture of the threat landscape.

Once the data sources are identified, organizations need to establish automated data collection mechanisms to gather information efficiently. Automation is crucial because the threat landscape is constantly evolving, and manual data collection may not keep pace with emerging threats.

The collected data is then processed to extract relevant information and indicators of potential threats. This process involves normalizing and enriching the data, making it more usable and meaningful. For example, IP addresses can be geolocated, domain names can be resolved to IP addresses, and malware samples can be analyzed to identify their characteristics.

After processing, the data is correlated and analyzed to identify patterns, trends, and potential threats. This analysis phase is where the true value of threat intelligence is realized. Analysts use various techniques, such as data mining, statistical analysis, and machine learning, to identify anomalies and potential threats.

Once threats are identified and assessed, organizations must decide on an appropriate response. Response options can vary from blocking malicious IP addresses and domain names to updating security policies and procedures. The choice of response depends on the severity of the threat and the organization's risk tolerance.

Threat intelligence frameworks also emphasize the importance of information sharing and collaboration. Organizations are encouraged to share threat intelligence with trusted partners, industry peers, and government agencies. This collective sharing of information helps create a more robust and up-to-date threat intelligence ecosystem.

A key aspect of threat intelligence frameworks is the concept of threat intelligence feeds. These feeds are sources of threat data that organizations subscribe to or purchase. Threat intelligence feeds provide a continuous stream of data on known threats and vulnerabilities, allowing organizations to stay informed in real-time.

Threat intelligence feeds can cover a wide range of threat categories, including malware, phishing, botnets, and vulnerabilities in software and hardware. Organizations can select feeds that align with their specific threat landscape and risk profile.

To make the most of threat intelligence feeds, organizations need to integrate them into their security infrastructure. This integration allows security tools and systems to automatically consume threat intelligence data and take action based on predefined rules and policies.

Many organizations also invest in threat intelligence platforms (TIPs) to streamline the collection, processing, analysis, and dissemination of threat intelligence data. TIPs provide a centralized repository for threat data, allowing analysts to collaborate more effectively and enabling automated responses to threats.

Threat intelligence frameworks also emphasize the importance of timely and relevant threat intelligence. Stale or outdated threat data can lead to false positives and unnecessary alerts, which can overwhelm security teams and dilute the effectiveness of threat detection and response efforts.

To address this issue, organizations need to establish a process for continuously updating and validating threat intelligence data. This involves verifying the accuracy and relevance of threat indicators and adapting security measures accordingly.

Moreover, organizations must also consider the ethical and legal aspects of threat intelligence sharing and collection. Adhering to privacy regulations and data protection laws is crucial when handling threat intelligence data, especially when sharing information with external parties.

Threat intelligence frameworks also advocate for proactive threat hunting. Threat hunting is the practice of actively searching for signs of malicious activity within an organization's network and systems, even when no specific threat is known. It involves a combination of manual and automated techniques to identify hidden threats that may have evaded detection.

Furthermore, organizations should establish a feedback loop to continuously improve their threat intelligence programs. This feedback loop includes evaluating the effectiveness of threat intelligence in reducing the organization's risk, improving detection and response capabilities, and refining threat intelligence collection and analysis processes.

In summary, threat intelligence frameworks are essential tools for modern cybersecurity. They provide organizations with a structured approach to collecting, processing, and analyzing threat data, enabling them to stay ahead of emerging threats and protect their digital assets effectively. By following best practices and continually evolving their threat intelligence programs, organizations can enhance their security posture and reduce the impact of cyber threats.

Analyzing cyber threats is a critical aspect of modern cybersecurity, and various models have been developed to help organizations understand, assess, and respond to these threats effectively. These models provide structured frameworks for comprehending the complex and evolving landscape of cyber threats.

One of the foundational models in cybersecurity threat analysis is the Cyber Kill Chain, which was introduced by defense contractor Lockheed Martin. The Cyber Kill Chain is a concept that breaks down the stages of a cyberattack into distinct steps, from initial reconnaissance to data exfiltration. This model helps organizations visualize how an attacker progresses through these stages and allows for proactive defense at each step.

The Cyber Kill Chain typically consists of seven stages: reconnaissance, weaponization, delivery, exploitation, installation, command and control, and actions on objectives. Understanding these stages enables organizations to develop strategies and defenses to detect and disrupt cyberattacks in their early stages, minimizing potential damage.

Another influential model is the Diamond Model of Intrusion Analysis, which focuses on four key attributes: adversary, infrastructure, victim, and capability. This model emphasizes the relationships among these attributes and how they can be used to gain insights into cyber threats. By examining these attributes, organizations can better understand the tactics, techniques, and procedures (TTPs) of adversaries and enhance their threat intelligence.

The Diamond Model provides a structured approach to analyzing incidents and attacks, helping organizations determine the who, what, where, when, why, and how of a cyber threat. This comprehensive understanding is crucial for making informed decisions about threat mitigation and response.

In addition to these models, the STIX/TAXII framework plays a vital role in threat analysis and information sharing within the cybersecurity community. STIX (Structured Threat Information eXpression) is a standardized language for describing cyber threats and incidents, while TAXII (Trusted Automated Exchange of Indicator Information) is a protocol for sharing threat intelligence. STIX/TAXII facilitates the exchange of threat information between organizations, allowing them to collaborate in real-time to detect and mitigate cyber threats. This framework has become a cornerstone of the threat intelligence community, enabling organizations to share actionable intelligence and improve their collective defense.

Another important model is the Diamond Threat Intelligence Model (DTIM), which provides a structured approach to collecting and analyzing threat intelligence data. DTIM focuses on four primary dimensions: tactical, operational, strategic, and geopolitical. Each dimension represents a different level of analysis and helps organizations tailor their threat intelligence efforts to their specific needs.

The tactical dimension involves real-time threat data, such as indicators of compromise (IoCs), and is focused on immediate threat detection and response. The operational dimension delves deeper into adversary TTPs and provides insights into ongoing campaigns and attacks. The strategic dimension examines long-term trends and threats that may impact an organization's overall security posture, while the geopolitical dimension considers broader global threats and their potential implications.

By using the DTIM, organizations can align their threat intelligence efforts with their strategic objectives and make informed decisions about resource allocation and threat mitigation.

The Diamond Model of Intrusion Analysis, the Cyber Kill Chain, STIX/TAXII, and the Diamond Threat Intelligence Model are just a few examples of the many models available for analyzing cyber threats. Each of these models has its strengths and weaknesses, and organizations may choose to adopt multiple models to gain a more comprehensive view of the threat landscape.

Furthermore, machine learning and artificial intelligence (AI) are increasingly being integrated into threat analysis models. These technologies have the potential to analyze vast amounts of data quickly and identify patterns and anomalies that may not be apparent to human analysts. Machine learning models can help organizations detect and respond to threats more rapidly and accurately.

While models and frameworks provide valuable guidance in the field of cyber threat analysis, it's important to recognize that the threat landscape is constantly evolving. New attack techniques and tactics emerge regularly, and threat actors adapt their strategies in response to defensive measures. Therefore, organizations must remain agile and continuously update their threat analysis approaches to stay ahead of cyber adversaries.

In summary, models for analyzing cyber threats are essential tools for organizations seeking to understand, assess, and respond to the ever-evolving landscape of cybersecurity threats. These models provide structured frameworks and methodologies for comprehending the intricacies of cyberattacks, enabling organizations to proactively defend their digital assets. As the threat landscape continues to evolve, organizations must adapt and leverage new technologies, such as machine learning and AI, to enhance their threat analysis capabilities and maintain effective cybersecurity postures.

Chapter 7: OSINT in Counterintelligence Operations

Counterintelligence is a crucial component of national security and defense strategies, and in the modern digital age, open-source intelligence (OSINT) plays a pivotal role in supporting counterintelligence efforts. Counterintelligence is the practice of detecting, preventing, and countering espionage, sabotage, and other intelligence activities conducted by foreign entities or adversaries. It aims to protect a nation's critical assets, secrets, and interests from threats posed by foreign intelligence services, cybercriminals, and other malicious actors.

OSINT, as a valuable source of information gathered from publicly available sources, contributes significantly to counterintelligence operations. It provides a broad and unclassified view of various aspects of an adversary's activities, intentions, and capabilities. OSINT can help identify potential threats, uncover vulnerabilities, and support decision-making processes in counterintelligence efforts.

One of the primary roles of OSINT in counterintelligence is to monitor and analyze publicly available information to detect early warning signs of espionage or covert activities. This can include tracking the online presence and behavior of individuals or organizations with suspicious or unauthorized access to sensitive information. OSINT analysts can examine social media posts, public records, news articles, and other open sources to identify patterns or anomalies that may indicate espionage or insider threats.

In addition to identifying potential threats, OSINT can also aid in understanding the motivations and objectives of foreign intelligence services or hostile actors. By analyzing publicly available information, counterintelligence professionals can gain insights into the strategic goals, areas of interest, and tactics employed by adversaries. This knowledge is essential for developing effective countermeasures and protective measures.

OSINT can also help assess the vulnerabilities and weaknesses within an organization or government agency that may be exploited by foreign intelligence services. This includes evaluating the security of physical facilities, information systems, and supply chains. By identifying vulnerabilities through OSINT, counterintelligence teams can take proactive steps to mitigate risks and enhance security.

Furthermore, OSINT plays a role in supporting counterintelligence investigations. When suspicions of espionage or insider threats arise, OSINT can be used to gather evidence and build a case against individuals or organizations involved in illicit activities. This may involve analyzing communication patterns, financial records, travel history, and other publicly available data to establish a timeline of events and connections.

Another crucial aspect of OSINT in counterintelligence is the monitoring of emerging threats and trends. The digital landscape is continually evolving, and new tactics and technologies are constantly emerging. OSINT analysts must stay vigilant and adapt to these changes to remain effective in their counterintelligence efforts. By keeping abreast of evolving threat vectors and techniques, counterintelligence professionals can develop strategies to detect and counter emerging threats.

Collaboration and information sharing are essential in counterintelligence, and OSINT can facilitate this by providing a common source of information that can be shared among government agencies, law enforcement, and private sector partners. Effective information sharing can help build a comprehensive understanding of threats and enhance the collective defense against espionage and other malicious activities.

Moreover, OSINT can support counterintelligence by contributing to threat assessments and risk analysis. By aggregating and analyzing open-source information, intelligence agencies and security organizations can produce assessments that inform policymakers and decision-makers about the level of threat posed by foreign intelligence services or other adversaries. These assessments are critical for allocating resources and prioritizing counterintelligence efforts.

In summary, the role of OSINT in counterintelligence is multifaceted and indispensable in today's digital age. OSINT provides valuable insights, early warning capabilities, and investigative support in identifying and countering espionage, insider threats, and other malicious activities. It aids in understanding the motivations and tactics of adversaries, assessing vulnerabilities, monitoring emerging threats, and facilitating collaboration among stakeholders. As technology continues to advance, OSINT will remain a vital tool in the ongoing effort to protect national security and defend against espionage and covert activities.

In the realm of cybersecurity and corporate security, one of the most significant and challenging threats that organizations face is the insider threat. Insider threats refer to security risks that originate from individuals within the organization, such as employees, contractors, or business partners, who have access to the organization's systems, data, and networks. These individuals, while granted legitimate access, may intentionally or unintentionally misuse their privileges to compromise the organization's security, steal sensitive information, or engage in malicious activities. The key challenge in identifying and countering insider threats lies in distinguishing between legitimate and malicious actions within an organization. It's important to recognize that not all insider threats are the result of malicious intent; some may arise from employee negligence, lack of awareness, or even coercion. However, organizations must remain vigilant in identifying and mitigating these threats to protect their data, intellectual property, and reputation. One crucial aspect of addressing insider threats is establishing a comprehensive insider threat detection program. This program involves the implementation of technical and procedural controls to monitor and analyze user activities and behavior within the organization's IT environment. Technological solutions, such as user and entity behavior analytics (UEBA) tools, can play a vital role in detecting anomalous or suspicious activities that may indicate an insider threat. UEBA tools analyze patterns of behavior and can trigger alerts or alarms when deviations from the norm occur, helping security teams investigate potential threats. In addition to technology, organizations should also focus on the human element of insider threat detection. Creating a culture of security awareness and accountability among employees is essential. Employees should be educated about the risks of insider threats and encouraged to report any suspicious behavior they encounter. Moreover, organizations can implement security policies and procedures that restrict access to sensitive information to only those individuals who require it for their job roles. This principle, known as the principle of least privilege (PoLP), limits the potential damage an insider threat can cause by limiting their access to critical systems and data. Effective access controls, like strong authentication and authorization mechanisms, further enforce PoLP and reduce the risk of insider threats. Another crucial aspect of insider threat detection is monitoring user activity and data access. Security information and event management (SIEM) systems, in combination with log analysis and monitoring, can help organizations keep a close watch on user actions. SIEM tools collect and analyze log data from various sources, enabling security teams to detect unusual or suspicious activities that may indicate insider threats. It's important to set up alerts and triggers within SIEM systems to notify security personnel when specific patterns of behavior occur. To further enhance insider threat detection, organizations can implement data loss prevention (DLP) solutions. DLP tools monitor and control the movement of sensitive data within and outside the organization. They can detect and prevent unauthorized data transfers, helping to thwart insider threats attempting to exfiltrate valuable information. User training and awareness programs are instrumental in preventing and countering insider threats. Employees should receive regular training on cybersecurity best practices, the risks of insider threats, and how to recognize and report suspicious activities. Organizations should also conduct simulated insider threat exercises to test their detection and response capabilities. These exercises help both security personnel and employees understand the potential risks and responses to insider threats. Employee assistance programs (EAPs) can provide a support system for employees who may be experiencing personal or professional difficulties that could lead to insider threats. By addressing underlying issues, organizations can help prevent employees from resorting to malicious actions. Additionally, organizations should establish clear and well-communicated insider threat policies and procedures. Employees should know the consequences of insider threats and the organization's commitment to investigating and addressing such incidents. In the event of an insider threat incident, a well-defined incident response plan should be in place. This plan should outline the steps to be taken, including isolating affected systems, conducting forensic analysis, and involving law enforcement if necessary. An important consideration is legal and ethical aspects when countering insider threats. Organizations must respect the privacy and legal rights of employees while investigating potential threats. This may involve collaborating with legal counsel to ensure that all actions are within the bounds of the law. It's essential to strike a balance between security and privacy to maintain trust within the organization. In summary, identifying and countering insider threats is a multifaceted challenge that requires a combination of technology, policies, procedures, and a security-aware culture. Organizations must remain vigilant in monitoring user activities, implementing access controls, and educating employees about the risks. By taking a proactive approach to insider threat detection and mitigation, organizations can better protect their valuable assets and maintain a secure environment in an ever-evolving threat landscape.

Chapter 8: Advanced OSINT Tools and Techniques

In the ever-evolving landscape of open-source intelligence (OSINT), staying up-to-date with cutting-edge tools and software is crucial. These tools are the backbone of OSINT operations, enabling analysts, investigators, and researchers to collect, analyze, and visualize vast amounts of publicly available information from the internet. One of the standout OSINT tools that has gained prominence in recent years is Maltego. Maltego is a powerful data mining and link analysis tool that assists in gathering information about individuals, organizations, or any online entity. It allows users to visualize complex relationships between data points and identify patterns that might be hidden in plain sight. The versatility of Maltego makes it an indispensable tool for OSINT professionals. Another noteworthy tool is OSINT Framework, a comprehensive collection of various OSINT resources and tools. It provides an organized and categorized list of online resources and tools, making it easier for OSINT practitioners to find what they need quickly. OSINT Framework covers a wide range of categories, including social media, domain research, IP address investigation, and much more. For those focusing on social media intelligence, tools like Sherlock and SherlockML can be invaluable. Sherlock helps identify social media profiles and accounts associated with a specific username across various platforms, while SherlockML takes it a step further by providing machine learning capabilities for the same purpose. These tools are particularly useful for tracking individuals or entities across different social media platforms. When it comes to monitoring web content, Feedly is a robust tool for aggregating and tracking information from multiple websites and blogs. It allows users to subscribe to specific RSS feeds or websites and receive real-time updates in one consolidated interface. This is particularly beneficial for OSINT analysts who need to stay informed about the latest developments in their areas of interest. For analyzing and visualizing data, Gephi is a powerful open-source tool that specializes in graph and network analysis. It is particularly useful for uncovering connections and relationships among data points, making it an excellent choice for OSINT investigations involving social networks, websites, or any data with complex interdependencies. Moreover, Gephi provides various layout algorithms and customization options for creating compelling visualizations. In the realm of image analysis, tools like EXIFPurge and Jeffrey's Exif Viewer are essential for extracting metadata from images. EXIFPurge allows users to remove sensitive metadata from images to protect their privacy, while Jeffrey's Exif Viewer provides a comprehensive view of the metadata contained within an image file. These tools are vital for understanding the context and origins of images encountered during OSINT investigations. For OSINT analysts who deal with geospatial data, Google Earth Pro remains a valuable resource. While Google Earth's free version offers basic functionality, the Pro version provides advanced tools for measuring distances, importing data from GPS devices, and creating high-resolution images and videos. This software is indispensable for mapping and geospatial analysis within the context of OSINT. On the communication front, Slack and Discord have become increasingly popular platforms for OSINT professionals to collaborate and share information. These chat applications offer real-time communication and the ability to create private channels, making them suitable for secure discussions and information sharing among OSINT teams. Furthermore, for those interested in exploring the deep and dark web, tools like Tor and Tor Browser are essential. The Tor network enables anonymous browsing by routing internet traffic through a series of volunteer-operated servers, effectively concealing the user's identity and location. The Tor Browser, based on Firefox, simplifies access to the Tor network and is an indispensable tool for OSINT professionals concerned with anonymity. When conducting OSINT investigations related to cybersecurity, the Shodan search engine is an invaluable resource. Shodan specializes in scanning and indexing devices connected to the internet, including routers, servers, webcams, and more. This information can help identify potential vulnerabilities and security risks, making it a critical tool for threat intelligence. Moreover, the continually evolving landscape of OSINT tools also includes paid services like Recorded Future and DigitalStakeout. Recorded Future is an advanced threat intelligence platform that aggregates and analyzes data from various sources to provide predictive insights on cybersecurity threats. DigitalStakeout, on the other hand, focuses on monitoring social media and the deep web to identify potential security risks and threats. These platforms offer OSINT professionals advanced capabilities for staying ahead of cyber threats. In addition to specialized tools, web scraping libraries like BeautifulSoup and Scrapy are indispensable for collecting data from websites. These Python libraries facilitate the extraction of structured information from web pages and enable automation of data collection processes. Web scraping is a fundamental technique in OSINT, enabling the retrieval of publicly available data from websites for analysis. While this list showcases some of the cutting-edge OSINT tools and software available today, it's essential to remember that the field is continually evolving. New tools and resources emerge regularly, reflecting the dynamic nature of the internet and the ever-expanding digital footprint. As such, OSINT professionals must stay proactive in exploring and adopting new tools to enhance their capabilities and adapt to evolving challenges. Ultimately, the effective use of these tools, coupled with analytical skills and a deep understanding of the digital landscape, empowers OSINT practitioners to uncover valuable insights and intelligence in today's information-rich environment. In the ever-evolving field of intelligence gathering, the need for advanced techniques has never been more critical. These techniques go beyond the basics, providing intelligence professionals with advanced tools and strategies to collect, analyze, and interpret data effectively. One of the fundamental concepts in advanced intelligence gathering is the principle of open-source intelligence (OSINT). OSINT refers to the practice of collecting and analyzing publicly available information from a wide range of sources to generate valuable intelligence. This approach leverages a vast array of data, including online news articles, social media posts, publicly accessible databases, and more, to gain insights into various subjects of interest. OSINT has become a cornerstone of modern intelligence gathering, offering a treasure trove of data that can be used to inform decision-making and strategic planning. To harness the power of OSINT effectively, intelligence professionals employ advanced search techniques to filter and refine their data collection efforts. Advanced search operators, such as Boolean operators and wildcards, allow analysts to craft precise queries that yield highly relevant results. These operators enable users to narrow down their search to specific keywords, phrases, or combinations of terms, significantly improving the efficiency of data collection. Additionally, advanced search operators enable the inclusion or exclusion of particular terms, ensuring that the results align with the intelligence objectives. While traditional search engines like Google are powerful, specialized OSINT search engines and databases have emerged to cater specifically to intelligence professionals. Platforms like Echosec and the IntelTechniques Search Tool offer advanced search capabilities tailored for OSINT purposes. They provide access to a wide range of online sources, including social media platforms, forums, and public records, making them indispensable tools for intelligence gathering. In addition to advanced search techniques, geospatial analysis plays a crucial role in intelligence gathering. Geospatial intelligence (GEOINT) involves the collection, analysis, and visualization of geospatial data to produce actionable intelligence. This approach allows analysts to incorporate location-based information into their assessments, offering insights into the spatial relationships between various data points. One of the key tools in GEOINT is geographic information systems (GIS), which enables the creation of detailed maps and spatial analysis. Intelligence professionals use GIS to visualize data in a geographical context, helping them identify patterns, trends, and potential areas of interest. For instance, analyzing the geographic distribution of social media posts during a protest can reveal valuable information about the movement's dynamics and participants. Another advanced technique in intelligence gathering is sentiment analysis, a natural language processing method used to determine the sentiment or emotion expressed in text data. Sentiment analysis algorithms assess the tone of a piece of text, categorizing it as positive, negative, or neutral. Intelligence professionals apply sentiment analysis to social media content, news articles, and online forums to gauge public opinion, identify potential threats, or track the sentiment surrounding a particular issue or event. This technique is particularly valuable in assessing the public's response to policies, events, or crises. Advanced intelligence gathering extends to the realm of data visualization, where analysts use sophisticated tools to create visual representations of complex data. Data visualization techniques allow intelligence professionals to convey information more effectively, making it easier for decision-makers to grasp the significance of the data. Tools like Tableau, Power BI, and D3.js enable the creation of interactive dashboards, charts, and graphs that help tell a compelling story with data. For instance, a data visualization dashboard could display real-time metrics related to cybersecurity threats, allowing security analysts to monitor and respond to emerging risks promptly. When dealing with large datasets, analysts turn to data mining and machine learning techniques to uncover hidden insights. Data mining involves the exploration and extraction of patterns, trends, and valuable knowledge from vast amounts of structured and unstructured data. Machine learning algorithms can be trained to identify anomalies, predict future events, or classify data points based on patterns. These advanced techniques are invaluable in identifying emerging threats or understanding evolving trends in areas such as cybersecurity, financial markets, or geopolitical developments. Additionally, social network analysis (SNA) is a powerful technique used in intelligence gathering to understand the relationships and connections between individuals or entities. SNA visualizes and analyzes the network structure, identifying key actors, influencers, and potential nodes of interest. By examining the structure of a social network, intelligence professionals can gain insights into organizational hierarchies, communication patterns, and potential vulnerabilities. For instance, SNA can reveal the key figures within a criminal organization or the social ties among individuals involved in a cyberattack. Advanced intelligence gathering techniques also encompass the use of specialized tools and software designed for specific tasks. For example, digital forensics tools enable investigators to recover, preserve, and analyze digital evidence from computers, mobile devices, and other digital media. These tools are crucial in criminal investigations, counterterrorism efforts, and cybersecurity incidents. Moreover, cyber threat intelligence platforms aggregate and analyze data from various sources to provide organizations with actionable insights into potential cyber threats. These platforms help organizations proactively defend against cyberattacks by identifying vulnerabilities and indicators of compromise. In the world of signals intelligence (SIGINT), advanced techniques involve intercepting and deciphering electronic communications. SIGINT analysts use sophisticated equipment and methods to intercept and decode signals, providing valuable intelligence on communications between foreign entities. This information can be critical in national security and military operations. Lastly, in the field of human intelligence (HUMINT), advanced techniques encompass covert operations, espionage, and human source development. HUMINT professionals employ a range of tactics to gather information from human sources, often in clandestine or sensitive environments. These techniques require a deep understanding of human psychology, as well as the ability to build rapport and trust with sources. In summary, advanced techniques for intelligence gathering encompass a wide range of tools, methods, and approaches that go beyond the basics. These techniques leverage advanced search operators, geospatial analysis, sentiment analysis, data visualization, data mining, social network analysis, specialized tools, and more. By mastering these advanced techniques, intelligence professionals can uncover valuable insights, detect emerging threats, and inform decision-making effectively. In an era of information overload and complexity, staying ahead of the curve in intelligence gathering is essential for national security, law enforcement, corporate intelligence, and various other domains where actionable intelligence is paramount.

Chapter 9: Predictive Analysis and Threat Assessment

In the ever-evolving landscape of open-source intelligence (OSINT), predictive analytics has emerged as a powerful tool for enhancing the capabilities of intelligence professionals. This advanced technique leverages historical data and statistical algorithms to make informed predictions about future events or trends. Predictive analytics in OSINT goes beyond traditional data analysis, enabling analysts to anticipate developments, identify potential threats, and make proactive decisions. At its core, predictive analytics relies on the principle that patterns and trends in historical data can offer insights into future behavior. By analyzing past events and their outcomes, intelligence professionals can build models that predict future occurrences with a degree of accuracy. These predictions can be invaluable in a wide range of applications, from national security and law enforcement to business intelligence and cybersecurity. One of the key components of predictive analytics is the availability of high-quality historical data. To make accurate predictions, analysts need access to comprehensive and reliable datasets. In OSINT, this data can come from various sources, including online news articles, social media posts, financial reports, and public records. For example, in the realm of cybersecurity, analysts may gather historical data on cyberattacks, including the methods used, the targets, and the outcomes. This data forms the foundation for predictive models that can identify potential cyber threats and vulnerabilities. Predictive analytics in OSINT often involves the use of machine learning algorithms. Machine learning is a subset of artificial intelligence (AI) that focuses on the development of algorithms capable of learning from data and making predictions or decisions. These algorithms can automatically identify patterns, relationships, and trends within large datasets. In the context of OSINT, machine learning models can be trained to recognize patterns in historical data that are indicative of specific events or behaviors. For example, a machine learning model can analyze social media posts to identify early indicators of civil unrest or protests in a particular region. Once trained, these models can then be applied to real-time data streams to make predictions based on incoming information. Natural language processing (NLP) is another crucial component of predictive analytics in OSINT. NLP techniques enable the analysis of text data, such as news articles, social media posts, and forum discussions. By extracting insights from unstructured text, NLP can help intelligence professionals understand public sentiment, detect emerging trends, and assess the credibility of sources. For instance, NLP algorithms can be used to analyze social media conversations surrounding a political event, providing insights into public opinion and potential risks. In addition to machine learning and NLP, geospatial analysis plays a vital role in predictive analytics. Geospatial data, which includes information about the location and spatial relationships of objects or events, can be integrated into predictive models. For example, analysts can use geospatial data to predict the movement of natural disasters, such as hurricanes or wildfires, by analyzing historical weather patterns and geographical features. Geospatial analysis can also aid in predicting the spread of infectious diseases, assessing the impact of urban development, and even anticipating traffic congestion based on historical traffic data. Time-series analysis is another technique commonly used in predictive analytics. This approach focuses on data that changes over time and aims to identify patterns and trends in sequential data points. For example, time-series analysis can be applied to financial data to predict stock market trends, to social media data to anticipate the popularity of a topic, or to weather data to forecast temperature fluctuations. Intelligence professionals often use a combination of these techniques to create robust predictive models. For instance, a cybersecurity analyst might develop a machine learning model that integrates historical cyberattack data with geospatial information and real-time network traffic data. This model can continuously analyze incoming data to detect potential cyber threats and provide early warnings to security teams. Furthermore, predictive analytics in OSINT is not limited to a single domain or application. It can be applied across various fields, including national security, law enforcement, financial markets, supply chain management, and more. In the realm of national security, predictive analytics can help identify potential terrorist threats by analyzing patterns in communication and travel data. In law enforcement, it can aid in predicting crime hotspots and allocating resources accordingly. In the business world, predictive analytics can optimize supply chain logistics, forecast customer demand, and improve marketing strategies. Despite its potential, predictive analytics in OSINT comes with its own set of challenges. One of the main challenges is the availability and quality of data. For predictive models to be accurate, they require large and reliable datasets, which may not always be accessible in the world of OSINT. Moreover, the dynamic and ever-changing nature of online data poses a challenge, as predictive models need to adapt to evolving circumstances. Privacy and ethical concerns also play a role in the application of predictive analytics. The use of personal data for predictive purposes raises questions about privacy, consent, and data protection regulations. Therefore, it is essential for intelligence professionals to adhere to ethical guidelines and legal frameworks when collecting and analyzing data. In summary, predictive analytics has become a valuable asset in the field of open-source intelligence (OSINT). By leveraging historical data, machine learning algorithms, natural language processing, geospatial analysis, and time-series analysis, intelligence professionals can make informed predictions about future events and trends. These predictions have wide-ranging applications, from enhancing national security to improving business strategies. However, the challenges of data availability, data quality, privacy, and ethics must be carefully navigated to ensure the responsible and effective use of predictive analytics in OSINT. As we delve into the complex world of cybersecurity and open-source intelligence (OSINT), one of the critical aspects is the assessment of future threats and vulnerabilities. This topic is of paramount importance in the ever-evolving landscape of digital security. In a digital age where technology is constantly advancing, it's essential to anticipate potential threats and vulnerabilities that may arise. By doing so, organizations and security professionals can proactively implement measures to safeguard their systems and data. Assessing future threats and vulnerabilities is not a crystal ball exercise but a systematic process based on analysis, intelligence, and staying ahead of emerging trends. To begin, it's crucial to understand that the threat landscape is constantly evolving. Cybercriminals are becoming increasingly sophisticated, and new attack vectors are emerging regularly. Therefore, what was secure yesterday may not be secure tomorrow. To assess future threats effectively, security professionals must adopt a forward-thinking mindset. One of the primary tools in this endeavor is threat intelligence. Threat intelligence involves the collection, analysis, and dissemination of information about potential threats and vulnerabilities. This information can come from various sources, including OSINT, proprietary data, government agencies, industry reports, and security research organizations. By harnessing the power of threat intelligence, organizations gain insights into emerging threats and can develop proactive strategies to mitigate risks. Machine learning and artificial intelligence (AI) are playing an increasingly significant role in predicting future threats. These technologies can analyze vast amounts of data and identify patterns and anomalies that human analysts might overlook. For example, machine learning algorithms can detect unusual network activity, which could be an early indicator of a cyberattack. They can also analyze malware samples to predict how threats might evolve and adapt over time. Furthermore, AI-powered chatbots and virtual assistants are being used to enhance security awareness and education within organizations, making employees more vigilant against potential threats. The analysis of historical attack data is another valuable method for assessing future threats. By studying past incidents, security professionals can identify common tactics, techniques, and procedures (TTPs) used by cybercriminals. They can then anticipate how these TTPs might be used in future attacks. For instance, if a certain malware strain has been used in previous attacks, it's likely that cybercriminals will continue to use and adapt it in the future. Moreover, the analysis of past incidents can reveal trends in attacker motivations and targets, shedding light on potential future targets. In addition to threats, it's crucial to assess vulnerabilities in systems, software, and infrastructure. Vulnerabilities are weaknesses or flaws that can be exploited by attackers to gain unauthorized access or compromise systems. Regular vulnerability assessments and penetration testing are essential for identifying and addressing weaknesses. By conducting these assessments, organizations can proactively patch vulnerabilities and reduce the attack surface. Furthermore, organizations should consider the human element when assessing future threats. Social engineering attacks, such as phishing and spear-phishing, are highly effective because they exploit human psychology. Security professionals need to continuously educate employees and raise awareness about the dangers of social engineering tactics. This human-centric approach is a critical component of future threat assessment. In a world where the Internet of Things (IoT) is becoming increasingly prevalent, the attack surface is expanding. IoT devices, from smart thermostats to connected vehicles, are potential entry points for cyberattacks. Assessing future threats in the context of IoT requires understanding the unique vulnerabilities and risks associated with these devices. For example, IoT devices often lack robust security features, making them attractive targets for attackers. In the coming years, we can anticipate more sophisticated attacks that leverage IoT vulnerabilities to gain access to critical systems. Another area of concern is the growing use of artificial intelligence and machine learning by both defenders and attackers. While AI can enhance security by automating threat detection and response, it can also be used by cybercriminals to create more advanced and adaptive attacks. Security professionals must assess how AI and machine learning will impact the threat landscape and develop strategies to stay one step ahead. The rise of nation-state actors in cyberattacks is also a significant concern. State-sponsored hackers have access to substantial resources and advanced techniques. Their motivations can range from espionage to disruption of critical infrastructure. To assess future threats, organizations must consider the potential involvement of nation-states and develop strategies to defend against their attacks. In summary, assessing future threats and vulnerabilities is a multifaceted and dynamic process. It requires a combination of threat intelligence, data analysis, human awareness, and a forward-thinking approach. As technology continues to advance, the threat landscape will evolve, presenting new challenges and risks. Security professionals must remain vigilant, adaptable, and well-informed to effectively anticipate and mitigate future threats in the ever-changing world of cybersecurity and OSINT.

Chapter 10: Case Studies in Expert Cyber Reconnaissance

Let's now delve into the intriguing world of cyber reconnaissance by exploring real-world examples of expert-level operations. Imagine a scenario where a large financial institution has fallen victim to a series of cyberattacks, resulting in the theft of sensitive customer data. In response, the organization calls upon a team of cyber reconnaissance experts to investigate the source of these attacks.

These experts begin by gathering OSINT from various online sources, including social media, forums, and hacker communities. They aim to identify potential threat actors who may have been involved in the attacks. Through meticulous analysis, they uncover a trail of digital breadcrumbs left by the attackers.

One of the key findings is the use of a previously unknown malware variant. To gain a deeper understanding of this threat, the experts turn to specialized malware analysis tools and sandbox environments. By dissecting the malware's code and behavior, they uncover valuable insights into the attacker's tactics and capabilities.

Next, the experts pivot their investigation towards the dark web, a shadowy realm notorious for hosting cybercriminal activities. Using specialized tools and techniques, they navigate the dark web's hidden marketplaces and forums, searching for any traces of the stolen customer data.

Their efforts pay off when they discover a listing on an underground marketplace offering the stolen data for sale. To infiltrate the seller's network and gather more evidence, the experts adopt sophisticated deception techniques. They create convincing personas and engage with the seller in a way that doesn't arouse suspicion.

As the investigation progresses, the experts encounter encrypted communications channels used by the cybercriminals. To decipher these messages, they employ advanced cryptography and decryption tools, gradually unraveling the web of secrecy surrounding the attackers' operations.

In parallel, the team conducts geospatial analysis to pinpoint the physical location of the attackers. By correlating IP addresses, domain registrations, and other metadata, they narrow down the potential geographical areas from which the attacks originated.

To further gather intelligence, the experts leverage human sources within the cybercriminal community. They cultivate relationships with informants who provide valuable insider information on the attackers' identities and motives. This human-centric approach proves instrumental in unraveling the mystery. Throughout the investigation, the experts constantly monitor social media platforms, searching for any inadvertent disclosures or clues left behind by the cybercriminals. They also employ sentiment analysis tools to gauge the mood and intentions of potential threat actors within the online forums. As the puzzle pieces fall into place, the cyber reconnaissance experts identify a group of hackers operating from a foreign country. These hackers had meticulously planned and executed the attacks on the financial institution, intending to profit from the stolen data.

With the gathered evidence in hand, the experts collaborate with law enforcement agencies, sharing their findings and assisting in the attribution of the cybercriminals. Legal actions are initiated against the threat actors, resulting in arrests and the dismantling of their criminal operation.

This real-world example highlights the intricate and multifaceted nature of expert-level cyber reconnaissance. It demonstrates how a combination of OSINT, malware analysis, dark web exploration, cryptography, geospatial analysis, human intelligence, and social media monitoring can be employed to track down cybercriminals and mitigate their activities.

Another compelling scenario involves a global corporation facing a persistent and highly sophisticated cyber espionage campaign. In this case, the organization's sensitive intellectual property and trade secrets are at risk, making it imperative to identify the perpetrators and their motives.

The cyber reconnaissance experts tasked with this investigation employ an array of advanced techniques to uncover the espionage operation's intricacies. They begin by dissecting the malware used in the attacks, revealing its advanced capabilities and connections to known state-sponsored threat actors.

To gain insights into the attackers' motives, the experts turn to psychological profiling. By analyzing the tactics, targets, and messages left behind by the threat actors, they build a psychological profile that helps predict future actions and motivations.

Simultaneously, the experts conduct deep dives into the digital footprints of the threat actors. They examine their online personas, social media activities, and affiliations, slowly piecing together the puzzle of who might be behind the espionage campaign.

As the investigation unfolds, the experts discover a complex network of compromised systems and command-and-control servers used by the attackers. To disrupt the espionage operation, they coordinate with international cybersecurity agencies to dismantle these infrastructure components.

The cyber reconnaissance team also engages in counterintelligence efforts to identify potential moles or insider threats within the organization. They conduct thorough background checks on employees with access to sensitive information and scrutinize their digital behaviors for signs of compromise or collusion.

To combat the sophisticated phishing campaigns employed by the threat actors, the experts employ advanced email analysis techniques. They trace the phishing emails back to their sources and identify the techniques used to evade traditional security measures.

In a surprising twist, the cyber reconnaissance team uncovers evidence of a double agent within the organization, leaking critical information to the threat actors. This revelation leads to a high-stakes internal investigation and the identification of the insider responsible for the security breach.

With a clearer picture of the threat landscape, the experts work closely with the organization's cybersecurity team to fortify its defenses. They recommend advanced threat detection systems, employee training programs, and enhanced security protocols to prevent future espionage attempts.

Ultimately, through their relentless pursuit of the truth, the cyber reconnaissance experts succeed in identifying the state-sponsored threat actors behind the espionage campaign. This information is crucial for the organization's legal and diplomatic efforts to hold the perpetrators accountable on the global stage.

These real-world examples underscore the critical role of cyber reconnaissance in today's digital age. They showcase the sophistication of expert-level operations and the diverse range of techniques and tools employed to uncover cyber threats, track down threat actors, and safeguard organizations and individuals from cyberattacks.

Let's next delve into the fascinating realm of cyber reconnaissance and learn from successful operations conducted by experts in the field. These real-world examples will provide valuable insights into the strategies and techniques employed to gather intelligence and protect against cyber threats.

Imagine a multinational technology corporation that becomes the target of a sophisticated cyber espionage campaign. In response, a team of cyber reconnaissance experts is brought in to investigate the source of the attacks and understand the motives behind them.

The experts begin their investigation by analyzing the malware used in the attacks. This malware exhibits advanced capabilities, indicating the involvement of a well-funded and highly skilled threat actor. By dissecting the malware's code and behavior, the experts gain valuable intelligence about the attacker's tactics and intentions.

To identify the threat actor responsible for the cyber espionage campaign, the experts turn to open-source intelligence (OSINT) techniques. They scour the dark web, hacker forums, and social media platforms for any traces of information related to the attackers. This meticulous OSINT gathering leads them to a series of online personas and affiliations associated with the threat actor.

One of the most critical aspects of successful cyber reconnaissance is attribution, or the process of identifying the individuals or groups behind cyberattacks. In this case, the experts employ a combination of technical analysis and human intelligence to attribute the attacks to a nation-state actor with a history of cyber espionage.

As the investigation progresses, the experts conduct geospatial analysis to pinpoint the geographical location of the threat actor's command-and-control servers. By correlating IP addresses, domain registrations, and other metadata, they narrow down the potential countries from which the attacks are originating.

Simultaneously, the cyber reconnaissance team engages in psychological profiling of the threat actor. They analyze the patterns of behavior, targets, and messaging left behind by the attacker to build a psychological profile. This profile helps predict future actions and motives, enabling the organization to better defend against future cyber threats.

To disrupt the espionage campaign, the experts collaborate with international cybersecurity agencies to dismantle the infrastructure used by the threat actor. This includes taking down compromised servers and disrupting the command-and-control channels, effectively cutting off the attacker's access to compromised systems.

In a surprising twist, the cyber reconnaissance team uncovers evidence of insider involvement. They identify an employee within the organization who had been unknowingly compromised by the threat actor and inadvertently provided access to sensitive information. This discovery highlights the importance of insider threat detection in cybersecurity.

With a clearer understanding of the threat landscape, the experts work closely with the organization's cybersecurity team to enhance its defenses. They recommend implementing advanced threat detection systems, conducting regular employee training on cybersecurity best practices, and fortifying security protocols to prevent future attacks.

Ultimately, the cyber reconnaissance experts succeed in identifying the nation-state threat actor behind the cyber espionage campaign. This attribution is critical for the organization's diplomatic and legal efforts to hold the perpetrators accountable on the global stage.

These real-world examples emphasize the vital role of cyber reconnaissance in modern cybersecurity. They illustrate the complexity of expert-level operations and the diverse range of techniques used to uncover cyber threats, attribute attacks to specific threat actors, and safeguard organizations and individuals from cyber espionage.

In another scenario, consider a large financial institution facing a series of cyberattacks resulting in the theft of sensitive customer data. The organization enlists the expertise of cyber reconnaissance professionals to investigate the source of these attacks and mitigate further risks.

The cyber reconnaissance experts initiate their investigation by collecting OSINT from various online sources, including social media platforms, hacker forums, and dark web marketplaces. Their goal is to identify potential threat actors responsible for the attacks.

Through meticulous analysis, the experts uncover a trail of digital breadcrumbs left by the attackers. They piece together information about the attackers' tactics, techniques, and infrastructure, gaining a deeper understanding of their modus operandi.

One of the key findings is the use of a previously unknown malware variant. To gain further insights into this threat, the experts employ advanced malware analysis tools and sandbox environments. By dissecting the malware's code and observing its behavior, they uncover valuable intelligence about the attacker's capabilities and intentions.

The investigation also leads the experts to the dark web, a hidden realm known for hosting cybercriminal activities. Using specialized tools and techniques, they navigate the dark web's underground marketplaces and forums in search of any traces of the stolen customer data.

Their efforts yield results when they discover a listing on an underground marketplace offering the stolen data for sale. To infiltrate the seller's network and gather more evidence, the experts adopt sophisticated deception techniques. They create convincing personas and engage with the seller without arousing suspicion.

Simultaneously, the experts encounter encrypted communication channels used by the cybercriminals. To decrypt these messages and gain access to critical information, they utilize advanced cryptography and decryption tools, slowly unraveling the web of secrecy surrounding the attackers.

As the investigation progresses, the team also engages in behavioral analysis and sentiment monitoring. They monitor the online activities and communications of potential threat actors within hacker communities, assessing their mood and intentions.

Ultimately, the cyber reconnaissance experts identify a group of hackers operating from a foreign country with the intent to profit from the stolen data. With the evidence gathered, they collaborate with law enforcement agencies to share their findings and assist in the attribution of the cybercriminals.

To mitigate the immediate threat, the experts work closely with the financial institution's cybersecurity team to strengthen its defenses. They recommend implementing robust intrusion detection systems, enhancing employee training on cybersecurity awareness, and continuously monitoring for signs of compromise.

These real-world examples highlight the critical role of cyber reconnaissance in uncovering cyber threats and attributing attacks to specific threat actors. They showcase the diverse array of techniques and tools employed by experts to protect organizations from data breaches and cybercriminal activities.

In yet another scenario, let's explore the case of a government agency facing a series of cyberattacks aimed at disrupting critical infrastructure and stealing classified information. To counter these threats, the agency turns to a team of cyber reconnaissance specialists.

The experts begin by conducting a comprehensive assessment of the agency's digital footprint. They analyze the organization's online presence, identifying potential vulnerabilities and entry points for attackers. This initial assessment provides a baseline for understanding the agency's cyber landscape.

As part of their investigation, the cyber reconnaissance team employs advanced network scanning tools to map out the agency's network architecture. They identify critical assets, assess their security posture, and pinpoint potential weaknesses that could be exploited by threat actors.

To gather intelligence on the attackers, the experts turn to open-source intelligence (OSINT) techniques. They scour the internet for any publicly available information related to the threat actors, including their online personas, affiliations, and past activities.

In parallel, the experts conduct deep web and dark web investigations to uncover hidden threat actor activities. They utilize specialized search engines and tools to access secretive online communities and forums where cybercriminals may be planning and coordinating attacks.

One of the significant challenges in this case is the use of anonymization technologies by the attackers. To overcome this obstacle, the cyber reconnaissance specialists employ advanced techniques for tracing digital artifacts to their sources. They follow the trail of breadcrumbs left by the attackers and gradually unmask their identities.

As the investigation unfolds, the team engages in behavioral analysis and sentiment monitoring to gain insights into the threat actors' motivations and intentions. They analyze the language, tone, and patterns of communication within hacker communities to anticipate future attacks.

The experts also recognize the importance of insider threat detection within the government agency. They conduct thorough background checks and security audits to identify any potential insider threats or compromised personnel.

To disrupt the attackers' operations, the cyber reconnaissance team collaborates with international cybersecurity partners and law enforcement agencies. They share intelligence findings, coordinate takedowns of malicious infrastructure, and work to neutralize the threat actors.

Throughout the investigation, the experts provide the government agency with actionable intelligence and recommendations to bolster its cybersecurity defenses. They advise on the implementation of advanced threat detection systems, employee training, and incident response protocols.

In the end, the cyber reconnaissance specialists successfully attribute the cyberattacks to a state-sponsored threat actor known for targeting critical infrastructure and government organizations. Their efforts contribute to the agency's ability to defend against future attacks and safeguard national security.

These real-world examples illustrate the pivotal role of cyber reconnaissance in identifying cyber threats, tracing attackers, and protecting critical infrastructure and sensitive information. They highlight the complexity of expert-level operations and the multifaceted approaches used to safeguard organizations and governments from cyberattacks.

Conclusion

In the pages of the "OSINT 101 Handbook: Expert-Level Intelligence Gathering," we've embarked on a journey through the intricate and dynamic world of Open Source Intelligence (OSINT). This comprehensive bundle, comprising four distinct volumes, has been meticulously crafted to empower both beginners and seasoned professionals with the knowledge and skills necessary to excel in the realm of intelligence gathering, reconnaissance, threat assessment, and counterintelligence.

In "BOOK 1 - OSINT Fundamentals," we laid the foundation, guiding beginners through the essential concepts and techniques of OSINT. It provided a gentle introduction to the art of open source intelligence, helping readers understand its significance in today's information-driven world.

"BOOK 2 - Advanced OSINT Strategies" elevated our understanding, delving deeper into the sophisticated strategies employed by experts in the field. Readers discovered advanced search techniques, explored the power of automation, and harnessed the full potential of OSINT tools to gather intelligence effectively.

With "BOOK 3 - Digital Footprint Analysis," we ventured into the intriguing realm of profiling and investigations. Expert-level OSINT techniques were unveiled, enabling readers to dissect digital footprints, conduct behavioral analysis, and extract valuable insights from social media activity.

Finally, "BOOK 4 - Expert OSINT" took us to the frontlines of cyber reconnaissance and threat intelligence. We examined real-world examples of expert-level operations, gaining insights into how OSINT experts attribute cyberattacks, disrupt malicious infrastructure, and protect critical assets.

As we conclude our journey through this book bundle, it's clear that OSINT is not merely a skill but a mindset—a mindset that embraces curiosity, adaptability, and a relentless pursuit of knowledge. The knowledge imparted in these volumes equips readers with the tools they need to navigate the complex landscape of information, uncover hidden threats, and protect against cyber adversaries.

But the world of OSINT is ever-evolving, and the quest for intelligence never truly ends. It's a field where continuous learning is paramount, where new tools and techniques emerge, and where adaptability is the key to success. As you close this bundle, remember that your journey in OSINT has only just begun.

Whether you're a novice eager to explore the fundamentals or an expert honing your skills, the "OSINT 101 Handbook" is a valuable resource that empowers you to excel in the realms of intelligence gathering, reconnaissance, threat assessment, and counterintelligence. The knowledge contained within these pages is a beacon guiding you through the labyrinth of data, revealing insights, and helping you make informed decisions.

In the world of OSINT, the pursuit of knowledge is unending, and the application of that knowledge is the essence of intelligence gathering. With each volume in this bundle, you've taken another step toward becoming an OSINT expert. As you continue your journey, may your curiosity be unceasing, your skills ever-sharpening, and your commitment unwavering.

Thank you for joining us on this exploration of OSINT, and may your future endeavors in the world of intelligence gathering be both rewarding and impactful.